D1756002

THE EUROPEAN UNION SERIES

General Editors: Neill Nugent, William E. Paterson

The European Union series provides an authoritative library on the European Union, ranging from general introductory texts to definitive assessments of key institutions and actors, issues, policies and policy processes, and the role of member states.

Books in the series are written by leading scholars in their fields and reflect the most up-to-date research and debate. Particular attention is paid to accessibility and clear presentation for a wide audience of students, practitioners and interested general readers.

The series editors are **Neill Nugent**, Emeritus Professor of Politics at Manchester Metropolitan University, UK, and **William E. Paterson**, Honorary Professor in German and European Studies, University of Aston. Their co-editor until his death in July 1999, **Vincent Wright**, was a Fellow of Nuffield College, Oxford University.

Feedback on the series and book proposals are always welcome and should be sent to Andrew Malvern, Palgrave, 4 Crinan Street, London N1 9XW, or by e-mail to **andrew.malvern@palgrave.com**

General textbooks

Published

Laurie Buonanno and Neill Nugent **Policies and Policy Processes of the European Union**
Desmond Dinan **Encyclopedia of the European Union**
[Rights: Europe only]
Desmond Dinan **Europe Recast: A History of the European Union (2nd edn)**
[Rights: Europe only]
Desmond Dinan **Ever Closer Union: An Introduction to European Integration (4th edn)**
[Rights: Europe only]
Mette Eilstrup Sangiovanni (ed.) **Debates on European Integration: A Reader**
Simon Hix and Bjørn Høyland **The Political System of the European Union (3rd edn)**
Dirk Leuffen, Berthold Rittberger and Frank Schimmelfennig **Differentiated Integration**
Paul Magnette **What is the European Union? Nature and Prospects**
John McCormick **Understanding the European Union: A Concise Introduction (6th edn)**
Brent F. Nelsen and Alexander Stubb **The European Union: Readings on the Theory and Practice of European Integration (4th edn)**
[Rights: Europe only]

Neill Nugent (ed.) **European Union Enlargement**
Neill Nugent **The Government and Politics of the European Union (8th edn)**
John Peterson and Elizabeth Bomberg **Decision-Making in the European Union**
Ben Rosamond **Theories of European Integration**
Sabine Saurugger **Theoretical Approaches to European Integration**
Ingeborg Tömmel **The European Union: What it is and How it Works**
Esther Versluis, Mendeltje van Keulen and Paul Stephenson **Analyzing the European Union Policy Process**
Hubert Zimmermann and Andreas Dür (eds) **Key Controversies in European Integration (2nd edn)**

Also planned

The European Union and Global Politics
The Political Economy of European Integration

Visit Palgrave Macmillan's
EU Resource area at
he.palgrave.com/companion/EU-Resource-Area/

The Trade Policy of the European Union

Sieglinde Gstöhl and Dirk De Bièvre

First published 2018 by
PALGRAVE

Palgrave in the UK is an imprint of Macmillan Publishers Limited, registered in England, company number 785998, of 4 Crinan Street, London, N1 9XW.

Palgrave® and Macmillan® are registered trademarks in the United States, the United Kingdom, Europe and other countries.

ISBN 978–0–230–27196–8 hardback
ISBN 978–0–230–27197–5 paperback

This book is printed on paper suitable for recycling and made from fully managed and sustained forest sources. Logging, pulping and manufacturing processes are expected to conform to the environmental regulations of the country of origin.

A catalogue record for this book is available from the British Library.

A catalog record for this book is available from the Library of Congress.

Contents

List of Features

Tables

Boxes

Preface and Acknowledgements

This book has taken a long time to take shape. A phone call from Sieglinde with the request to join her initiative to write a first real political science textbook on European trade policy kicked off the process. Having taught a broad course on the European Union's common commercial policy for some time at the College of Europe, she considered it time to fill this glaring gap in the literature. Combined with teaching, faculty responsibilities, directing a study programme, the organization of conferences, peer review article publishing and working on other book projects, the challenge of writing this book was often exercising the necessary calm and time to concentrate and distil which topics to include and which to skirt over. In the end, it seems we equalled the duration of EU trade agreement negotiations – that is, far longer than announced and far longer than expected. Despite our exasperation at the long periods of interruption, we thoroughly enjoyed the process of writing together, combining our expertise, acting as each other's constructive critic and bringing together a host of literature and insight into this political science–based yet pluridisciplinary book on a topic that has galvanized the attention and curiosity of both of us since the 1990s. After all, writing an overview textbook – a genre that we learned to appreciate ever more as we went along – is a wholly different intellectual endeavour than writing a research monograph or a theory-guided piece of empirical research. We hope readers will equally enjoy the product of our work and will like our choices of what to include and what to forego while being forgiving for our less lucky strikes.

We have received many encouragements and/or detailed and incisive comments from close colleagues to persevere in this long-term project, especially Tomas Baert, Ferdi De Ville, Pierre Defraigne, Andreas Dür, Jappe Eckhardt, Michael Geelhand, Inge Govaere, Frank Hoffmeister, Bart Kerremans, James Mackie, Petros Mavroidis and Arlo Poletti, as well as Neill Nugent and the Palgrave reviewers. Dirk is particularly grateful to Manfred Elsig for hosting him for a brief but intensive writing period at the World Trade Institute at the University of Bern in late 2014, as well as to Mathias Koenig-Archibugi and the Department of Government of the London School of Economics and Political Science for hosting him as a visiting fellow in the academic year of 2014–2015, creating the preconditions for that quiet environment so conducive to concentrated work. He also gratefully acknowledges funding from the Research Fund of the University of Antwerp and the Research Foundation Flanders FWO to pay for his replacement in teaching at the Antwerp faculty during that academic year. Sieglinde would like to acknowledge the assistance of the Research Support Fund of the College of Europe for the indexing.

Last but not least, we both would like to thank our graduate students, who come from many different backgrounds, for continuously asking questions. We hope that they will find some answers in this book, but also new, interesting and critical questions. The book aims to explain the workings of the common commercial policy in detail, yet in an accessible way, to anyone interested in it. While considerably gaining in importance, the EU's trade policy has for far too long remained insufficiently known and understood.

Bruges and Antwerp,
June 2017

List of Abbreviations

ACEA	European Automobile Manufacturers Association
ACTA	Anti-Counterfeiting Trade Agreement
Art.	Article
ACP	African, Caribbean and Pacific countries
ASEAN	Association of Southeast Asian Nations
BIPAVER	European Retread Manufacturers Association
BRIC	Brazil, Russia, India and China
BRICS	Brazil, Russia, India, China and South Africa
CAP	Common Agricultural Policy
CEFIC	European Chemical Industry Council
CETA	Comprehensive Economic and Trade Agreement
CFSP	Common Foreign and Security Policy
CJEU	Court of Justice of the European Union
COREPER	Committee of Permanent Representatives
DCFTA	Deep and Comprehensive Free Trade Area
DCI	Development Cooperation Instrument
DDB	Duty Drawback
DEVCO	DG International Cooperation and Development
DEVE	Development Cooperation Committee
DG	Directorate-General
DSB	Dispute Settlement Body
EAC	East African Community
EAMA	*Etats africains et malgache associés*
EBA	Everything-But-Arms initiative
EBMA	European Bicycles Manufacturers Association
EC	European Community
ECHO	DG International Cooperation, Humanitarian Aid and Crisis Response (formerly European Community Humanitarian Office)
ECR	European Court Reports
ECOWAS	Economic Community of West African States
ECSC	European Coal and Steel Community
EDF	European Development Fund
EEA	European Economic Area

EEAS	European External Action Service
EEC	European Economic Community
EESC	European Economic and Social Committee
EFTA	European Free Trade Association
EIDHR	European Instrument for Democracy and Human Rights
ENI	European Neighbourhood Instrument
ENP	European Neighbourhood Policy
ENPI	European Neighbourhood and Partnership Instrument
EPA	Economic Partnership Agreement
ERTA	European Road Transport Agreement
ESF	European Services Forum
EU	European Union
FAC	Foreign Affairs Council
FDI	foreign direct investment
FPI	Foreign Policy Instruments
FTA	free trade agreement
GATS	General Agreement on Trade in Services
GATT	General Agreement on Tariffs and Trade
GCC	Gulf Cooperation Council
GDP	gross domestic product
GNI	gross national income
GPA	Government Procurement Agreement
GSP	Generalized System of Preferences
HR/VP	High Representative of the Union for Foreign Affairs and Security Policy/Vice-President of the European Commission
IHA	Instrument for Humanitarian Aid
IfS	Instrument for Stability
ILO	International Labour Organization
INSC	Instrument for Nuclear Safety Co-operation
INTA	International Trade Committee
IPA	Instrument for Pre-accession Assistance
IPI	International Procurement Instrument
ISDS	investor-to-state dispute settlement
ITA	Information Technology Agreement
ITO	International Trade Organization
ITTO	International Tropical Timber Organization
LDC	least developed country

LRRD	linkage between relief, rehabilitation and development
MDG	Millennium Development Goals
MEP	Member of European Parliament
MFN	most-favoured nation
NAFTA	North American Free Trade Agreement
NGO	non-governmental organization
NTBs	non-tariff barriers to trade
ODA	official development assistance
OECD	Organization for Economic Co-operation and Development
PCA	Partnership and Cooperation Agreement
PI	Partnership Instrument
SACU	Southern Africa Customs Union
SADC	Southern African Development Community
SCA	Special Committee on Agriculture
SCM	Agreement on Subsidies and Countervailing Measures
SDG	Sustainable Development Goals
SDT	special and differential treatment
SEA	Single European Act
SIA	Sustainability Impact Assessment
SPS	sanitary and phytosanitary measures
STABEX	Stabilization of Export Earnings
STIS	Steel, Textiles and other Industrial Sectors
SYSMIN	System of Stabilization of Export Earnings from Mining Products
TBR	Trade Barriers Regulation
TBT	technical barriers to trade
TDCA	Trade, Development and Cooperation Agreement
TDI	trade defence instrument
TEC	Treaty establishing the European Community
TEU	Treaty on European Union
TFA	Trade Facilitation Agreement
TFEU	Treaty on the Functioning of the European Union
TiSA	Trade in Services Agreement
TPC	Trade Policy Committee
TRIMs	Agreement on Trade-Related Investment Measures
TRIPs	Agreement on Trade-Related Intellectual Property Rights
UK	United Kingdom

UN   United Nations
UNCTAD   United Nations Conference on Trade and Development
UNESCO   United Nations Educational, Scientific and Cultural
            Organization
US   United States
WTO   World Trade Organization

Chapter 1

Introduction: Why Study EU Trade Policy?

From the creation of the European Economic Community (EEC) in 1958 until today, the member states of the European Union (EU) have crafted a common commercial policy. With this momentous decision embodied in the Treaty of Rome, within a few years they abolished tariffs and other barriers to trade between themselves, and they delegated the setting of external tariff levels and of rules regulating trade with the rest of the world to the supranational, European level. Member states thus granted the Union exclusive competence in the conduct of external trade policy. Along with only a few other policy fields, such as the regulation of the internal market, competition policy or monetary policy, trade policy is one of the outright most important exclusive competences of the EU. This makes the Union similar to a country in the realm of trade policymaking and international trade law.

Although EU trade policy has enjoyed this position of primordial importance in overall European policymaking for over six decades now, the trade policy of the EU has attracted much more attention in recent years, from both the public and scholars. The Doha Round negotiations in the World Trade Organization (WTO) have been facing a stalemate: new trading powers besides the United States, Japan, Canada and the EU – formerly known as the Quad – have entered the world stage, and the trade agenda has broadened, mobilizing more, and more diverse, stakeholders. Despite the rise of emerging economies like Brazil, India and particularly China, the EU's trade policy still matters in world politics because it remains the largest single market, trader and investor. Due to its sheer market size and its pivotal role in world trade, the EU is an economic and political powerhouse to be reckoned with by all other countries. Although the common commercial policy is the oldest and most integrated external policy of the EU, and a field in which the EU actually wields considerable power, it has – compared to EU foreign

policy – not been the subject of many dedicated textbooks. This introductory chapter sets the scene by asking why countries trade, to what
extent the EU is a trade power and what factors other than legal competence shape EU trade policy.

Why do countries trade?

One of the most standard economic explanations for why countries trade
is because they expect gains from a favourable trade policy. Economies
can gain by specializing in the sectors in which they have a comparative
advantage – that is, activities in which they encounter lower opportunity
costs (in terms of how much of a good country has to give up in order
to release enough resources to produce more of another good). It can be
efficient to specialize in a narrow range of activities so as to earn income
to buy a wide range of goods and services from abroad. Comparative
advantage can explain inter-industry trade between countries that are
different in terms of technology or how they have been endowed with
factors of production.

Countries can also gain from trade due to the existence of economies
of scale in production – that is, when a larger amount of production can
be achieved at a lower cost. Economies of scale can be found particularly
in industries that have large fixed costs in production (e.g. chemicals, steel
and automobiles). The larger the output, the more the costs of the equipment can be spread out among more units of the good. In the presence
of economies of scale, specialization and trade can increase productive
efficiency. Economies of scale can explain intra-industry trade between
similar countries (e.g. trade of different types of cars between the EU and
the United States).

Besides allocative gains, technical efficiency gains are considered one
of the most desirable effects of trade liberalization because exposure to
foreign competition can function as an incentive for technological progress and access to innovation. It is thus potentially beneficial to have
a trade policy to reap such gains; to obtain market access for domestic
exporters, low-cost inputs for importers and larger varieties of goods
and services for consumers; or to protect domestic producers and consumers if necessary. The fundamental changes in global supply chains,
where companies participate in dynamic worldwide networks involving
people, information, processes and resources in the production, handling
and distribution of materials and finished products or providing services
to the customers, have made it less important where exports are officially

recorded compared to where value added is in fact created. Trade is thus more and more about adding value from research and design to manufacturing of components, logistics or other services. This has made the protection of intellectual property and investments abroad more essential. As companies become more dependent on the protection of their patented products or copyrights, their governments are more inclined to ensure this protection through international law. Similarly, companies may attach greater importance to the legal status of their investments abroad since global supply chains have become pivotal to their survival and success, incentivizing governments to enlarge the international legal framework. At the same time, public authorities are also likely to turn more to ensuring fair and equal access to other markets as well as other countries' public procurement and to defend their companies against unfair competition.

Why do EU member states trade under a common policy?

The EU has in the first place a common commercial policy because it was and is a customs union. This means that custom tariffs levied at the EU external borders are exactly the same, regardless of which member state they enter the territory of the EU through. The same basic principle applies to providers of foreign services that want to engage in business within the EU. The advantage of this internal unification and liberalization has been and still is that it is relatively easier for the EU to open up markets abroad for European exports and investments. Although the economies of the EU member states also compete with each other when it comes to promoting exports or attracting foreign investment, together the Union has much more bargaining leverage for defending the interests of EU companies and citizens. A customs union constituted an important step in the European project, and it ensured the closer economic and political integration of West Germany. In addition, this step created necessary revenue for the EU. Finally, the common commercial policy can flank and assist other EU policies, notably development cooperation and foreign policy (see also Buonanno and Nugent, 2013, pp. 251–254).

What is thus commonly called 'trade policy' are those public policies that regulate the trans-border movement of goods and services. Generally, this concerns states, but in the case of the EU, this policymaking capacity is located entirely at the supranational, European level. The member states of the EU have liberalized trade in goods and services internally and established external tariffs for goods and uniform rules for the conduct of their trade policies towards the EU's trade partners. In comparison to most other public policy fields, like welfare state policies or the provision of public health, education, justice and policing, trade policy is one of the very few policy fields in which the EU has state-like competences – along with a monetary policy in the eurozone or a competition policy against anti-competitive behaviour by firms.

Trade policy has a direct impact on EU companies and citizens. Millions of European jobs depend on exports and on foreign direct investment (FDI). In a special 2010 Eurobarometer, 44 per cent of respondents across the EU said that they personally benefited from international trade, in particular by cheaper products and wider choice, whereas 39 per cent said that they did not benefit (European Commission, 2010c). Moreover, two-thirds (65 per cent) of Europeans thought that the EU was benefitting a lot from international trade. For the future, in light of the recent economic crisis, the creation of jobs in the EU was considered the most important priority for trade policy. Although trade is not directly associated with social and environmental standards, almost 40 per cent of respondents said that they were willing to pay more for goods and services that support certain values (ibid.).

Apart from this internal importance of trade policymaking for the member states, trade policy decisions of the EU have always been of considerable significance for its trading partners. The EU very much acts as any other state within the international trading system, and it 'speaks with one voice' to the outside world. Whether for developed countries, other regions, developing countries or least developed countries, EU decisions affect them due to the sheer size of the EU internal market.

The EU as a trade power

Table 1.1 compares the EU with other major established or emerging economies in the world, including the Quad and the BRICS countries (Brazil, Russia, India, China and South Africa): their relative shares of global domestic product (GDP), of trade in goods and services and of FDI inward and outward stocks.

China has in recent years started to bypass the EU and the United States in terms of its share of GDP and its share of trade in goods. Yet, the EU is still the biggest trader in services as well as the most important provider and host for FDI.

TABLE 1.1   *The EU in the World Economy (in per cent, 2016)*

	Share in world GDP	*Share of trade in goods*	*Share of trade in services*	*Share of FDI inward stocks 2015*	*Share of FDI outward stocks 2015*
EU-28	16.7	15.1	22.5	37.8	48.0
US	15.5	14.4	17.0	33.2	37.7
Canada	1.4	3.2	2.4	4.6	7.0
Japan	4.4	5.0	4.8	1.0	7.8
Brazil	2.6	1.3	1.3	2.9	1.1
Russia	3.2	1.9	1.7	1.5	1.6
India	7.2	2.5	4.0	1.7	0.9
China	17.8	14.8	9.0	7.2	6.3
South Africa	0.6	0.6	0.4	0.7	1.0
South Korea	1.6	3.6	2.8	1.1	1.8

Source: Based on European Commission (2017b, pp. 20, 30, 31, 68).

Table 1.2 ranks the 20 major trading partners of the EU in terms of export and imports of goods. When it comes to trade in services, the largest partners by far are the United States (27.2 per cent of EU exports and 31 per cent of EU imports in 2015), followed by neighbouring Switzerland and then China, China with a considerably lower share of 4.5 per cent in exports and 3.8 per cent in imports (European Commission, 2017b, p. 59). The transatlantic relationship is still crucial for the EU, although China has been catching up in its bilateral trade with the EU.

The EU is thus a trade power and of systemic importance for the world trading system. For example, the active support of the EU for the multilateral negotiations on trade liberalization from 1986 to 1994, at a time when the EU was completing its own internal market, was vital for the establishment of the WTO in 1995. The EU's longstanding relationship with some of the poorest developing countries, first and foremost the African, Caribbean and Pacific (ACP) states, has had a lasting impact on the global trade regime, as has its decision in 2001 to

TABLE 1.2   *The EU's Major Trading Partners: Trade in Goods (2016)*

EU exports to ... (in per cent)		EU imports from ... (in per cent)	
1. United States	20.8	1. China	20.2
2. China	9.7	2. United States	14.5
3. Switzerland	8.2	3. Switzerland	7.1
4. Turkey	4.5	4. Russia	7.0
5. Russia	4.1	5. Turkey	3.9
6. Japan	3.3	6. Japan	3.9
7. Norway	2.8	7. Norway	3.7
8. United Arab Emirates	2.6	8. South Korea	2.4
9. South Korea	2.6	9. India	2.3
10. India	2.2	10. Vietnam	1.9
11. Canada	2.0	11. Brazil	1.7
12. Hong Kong	2.0	12. Canada	1.7
13. Mexico	1.9	13. Taiwan	1.5
14. Saudi Arabia	1.9	14. South Africa	1.3
15. Australia	1.9	15. Malaysia	1.3
16. Singapore	1.8	16. Thailand	1.2
17. Brazil	1.8	17. Mexico	1.2
18. South Africa	1.3	18. Singapore	1.1
19. Israel	1.2	19. Saudi Arabia	1.1
20. Morocco	1.2	20. Hong Kong	1.1

Source: Based on European Commission (2017b, p. 58).

grant duty- and quota-free access for all goods (except arms) coming from the least developed countries. The EU is a champion of the rules-based multilateral trading system, and it was a pace setter in the late 1990s for the WTO's first trade round. Only when it became evident that the Doha Round, launched in 2001, would not deliver the expected results in a reasonable period of time did the EU revert to engaging in an extensive and growing network of bilateral preferential trade agreements. To take another example, the EU's decision in 2013 to impose so-called anti-dumping measures against heavily subsidized and under-priced solar panels manufactured in China affected the structure of the world market for this good, and it shaped Europe's relationship with the new commercial powerhouse of the world, which had joined the WTO in 2001.

Furthermore, the significance of the EU's common commercial policy becomes eminently clear when considering how very recent developments in world politics have been crucially intertwined with questions of trade policy. For instance, since 2013, the EU had been engaged in bilateral trade and investment agreement negotiations with the United States. With the arrival in office of the new US Administration under President Trump in January 2017, however, these bilateral negotiations were put on ice. As a first act in trade policy, the US President withdrew the United States from the Trans-Pacific Partnership signed in 2016. The announcement that the United States may deviate from its free trade policy and support of the WTO poses serious challenges to EU trade policy.

In times of internal and external crises, open markets often come under (protectionist) pressure. The EU has in recent years been facing multidimensional challenges. First of all, the EU had to deal with economic and financial challenges as a result of the banking and ensuing sovereign debt and eurozone crises that hit Europe since 2008. Second, the EU faced a governance crisis in the wake of what was often referred to as a 'refugee or migration crisis' during 2014–2015, when hundreds of thousands of asylum seekers from Syria and other conflict countries as well as irregular migrants arrived in the EU and at its borders. Third, protests against deep and comprehensive free trade agreements and a wave of right-wing populism and increased Euroscepticism have been on the rise in many EU member states, undermining European solidarity and common policies. A major fracture in this regard was the decision by referendum in June 2016 that the United Kingdom, one of the largest and most important EU member states with regard to international trade, would leave the EU. 'Brexit' means that the United Kingdom will forsake its free access to the European internal market and will become subject to some of the restrictions that many other countries face when they want to trade with the EU. After agreeing on the terms of withdrawal, the United Kingdom and the EU will have to negotiate a new trade relationship, and the EU's relative position in the world economy will weaken.

Questions of trade policymaking are of course embedded in the broader framework of the EU's external policies in the field of development, environmental cooperation, security and human rights, to name but some of the most important ones. In contrast to EU trade policy, though, these policy fields are governed by another set of decision-making rules. Nevertheless, the scope of what is commonly called 'trade policy' or 'commercial policy' has gradually been widened to cover a vast array of policy measures on regulatory affairs. This gradual expansion of the remit of trade policy was primarily driven by the requirement to start coordinating standards such as those on public health or environment, the standardization of customs valuation methods, the gradual integration of trade in services into international economic agreements, the growing importance of intellectual property rules, rules of origin or public procurement, attempts to limit ruinous subsidy races and many more regulatory matters. Since the 1980s, these issues have taken centre stage in the multilateral negotiations taking place within the framework of the General Agreement on Tariffs and Trade (GATT)/WTO.

The founding members of the EEC were also early contracting parties to the 1947 GATT, and soon after the completion of the customs union, the EEC de facto acquired member status (see Box 1.1 and Chapter 5). The 1994 WTO Agreement (Art. XI) stipulates that all contracting parties to GATT and the European Communities become founding members of the WTO. EU membership of the WTO is possible because any customs territory having full autonomy in the conduct of its trade policies can join the organization. In a nutshell, the WTO is an international organization operating a system of trade rules guaranteeing the stability and predictability of tariff levels granted on a non-discriminatory basis, a forum for negotiating further trade liberalization agreements and an institution to settle trade disputes at the global level.

The gradual expansion of international cooperation in the area of trade and the negotiation of new regulatory agreements on trade-related topics constituted one of the major developments to which the EU contributed and to which EU trade policy had to adapt over time. While being an important member of the WTO, the EU in parallel has been engaging in the conclusion of bilateral and/or regional trade agreements, in turn creating new challenges to EU trade policy (see Chapter 7).

This book deliberately refrains from the formulation of broad sweeping statements of what the EU *should* do, nor does it engage in the formulation of bold predictions of how the EU is likely to act *in the future*. Rather, this book intends to explain how the institutions and

Box 1.1 Global multilateral trade regime: GATT/WTO

Next to the creation of the World Bank for Reconstruction and Development and the International Monetary Fund for international monetary cooperation, the United States of America and the United Kingdom rallied countries around their initiative to create a third international institution for trade. Over 50 countries participated in negotiations to create an International Trade Organization (ITO) as a specialized agency of the United Nations. An ambitious ITO Charter was agreed in 1948, but ratification proved impossible in some national legislatures, especially in the US Congress. However, the GATT, signed in 1947, was already provisionally applied. This agreement then provided the rules for much of world trade for almost 50 years, and member states used the GATT forum to reduce tariffs step by step in most economic sectors, in a series of multilateral negotiations known as 'trade rounds'. The economic recessions in the 1970s drove many governments to devise other forms of protection for sensitive sectors. By the end of the Cold War, tariff liberalization in international trade in goods had become very substantial, yet new forms of non-tariff barriers – large-scale negotiated exceptions for developing countries and for some economic sectors, notably textiles and agriculture – had come to characterize the global trade regime. On the other hand, trade in services and international investment had expanded with the globalization of the world economy. These developments contributed to member states' willingness to reinforce the multilateral trading system. The GATT Uruguay Round, which lasted from 1986 to 1994, led to the creation of the WTO. Whereas GATT had dealt with trade only in goods, the WTO agreements also covered trade in services, trade-related intellectual property rights and investment measures. Moreover, the organization acquired more clout through the reinforcement of its dispute settlement procedures.

Source: Based on WTO website.

decision-making processes are organized and how this setup fosters particular policy outcomes at the detriment of others. On the broadest level, perhaps the most important characteristic of European trade policymaking is that it is governed by super-majorities. All key decisions, as well as non-decisions, come about only when there is qualified majority or even consensus support from the 28 (soon 27) governments of the EU member states, an absolute majority in the European Parliament and often also the approval of national parliaments. The consensual or super-majoritarian nature of EU decision-making, and of trade policy-making in particular, often bewilders observers alleging that it is elitist, bureaucratic, protectionist, insufficiently transparent or too neoliberal. However, this book contends that none of these allegations really do justice to EU trade policymaking, since consensual political systems are in the first place characterized by a great deal of stability, making them prone to conservatism and the continuation of policies that were in place before. Consensual political systems generate their policy effects in a structural fashion, reproducing certain policy practices over a long period of time and allowing for gradual changes only when these gain support from a wide variety of actors.

Given that trade policy touches on many legal, economic and political questions, this textbook takes a rather pluridisciplinary approach. In the study of EU trade policy, lawyers tend to focus on the competence allocation between the EU and its member states; economists on the economic benefits of trade and their distribution; political scientists on the competition of interest groups and their access to policymakers; and international relations specialists on the role of the EU as a global player. Each of these perspectives makes a contribution to understanding EU trade policy.

Beyond the distribution of legal competences, which will be set out in Chapter 2, many other factors have an impact on the contents of EU trade policy. Economic and societal stakeholders, developments in other policy fields, trade policies of non-EU states and international political developments all play a role in shaping decisions.

Shaping the contents of EU trade policy

This section deals briefly and in a cursory manner with some major elements that influence the contents of the common commercial policy. Each of them will be elaborated in greater detail in the subsequent chapters.

Aggregating preferences

In pluralist societies the preferences of the negotiator usually reflect the aggregation of different domestic constituencies mediated through domestic and European institutions (see Chapter 4). For the conclusion of trade agreements and the adoption of unilateral measures, the decision-making processes set the arena for the various actors to influence the policy outcome. In other words, the institutional framework has an impact on the EU's role in international trade negotiations (see Chapter 3). Sectoral interests and other actors lobby the decision-makers on the national and European levels at different stages of the policy process.

Trade policy usually generates diffuse costs and benefits for the general public in their role as consumers, but it generates concentrated costs and benefits for exporters or import-competing producers. While exporting sectors seek better access to foreign markets, nowadays often seconded by import-dependent industries, import-competing sectors prefer protection from foreign competition. Such constituencies usually have clear incentives to engage in lobbying activities, whereas diffuse interests (e.g. environmental, consumer, human rights or development non-governmental organizations) find it more difficult to mobilize autonomously due to problems such as lack of resources and free riding. Free riders enjoy the benefits of collective-action efforts without contributing to their provision. One consequence of this constellation of interests is that political actors tend to implement policies that are more in line with producer interests (Dür and De Bièvre, 2007, p. 82). This bias in favour of concentrated interests benefits both exporters as well as producers that compete with imports from outside the Union. The delegation of trade competence from the member states to the European level does not necessarily lead to the insulation of policy makers from societal interests, be they protectionist or liberal (De Bièvre and Dür, 2005).

Whether economic interests can be usefully conceived of as the principal drivers of trade policy is subject to some controversy. It is often said that political motivations may play a prominent role as well. Many observers assign a large degree of autonomy to EU institutions in determining trade policy (see Chapter 4). Hence, in addition to lobbying, institutional interests have to be taken into account. The European Parliament and/or the Council are commonly said to show more protection-oriented tendencies and to link commercial relations to non-trade concerns, such as environmental issues or human rights. By contrast, the European Commission is generally viewed as a more liberal, free-trade-oriented actor. Yet the Commission's position is often shaped by diverging views among different organizational units, in line with their functional remits: the Directorate-General (DG) International Cooperation and Development may take a more development-friendly stance than DG Trade, and DG Agriculture may be more protectionist than DG Trade. Within DG Trade, the Directorate of Trade Defence takes protection-oriented interests into account more than DG Trade does, overall.

The Treaty of Lisbon added new institutional players in the field of external action in the guise of the double-hatted High Representative and Vice-President of the Commission, assisted by the newly created European External Action Service (EEAS) and the permanent President of the European Council. The Commission has often viewed the Court of Justice of the EU (CJEU) as an ally in favour of consolidating – or, in the view of some, expanding – EU competences, but to the Commission's surprise, the Court has also sided with the Council, as the Court's opinions during the 1990s show (see Chapter 2). Finally, the European Parliament was formally excluded from the conclusion of trade agreements before entry into force of the Lisbon Treaty in 2009, even though practice since 1973 has been that the Commission regularly informs it about ongoing trade negotiations.

From the Community's inception, a simplifying distinction has often been made between a group of liberal Northern member states, allegedly led by Germany and the Netherlands, and a more protectionist Southern group, led by France and Italy, which was above all concerned about maintaining protection for agriculture and textiles (Johnson and Rollo, 2001). This balance shifted with each enlargement round. The so-called free traders were joined by the United Kingdom, Ireland, the Nordic member states and Austria, and the Southern group welcomed Greece, Spain and Portugal. Eastern enlargement, by contrast, may have been a more even package, although with a slight protectionist turn (Elsig, 2010). However, individual member states do not always live up to these labels, and coalitions in the Council tend to change from issue to issue, often due to whether or not the particular sector at stake has large production, employment and investment in a particular member state. Also, it remains to be seen what the United Kingdom's withdrawal from the EU, foreseen for 2019, will imply for the EU's trade policy in this regard. The United Kingdom having become far more of an economy dominated by (especially financial) services than industrial manufacturing will certainly play a role in that process.

Overall, the EU's trade stance is generally liberal, with a few glaring exceptions, such as the Common Agricultural Policy (CAP) or the use of anti-dumping measures, especially against Asian countries. Despite the rapidly changing international trade agenda, the member states remained reluctant to cede broader competence to the EU for a long time. The legal provisions of the common commercial policy have been tackled by the Treaty reforms only since the late 1990s (see Chapter 2). The new trade issues extended 'behind the borders' into the realm of domestic regulation and are thus generally regarded as more politically sensitive than the traditional 'at the border' issues, even though the latter have continued to generate controversy in the sectors of agriculture or textiles and clothing. Some governments did not always fully trust the Commission to represent their interests. During the Uruguay Round negotiations, for instance, the French conservative government claimed that the Commission had gone too far in the 1992 'Blair House Agreement' while a socialist French government had been in place. In this agreement, the EU and the United States settled most of their differences on agriculture. The Italian and Portuguese governments objected to the Commission's Uruguay Round deal on the phase-out of quotas in textiles and clothing. There have been similar allegations of 'defection' by the Commission voiced by national governments, especially during the negotiation of the more recent bilateral trade agreements with major industrialized countries such as South Korea, Canada and the United States.

A telling example from an intergovernmental conference with regard to 'behind the borders' measures is France's insistence during the Nice negotiations in 2000 that there should be an exception for trade in cultural and audio-visual services. Cross-border services are often closely linked to the free movement of persons, the right of establishment or the liberalization of capital movement. Due to the heterogeneity of services and their regulation, liberalizing trade in services is more complex and difficult than liberalizing trade in goods. Efforts to achieve further integration of the services market within the Community itself began only in the mid 1980s. Since the mid 1990s, the scope of the common commercial policy with regard to trade in services developed rapidly.

Next to lobbying groups and internal institutional dynamics, the direction of EU trade policy is also shaped by external aspects, such as the demands from the EU's trading partners and structural pressures emanating from the international level.

International developments

Since the founding of the EEC in 1958, the nature of international trade has changed dramatically. As long as the main form of economic interaction between countries was trade in goods, international negotiations focused on tariffs and quantitative restrictions. The Commission's role as negotiator on behalf of the Community had already developed with the GATT Dillon and Kennedy Rounds in the 1960s. In reaction to the threat of discriminatory effects resulting from the creation of the EEC, the United States had adamantly called for multilateral trade negotiations in the GATT (Dür, 2010, pp. 101–130). American exporters indeed feared that the internal liberalization of trade among the six founding members of the EEC would jeopardize their market share in exports to Germany, Italy, France and the Benelux countries. In effect, they feared their exports would be replaced and diverted by the trade creation within the EEC (see Chapter 4). Simultaneously, President de Gaulle exploited Germany's support for industrial tariff liberalization to secure a Common Agricultural Policy in favour of French farm policy by linking his approval for GATT negotiations to the German approval of the CAP (Moravcsik, 1998, pp. 159–237). Once all agricultural producers in EEC member states started to benefit from the CAP, member states that initially had been lukewarm regarding its creation supported the policy, despite its downsides (Scharpf, 1988). With the rise of non-tariff barriers to trade, cross-border services and FDI, as well as the growing importance of intellectual property rights, the international trade agenda changed considerably. One outcome of the Kennedy Round was the GATT Anti-Dumping Code adopted in 1967. The EEC, in turn, formalized its anti-dumping policy in its first anti-dumping regulation following year.

Many trade agreements were initiated at the demand of third countries, for instance neighbouring countries in search of secure access to the European market or potentially even EU membership. The EU's internal market, which grew with each enlargement round, represents considerable purchasing power. It thus constitutes an attractive export market for companies from third countries, holds a significant potential for trade diversion in case of exclusion and generates sizeable bargaining leverage for the EU. Various economic and political reasons may explain the EU's motivation to initiate, or to reacts to requests for, trade agreements (see Chapter 7).

The EU also responds in the name of all member states to cases brought to the attention of the WTO's Dispute Settlement Body (see Chapter 5). For example, the (in)famous 'bananas cases' have since 1993 opposed the EU and the United States – neither of which have significant banana industries – along with some Latin American countries in a series of disputes in the GATT/WTO, where the EU's failure to adequately implement the rulings in this multi-layered conflict fuelled retaliation and new legal challenges (see Chapter 6).

The EU also needs to react to external political events. When the United Nations impose economic or financial sanctions on a trading partner, the EU and its member states are to implement the binding resolutions of the Security Council (e.g. the trade sanctions against Iraq after its invasion of Kuwait in 1990 or the arms embargo against Sudan in 2005). The EU sanctioning practice follows at least three different logics: coercing, constraining and signalling (Giumelli, 2010). Sanctions seek to change the behaviour of targets, limit their capabilities and prevent them from taking certain actions, or they express the EU's disapproval without necessarily imposing direct material costs. The EU may adopt its own restrictive measures in reaction to violations of international law, human rights or democratic principles (see Chapter 7). It has, for instance, done so since March 2014 in response to Russia's annexation of Crimea and deliberate destabilization of Ukraine.

Another significant international development was the introduction of the Generalized System of Preferences (GSP) in 1971, in line with a recommendation by the United Nations Conference on Trade and Development in the context of the North–South debate. In a nutshell, the GSP system grants preferences to developing countries that are not accorded to developed countries, so as to facilitate exports for them and try and contribute to their more rapid economic development. Three decades later, the EU's 'Everything-But-Arms initiative', which grants duty- and quota-free access to imports of all products from least developed countries, except arms and ammunitions, developed in the context of the UN Millennium Development Goals and the launch of the WTO Doha Development Round in 2001. This initiative was then incorporated into the GSP (see Chapter 6).

Complying with other EU policies

Trade liberalization raises questions as to its relationship with other Union policies and the compatibility of their respective goals. Trade policy in particular may be connected to agricultural, competition, public health, development, environmental and foreign policies, and the objectives of these policies may also have an impact on trade liberalization. The interaction of these policies has increasingly gained in importance, and the boundaries between many policy areas become increasingly blurred (see Chapters 6 and 7). The EU Global Strategy calls upon the EU to become more joined up across external policies, between internal and external policies and between EU institutions and member states (European External Action Service, 2016).

On the one hand, the requirements of freer trade are not always easily reconciled with the requests for guarding non-trade concerns. Since there often is no clear line between the legitimate safeguarding of such values and interests and the protection of the domestic market against foreign competition, it befalls to political decisions to draw such lines. For example, the EU justifies its ban on imported beef produced from cattle treated with growth hormones with the need to protect consumers; yet clearly, European cattle farmers that do not use hormones benefit from protection against US competition on the EU beef market.

On the other hand, other policies may trump commercial considerations for political reasons. For example, human rights concerns may prevent the conclusion or lead to the suspension of a trade agreement, or a trade agreement may be sought with an economically negligible but strategically important country. Economic sanctions may serve to exercise pressure on countries for political or security reasons, such as in the case of South Africa's apartheid regime from 1985 to 1994 or the arms embargo against China since the 1989 massacre in Tiananmen Square. The restrictive measures thus connect the common commercial policy with the Common Foreign and Security Policy and with member states' national competences.

Complying with other EU policies has increasingly become a challenge for the common commercial policy, as indeed for the EU's external relations in general. This challenge was taken up by the Lisbon Treaty by explicitly enshrining the aim to ensure consistency between all areas of the EU's external actions and between these and its other policies in several Treaty articles.

All these internal and external factors shaping the common commercial policy will be addressed in the following chapters of this book.

Outline of the chapters

This book aims to shed light on the way in which EU trade policymaking is organized in order to provide the reader with the tools to make assessments of the EU's capacity to cope with these challenges. Chapter 2 sketches the legal development of the EU's common commercial policy over time. Agreeing on the scope of this policy while the global trade agenda has undergone significant changes has been one of the challenges for the member states. Tracing the major steps of this process, which has involved interpretations of the CJEU as well as Treaty amendments, is important in order to understand how and why the EU arrived at the current situation. Based on this historical analysis, Chapter 3 identifies the main actors and decision-making processes for the different trade policy instruments in order to explain who makes trade policy when the EU negotiates trade agreements; when it implements the common commercial policy; or when it applies unilateral trade policy measures, such as anti-dumping, or pursues complaints at the WTO.

Chapter 4 reviews major theoretical perspectives on the political economy of trade policymaking that help explain EU trade policy. The factors shaping trade policy can be located mainly on the levels of the international system, the society and the state. Each approach stresses different explanatory factors. The chapter also presents analytical tools which take into account the interaction between the levels of analysis when analysing the negotiation dynamics in EU trade policy.

Chapter 5 deals with the role of the EU within the WTO as one of its most prominent members when it comes to both the negotiation of trade rules as well as participation in the dispute settlement mechanism. Chapter 6 explores the relationship between the common commercial policy and European development policy. The EU's trade with developing countries has long been dominated by the historical 'bloc-to-bloc' relationship with the group of African, Caribbean and Pacific countries and by the unilateral GSP. This has changed with the global power shifts in the past two decades, but the trade-development nexus is arguably still the most important nexus between two external policies. Chapter 7 discusses some of the main challenges that EU trade policy currently faces: how the EU re-orientated its trade policy in recent years in terms of partners, deeper and more comprehensive free trade agreements, and the interconnection between trade and other external or internal EU policies, as well as the new institutional and political challenges that resulted from these changes. Finally, Chapter 8 concludes by outlining important future prospects of EU trade policy.

Further reading

Buonanno, L. and N. Nugent (2013) *Policies and Policy Processes of the European Union* (Basingstoke: Palgrave Macmillan), 251–272.

Woolcock, S. (2012) *European Union Economic Diplomacy: The Role of the EU in External Economic Relations* (Farnham: Ashgate).

Chapter 2

The Legal Development of the Common Commercial Policy

The common commercial policy has played an important part in the process of European integration, and today trade policy is crucial for the role of the European Union (EU) as a global actor. How did EU trade policy develop over time, and which factors have shaped it? This chapter provides an overview of the main steps in the legal development of the common commercial policy. It starts out with the origins and goals of EU trade policy and then analyses the expansion of legal competences through the interpretations of the Court of Justice of the EU (CJEU) as well as Treaty amendments. Agreeing on its scope has always been one of the challenges for the member states in developing the common commercial policy. Tracing the landmarks of this process is important in order to understand how and why the EU arrived at the current situation.

Creating a customs union: the need for a common commercial policy

This section introduces the roots and objectives of the common commercial policy.

The origins

In 1951, six West European countries (France, West Germany, Italy and the Benelux countries) signed the Paris Treaty, establishing the European Coal and Steel Community (ECSC), creating a customs union for coal, iron and steel for 50 years. This same group of countries established the European Economic Community (EEC) in 1957 (see De Bièvre and Poletti, 2013). The Rome Treaty very much followed the blueprint of the ECSC – a supranational Community based on a customs union, but this time for all goods and without an expiry date. The creation of a customs union required the removal of tariffs among the member states, the harmonization of external tariffs and a common commercial policy for negotiations with third parties.

From the very beginning, the common conduct of trade relations with third countries distinguished the ECSC and EEC customs unions from a simple free trade area (see Table 2.1). A customs union ensures legal certainty, strengthens bargaining power in international trade negotiations and avoids distortions of competition that would result from different national trade policies within a market with free movement of goods. The decision of the founding members to set up a customs union, with the further aim of building a common market, is at the origin of the common commercial policy. In other words, common external tariffs also imply a common trade policy vis-à-vis third parties, and trade was one of the first policy areas where member states granted the EEC exclusive competence. In areas of exclusive competence, the Community is able to adopt legally binding acts alone, while the member states may intervene only if it empowers them to do so. Member states cannot adopt any trade policy measure, like raising or lowering a tariff unilaterally, except in circumstances explicitly approved by the EEC decision-making procedures (see below). In addition to the principle of uniformity, aiming at a uniform regime for imports and exports, the principle of assimilation

TABLE 2.1 *Stages of Regional Economic Integration*

Preferential trade agreement	Member countries grant preferential market access (lower trade barriers) for certain products
Free trade area	Member countries agree to eliminate substantially all tariffs and quotas on imports from area members
Customs union	Free trade area & member countries set up a common external trade policy
Common (or internal) market	Customs union & free movement of capital, labour and services between the member countries
Economic [and monetary] union	Common market & harmonization of national economic policies (i.e. coordinated policies) [and a common currency]
Total economic integration	Economic [and monetary] union & unification of economic policies (i.e. single policies)

Source: Adapted from Balassa (1961).

implies that once goods have been imported into the Union, they fully benefit from the internal market (Eeckhout, 2011, pp. 440–446).

Although the stages in Table 2.1 present a sequence of increasing ambition in regional economic integration, this does not mean that member countries have to follow these steps in all cases or that other forms of regional economic integration are not possible. For example, the creation of a customs union was a primary objective of the EEC, thus skipping the step of a free trade area, while the European Free Trade Association (EFTA) founded in 1960 never aimed at more than a free trade area. Since in a free trade area products from third countries are still subject to (disparate) national trade policies, administrative controls such as certificates of origin can make sure that trade is not deflected via a low-tariff member into the market of a high-tariff member. For the politically more ambitious EEC, the customs union and common market were seen as a primary means to achieve the Treaty's economic aims, such as the harmonious development of economic activities or the raising of the standard of living. The European Economic Area (EEA) between the EU and some EFTA countries is an enhanced free trade area with free movement of goods, services, capital and persons.

In general, the transition to a customs union entails effects of trade creation, trade diversion and trade expansion. Trade creation results, on the supply side, from the replacement of the more expensive domestic production by the cheaper imports from the partner countries. Trade diversion results from the replacement of imports from lower-cost producers outside the customs union by relatively more expensive imports from less-efficient partner countries. Trade expansion can – as the demand side of trade creation – occur when, due to the removal of tariff barriers, prices in the customs union are lowered, leading to an increase in demand that is met by increased trade within the trade bloc or even beyond. Box 2.1 illustrates these effects with a simple three-country model: the creation of a customs union leads to the elimination of tariff t for member M (price P^M + t lies above P^N + t), while tariff t remains for non-member N. The goods previously imported from the lower-cost producer N (in quantity $Q^1 - Q^2$) will now be replaced by the cheaper imports from partner country M (in quantity $Q^3 - Q^4$). In addition to these static effects, integration will result in – usually more important – dynamic benefits resulting inter alia from increased competition, economies of scale, a stimulus to investment and the better use of economic resources. The overall welfare effect of a customs union or free trade area depends on whether its implications are mainly trade creating or trade diverting.

Box 2.1   Trade effects: trade creation, diversion and expansion

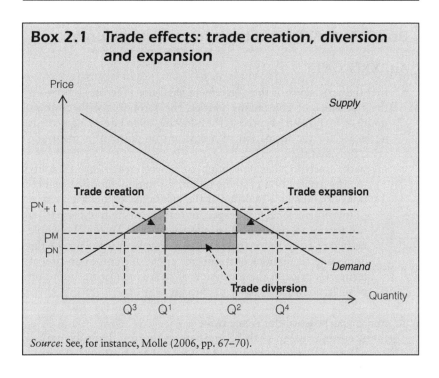

Source: See, for instance, Molle (2006, pp. 67–70).

The General Agreement on Tariffs and Trade (GATT) of 1947, incorporated as the so-called GATT 1994 in the bundle of treaties under the World Trade Organization (WTO), stipulates that a customs union should have a common external tariff and not erect higher trade barriers vis-à-vis non-members (Art. XXIV GATT, see Box 2.2). This provision aimed at preventing a customs union or free trade area from hindering multilateral trade liberalization. It prohibits the formation of a 'fortress' and encourages liberalization not just within a customs union but also beyond. In order to be GATT compatible, the EEC Treaty (Art. 9:1 which today corresponds to Art. 28:1 Treaty on the Functioning of the European Union, TFEU) provided that

[t]he Community shall be based upon a customs union covering the exchange of all goods and comprising both the prohibition, as between Member States, of customs duties on importation and exportation and all charges with equivalent effect and the adoption of a common customs tariff in their relations with third countries.

Box 2.2   GATT conditions for a customs union

Art. XXIV GATT

5. [...] the provisions of this Agreement shall not prevent, as between
the territories of contracting parties, the formation of a customs
union or of a free-trade area or the adoption of an interim agreement
necessary for the formation of a customs union or of a free-trade
area; *Provided* that:
   (a) with respect to a customs union, or an interim agreement leading
   to a formation of a customs union, the duties and other regulations of commerce imposed at the institution of any such union
   or interim agreement in respect of trade with contracting parties
   not parties to such union or agreement shall not on the whole
   be higher or more restrictive than the general incidence of the
   duties and regulations of commerce applicable in the constituent
   territories prior to the formation of such union or the adoption
   of such interim agreement, as the case may be; [...]

8. For the purposes of this Agreement:
   (a) A customs union shall be understood to mean the substitution
   of a single customs territory for two or more customs territories,
   so that
      (i) duties and other restrictive regulations of commerce [...] are
      eliminated with respect to substantially all the trade between
      the constituent territories of the union or at least with respect
      to substantially all the trade in products originating in such
      territories, and,
      (ii) [...] substantially the same duties and other regulations of
      commerce are applied by each of the members of the union
      to the trade of territories not included in the union;

Source: GATT (1947).

According to the Rome Treaty, the removal of intra-Community tariffs among the then six member countries and the setting of common
external tariffs was expected to take 12 years. The customs union was
completed by 1 July 1968, two years ahead of schedule. It included an
agreement on the establishment of a Common Agricultural Policy (CAP),

as required by the Treaty. The founding members of the EEC still had a large part of their workforce in the agricultural sector, whose income member states endeavoured to protect and further while also aiming at a largely self-sufficient food supply. The CAP was based on a single agricultural market, implying common prices for products, on Community preference and on financial solidarity among the member states, sharing the revenues and intervention costs (Ackrill, 2000, pp. 20–42). The Community preference meant that high trade barriers around the single market made imports more expensive and thus favoured the consumption of goods produced within the customs union.

At the same time, the development of a truly uniform trade policy faced certain challenges, as member states retained a long list of import restrictions and non-tariff barriers to trade (NTBs). The international economic climate in the 1970s and 1980s, which witnessed two oil crises with subsequent recessions and the emergence of new competitors, such as Japan, helped keep national protection measures alive. The GATT Tokyo Round went beyond tariff concessions by concluding new Codes of Conduct to tackle NTBs and revising the Anti-Dumping Code. Some of these agreements were signed as so-called mixed agreements by both the Community and the member states (Bourgeois, 1982, pp. 21–22).

Full uniformity of import conditions was only achieved with the completion of the internal market in 1993. Art. 115 of the Rome Treaty had still allowed individual member states to apply for an exemption from the common external tariff and to restrict, upon authorization by the Commission, imports of certain non-regulated goods from third countries that otherwise should be circulating freely within the customs union. Member states used this procedure to enforce national quotas and protect their car, textile and consumer electronics industries from being 'inundated' by goods deflected from another member state (Schuknecht, 1992, pp. 73–97). Since the implementation of the Single European Act (SEA), national measures are only possible on non-economic grounds, such as public health or security.

Goals of EU trade policy stipulated in the Treaty

The Treaty of Rome provided only an ad hoc definition of trade and did not specify the issues covered by the common commercial policy. It only enumerated some trade policy instruments in an illustrative, non-exhaustive list. Art. 113:1 EEC Treaty stipulated that after the expiry of the transitional period, the common commercial policy shall be based on uniform principles, particularly in regard to changes in tariff rates, the conclusion of tariff and trade agreements, the achievement of uniformity in measures of liberalisation, export policy and measures to protect trade such as those to be taken in case of dumping or subsidies.

This provision left the exact scope of the common commercial policy open for interpretation. From a narrow perspective, liberalization obligations were provided for goods but not for the more complex services, an economic sector that was not even considered to be 'trade' in the 1950s. The opposite, extensive reading was that the article could cover the entire external dimension of internal market integration, including trade in services. As member states had pragmatically delegated negotiation authority to the European Commission beyond a strict reading of the provisions of Art. 113:1, an opinion of the Court of Justice settled the question in between these two positions (see *Opinion 1/94* below).

Despite its vagueness, or perhaps because of its pragmatic generality, the above definition remained unchanged for 40 years, until the entry into force of the Lisbon Treaty in 2009. Art. 207:1 TFEU now specifies that

> [t]he common commercial policy shall be based on uniform principles, particularly with regard to changes in tariff rates, the conclusion of tariff and trade agreements *relating to trade in goods and services, and the commercial aspects of intellectual property, foreign direct investment*, the achievement of uniformity in measures of liberalisation, export policy and measures to protect trade such as those to be taken in the event of dumping or subsidies. *The common commercial policy shall be conducted in the context of the principles and objectives of the Union's external action.*

In general, EU trade policy has been characterized by a liberal aspiration. The provision of this goal stayed the same throughout the years (ex-Art. 131 of the Treaty establishing the European Community, TEC, respectively 110 EEC Treaty), except that the Lisbon Treaty in Art. 206 TFEU added foreign direct investment (FDI):

> the Union shall contribute, in the common interest, to the harmonious development of world trade, the progressive abolition of restrictions

on international trade *and on foreign direct investment*, and the lowering of customs and other barriers.

At the same time, the Lisbon Treaty for the first time placed the common commercial policy under the part on the Union's external action to which the general provisions of Art. 21 of the Treaty on European Union (TEU) apply (see Box 2.3). EU trade policy – as well as EU development

---

Box 2.3   Objectives of EU external action (including trade policy)

Art. 21 TEU (Lisbon)

2. The Union shall define and pursue common policies and actions, and shall work for a high degree of cooperation in all fields of international relations, in order to:
    (a) safeguard its values, fundamental interests, security, independence and integrity;
    (b) consolidate and support democracy, the rule of law, human rights and the principles of international law;
    (c) preserve peace, prevent conflicts and strengthen international security, in accordance with the purposes and principles of the United Nations Charter, with the principles of the Helsinki Final Act and with the aims of the Charter of Paris, including those relating to external borders;
    (d) foster the sustainable economic, social and environmental development of developing countries, with the primary aim of eradicating poverty;
    (e) encourage the integration of all countries into the world economy, including through the progressive abolition of restrictions on international trade;
    (f) help develop international measures to preserve and improve the quality of the environment and the sustainable management of global natural resources, in order to ensure sustainable development;
    (g) assist populations, countries and regions confronting natural or man-made disasters; and
    (h) promote an international system based on stronger multilateral cooperation and good global governance.

Source: TEU, Lisbon version.

cooperation – is now placed in the context of broader principles and objectives than simply the conduct of trade policy in a strict economic policy sense. According to the Treaty, the Union shall promote its values and interests in its relations with the wider world by contributing

> to peace, security, the sustainable development of the Earth, solidarity and mutual respect among peoples, free and fair trade, eradication of poverty and the protection of human rights, in particular the rights of the child, as well as to the strict observance and the development of international law, including respect for the principles of the United Nations Charter (Art. 3:5 TEU, see also Art. 21:1 TEU).

The EU shall thus combine economic interests and political values in its external action, yet the Treaty does not establish priorities among these objectives.

Although the 1992 Maastricht Treaty had already stipulated that the Union shall ensure the consistency of its external activities as a whole (ex-Art. 3 TEU), the Lisbon Treaty's new 'quasi-constitutional' framework for EU external action created a legal foundation for coordinating the common commercial policy with other external policies and for pursuing non-trade objectives through trade (Dimopoulos, 2010, p. 161).

From the outset, the European Community (EC) and later the EU have often concluded trade agreements for more than merely commercial purposes, especially with neighbouring and developing countries. Yet, in its 2006 'Global Europe' trade strategy (see Chapter 7), the Commission asserted that it aimed more overtly at reinforcing the EU's competitiveness by opening up new markets through free trade agreements (FTAs) with partners of significant market potential and levels of protection against EU exports (European Commission, 2006). These 'new generation' FTAs go beyond trade in goods and services and also cover issues such as investment, public procurement, competition or enforcement of intellectual property rights. These bilateral agreements thus also allow the EU to go beyond what has so far been achieved in the WTO.

With the expansion of the international trade agenda, both within the multilateral framework of the GATT/WTO and of the EU's bilateral trade relations, came also a legal debate on the exact scope of the common commercial policy, resulting in case law and Treaty amendments (see next section; Young, 2002). The legal competences (Community/ Union or member states) and the applicable decision-making procedures (qualified majority voting or unanimity) in trade policy have been part of the struggle between supranational and intergovernmental methods inherent in the process of European integration.

As the next section will show, the EU's competence to conclude international agreements may arise from express attribution in the Treaty or flow implicitly from Treaty provisions, confirmed by the jurisprudence of the Court of Justice.

Clarifying competences: the role of the Court of Justice

Through its rulings and opinions, the Court of Justice has played an important role in the clarification, sometimes the expansion, sometimes the restriction, of the Union's legal competences regarding trade. Especially in the early phases, the link between the common commercial policy and the building of the common market may help explain the Court's and the Commission's resolve to establish and expand exclusive EC competence.

1971 ERTA case: implied powers

The Treaty of Rome did not contain many provisions expressly referring to external action, although it established that the Community shall have legal personality. Legal personality means that the Community can negotiate, conclude and implement international agreements and that it has the right of legation and to present international claims as well as liability for the breach of international law. Besides the common commercial policy, there were provisions on the conclusion of association agreements and the maintenance of 'appropriate relations' with other international organizations. The question thus arose whether the Community's external powers were confined to these areas or whether the Treaty contained 'implied' external powers.

In 1970, the European Commission brought a case to the Court of Justice on the European Road Transport Agreement (ERTA). In its ensuing ruling, the Court of Justice developed the 'doctrine of implied powers' by stating that

> each time the Community, with a view to implementing a common policy envisaged by the Treaty, adopts provisions laying down common rules, whatever form these may take, the member states no longer have the right, acting individually or collectively, to undertake obligations with third countries which affect those rules. [...] With regard

to the implementation of the provisions of the Treaty the system of internal Community measures may not therefore be separated from that of external relations. (Case 22/70 *Commission v. Council* [1971] ECR 263).

This landmark ruling extended the external powers of the Community beyond those expressly established in the Treaty, allowing the EEC institutions to act externally in matters which they may regulate internally. Once Community rules for the attainment of Treaty objectives were adopted, the competence was exclusive and the member states could not enter international commitments which might affect or alter the scope of those internal rules. To some extent the ERTA doctrine thus established a parallelism between Community internal and external jurisdiction, a legal principle that is commonly referred to as *in foro interno, in foro externo*.

The subsequent Treaty amendments specified the scope of the areas where the Community is expressly competent to act externally. The Lisbon Treaty has codified the ERTA doctrine and introduced 'implied powers' as a general rule (Art. 3:2 and 216:1 TFEU). It also gave the EU an express legal personality (Art. 47 TEU). The single legal personality allows the EU to represent the member states in negotiations with third countries or international organizations in all areas where it can legislate internally. The Union may conclude international agreements where the Treaty so provides or where the conclusion of an agreement is necessary in order to achieve one of the objectives referred to in the Treaty or is provided for in a legally binding Union act or is likely to affect common rules or alter their scope.

The controversy over exclusive EC/EU competence versus member state competence in the field of trade has also led to several opinions of the Court of Justice on envisaged trade agreements. Three particularly relevant opinions – reaffirming, extending exclusivity and/or outlining some of its limits – are briefly set out below.

Opinion 1/75: exclusivity

In 1975, the Court of Justice delivered its first opinion on an international agreement, the 'Understanding on a Local Cost Standard', which was to be adopted within the Organization for Economic Co-operation and Development (OECD). Since there was no consensus in the Council on who was competent to conclude this OECD agreement, which regulated governments' export credits, the Commission asked the Court whether the Community had the power to do so.

The Court pointed out that the common commercial policy, which was being built gradually through the adoption of internal legislation and the conclusion of international agreements, was conceived 'in the context of the operation of the common market, for the defence of the common interests of the Community, within which the particular interests of the member states must endeavour to adapt to each other' and that the Treaty provisions on the conclusion of trade agreements 'show clearly that the exercise of concurrent powers by the Member States and the Community in this matter is impossible' (Opinion 1/75 *Understanding on a Local Cost Standard* [1975] ECR 1355).

The Court thus underlined the link between the unity of the common market and a uniform trade policy. Member states could not legislate in an area which would affect the operation of the common commercial policy – at the time meaning trade in goods – even if the Community had not yet taken any action. In the following years, however, the development of international trade led to the extension of trade policy far beyond the reduction of tariffs and quotas.

Opinion 1/94: joint competence

The scope of the common commercial policy faced a major challenge when the GATT Uruguay Round, which had been launched in 1986, came to an end. The negotiating agenda included new topics such as trade in services, trade-related intellectual property rights and investment measures. During the negotiations, a pragmatic arrangement had been in place with the Commission as the sole negotiator under close supervision of the Council. When the Uruguay Round agreements, which resulted in the establishment of the WTO, had to be signed and concluded in 1994, the Commission requested the Court's opinion, claiming that the EC had exclusive competence to sign the agreements. The Commission's standpoint was disputed by all member states except for Belgium, Luxembourg, Ireland and Italy.

The Court of Justice reaffirmed in *Opinion 1/94* the dynamic character of the common commercial policy but rejected the Commission's view that all areas negotiated in the Uruguay Round fell under the policy's scope or were covered by implied powers. It concluded that all WTO agreements on trade in goods (e.g. the Agreement on Agriculture, the Agreement on Sanitary and Phytosanitary Measures, the Agreement on

Technical Barriers to Trade) did indeed fall within exclusive Community competence. With regard to trade in services, however, the Court issued a partly negative opinion. WTO members had identified four modes of supply of services in the General Agreement on Trade in Services (GATS): cross-border trade, consumption abroad, commercial presence and presence of natural persons. The Court was of the opinion that the Community generally had external competence over cross-border services not involving the movement of (natural and legal) persons, while the member states retained competence over the other three modes of supplying services (see Box 2.4). The treatment of nationals of non-member countries on crossing the external borders of member states could not be regarded as falling within the common commercial policy, as the EC Treaty dealt with such movement in different chapters.

Transport services were considered separately, as the EC Treaty contained a specific chapter on the common transport policy. A common

---

Box 2.4   Opinion 1/94: trade in services

As regards cross-frontier supplies not involving any movement of persons, the service is rendered by a supplier established in one country to a consumer residing in another. The supplier does not move to the consumer's country; nor, conversely, does the consumer move to the supplier's country. That situation is, therefore, not unlike trade in goods, which is covered by the common commercial policy within the meaning of the Treaty. There is thus no particular reason why such a supply should not fall within the concept of the common commercial policy.

The same cannot be said of the other three modes of supply of services covered by GATS, namely:

- consumption abroad, which entails the movement of the consumer into the territory of the WTO member country in which the supplier is established;
- commercial presence, that is to say, the presence of a subsidiary or branch in the territory of the WTO member country in which the service is to be rendered;
- the presence of natural persons from a WTO member country, enabling a supplier from one member country to supply services within the territory of any other member country.

Source: Opinion 1/94 *WTO Agreement* [1994] ECR I-5267.

European transport policy was already proposed in the Treaty of Rome, but member states had initially been very unwilling to give up national control of the transport sector, which at the time was still almost entirely under state control. Only the SEA laid down a more concrete plan for an opening and integration of the internal market for road, rail, air and water transportation. The Court did not follow the Commission's argument that international transport agreements of a commercial nature (as opposed to those relating to safety rules) fell within the common commercial policy. Instead, it further developed its 'ERTA doctrine' by pointing out that even in the field of transport,

> the Community's exclusive external competence does not automatically flow from its power to lay down rules at internal level. The Member States, whether acting individually or collectively, only lose their right to assume obligations with non-member countries as and when common rules which could be affected by those obligations come into being. Only in so far as common rules have been established at internal level does the external competence of the Community become exclusive. (Opinion 1/94 *WTO Agreement* [1994] ECR I-5267)

Since not all transport matters are covered by common rules, the member states had not lost their competence to conclude international transport agreements.

With regard to intellectual property rights affecting trade, the Court also concluded that, apart from the provisions on the prohibition of circulating counterfeit goods, the Agreement on Trade-Related Intellectual Property Rights (TRIPs) did not fall within the scope of the common commercial policy. The main reasons were the insufficient link between intellectual property and trade in goods, as well as the fact that recognizing exclusive competence would make it possible to achieve further harmonization within the Community by circumventing the voting procedures and rules to which the institutions would normally be subject when seeking to harmonize intellectual property law.

As a result, the Community was competent to conclude alone the WTO agreements on trade in goods, while the Community and the member states were, as a result of shared competence, only together competent to conclude both the GATS and the TRIPs Agreement. Agreements that are concluded jointly by the Community/Union and the member states are referred to as mixed agreements.

Opinion 2/15: reaffirming exclusive competences

In addition to developments on the global trade agenda, the changes
brought about by the Lisbon Treaty recently triggered an important ruling. In 2014 the European Commission requested an opinion from the
CJEU on the EU–Singapore FTA in order to clarify the scope of the
new EU competences, in particular with regard to FDI. While the Commission argued that the EU had exclusive competence to conclude the
agreement, the Council and some member state governments contended
that certain parts might arguably not fall under exclusive but shared
competence, resulting in a mixed agreement: certain transport services
and types of investment, non-commercial aspects of intellectual property
rights, or labour and environmental standards.

In its *Opinion 2/15*, the Court in May 2017 issued a new landmark ruling for trade policy (Opinion 2/15 *Singapore Free Trade
Agreement*, not yet reported). The Court confirmed the Commission's
view that the EU enjoys exclusive competence regarding market access
for goods and services (including all transport services), public procurement and energy generation from sustainable non-fossil sources,
provisions concerning intellectual property rights, competition policy,
the protection of FDI, dispute settlement other than non-direct FDI
and sustainable development. The Court argued that the transport
services covered in the agreement could affect common rules in secondary EU legislation or alter their scope and thus fall under implied
exclusive external competence ('ERTA doctrine'). The purpose of the
references to moral (as opposed to commercial) intellectual property
rights was not their regulation but the realization of a level playing
field for trade. Moreover, the Court found that the social protection
of workers and environmental protection form an integral part of
the common commercial policy because of their 'direct and immediate effects on trade'. That is, the sustainable development provisions
were not a standalone competence, aiming to regulate the level of protection in the parties' respective territory, but rather governing their
trade in order to achieve the objectives of trade liberalization and the
coherence of EU external action. The Court's reasoning thus relied
on a criterion which it had developed in recent case law: 'a European
Union act falls within the Common Commercial Policy if it relates
specifically to international trade in that it is essentially intended
to promote, facilitate or govern trade and has direct and immediate
effects on trade' (Larik, 2015, p. 783).

However, the Court also declared that the agreement cannot be concluded by the EU alone because two kinds of provisions fall within the competences shared between the Union and the member states. The CJEU stated that the EU is not endowed with exclusive competence in the field of non-direct foreign investment (so-called portfolio investment, which does not aim to influence the management of an enterprise) and with regard to the regime governing dispute settlement between investors and states. Investment protection is covered by the exclusive competence of the common commercial policy insofar as it relates to FDI, while non-direct foreign investment – based on the implied powers doctrine – falls within shared competence. Also, the investor-to-state dispute settlement remains within shared competence because it would remove a dispute from the domestic courts of the member states if a claimant investor submits it to arbitration. The establishment of such a mechanism thus requires member states' consent.

As a result of this ruling, the EU–Singapore FTA, as well as other FTAs already concluded – like the Comprehensive Economic and Trade Agreement (CETA) with Canada – or under negotiations (such as with Japan) are to be considered mixed agreements and consequently have to be ratified by all EU member state parliaments. In Belgium, this even means regional parliaments as well because of the peculiar constitutional prerogatives of Belgian regions in the field of external trade. Hence, if an agreement does not cover portfolio investment and investor–state dispute settlement, the EU can conclude FTAs alone based on qualified majority voting (with a few exceptions) in the Council and a simple majority in the European Parliament, without risking jeopardizing the negotiated outcome by numerous additional national parliamentary ratification procedures. The CJEU rendered a broad interpretation of the EU's post-Lisbon trade competences, which facilitates deep and comprehensive FTAs in line with the global trade agenda. The EU could thus develop ambitious sustainable development chapters in trade agreements to respond to some of the concerns voiced, in particular by civil society. By contrast, the EU and its partners might be less inclined to include investment arbitration, an area that has been particularly controversial.

The Court was asked to rule only on the nature of the competence when it comes to investor–state dispute settlement and not on its compatibility with EU law. In the context of the CETA controversy, Belgium is seeking an opinion of the Court on the latter question – that is, whether the new International Court System violates the principle of equality in EU law, since foreign investors but not domestic investors have the right to table complaints, as well as on the question whether the system would not infringe on the monopoly of the CJEU to interpret EU law.

Many developments in the case law of the Court of Justice, such as *Opinion 1/94*, were later reflected in EU Treaty amendments.

Responding to challenges: Treaty reforms

At intergovernmental conferences leading to Treaty revisions, member states agreed on responding to internal or external challenges by adapting the legal provisions on the common commercial policy.

Single European Act and Maastricht Treaty: completing the internal market

After the completion of the customs union in 1968, the breakdown of the fixed-exchange-rate regime in 1971, the oil crises of 1973 and 1979, rising inflation and unemployment, as well as growing competition from overseas, such as from Japan and the United States, led to rising protectionist pressures. NTBs in the form of technical regulations and standards, sanitary and phytosanitary measures, burdensome customs procedures or quantitative restrictions mushroomed both inside and outside the Community, challenging its liberal objectives. The attention to NTBs can partly also be explained by the fact that, as GATT member states had reduced tariff levels in the Kennedy (1964–67) and Tokyo Rounds (1973–79), barriers to trade that had hitherto been hidden became more visible. Furthermore, national measures such as Art. 115 restrictions or bilaterally negotiated Voluntary Export Restraints (e.g. for car imports from Japan) persisted and collided with the requirement to conduct uniform policies.

In 1985, the Commission's 'White Paper on the Internal Market' identified 279 legislative measures needed to complete the internal market (European Commission, 1985). Two years later, the SEA entered into force, which set the end of 1992 as the target for completion. Among other things, this Treaty reform increased the areas in which the Council could take decisions by qualified majority voting instead of unanimity and thus facilitated the establishment of the internal market. The Commission also relied on the *Cassis de Dijon* judgement of 1979, in which the Court of Justice had ruled that any product lawfully produced and marketed in a member state was in principle entitled to free circulation within the Community (Case 120/78 *Rewe v. Bundesmonopolverwaltung für Branntwein* [1979] ECR 649). This principle of mutual recognition became a cornerstone of the internal market, which the Treaty defined as 'an area without internal frontiers in which the free movement of goods, services, persons and capital is ensured' (now Art. 26:2 TFEU).

The White Paper did not directly address the external dimension of the internal market. The Community's general attitude was inward-looking because European governments and business had to be convinced that the project could be realized. The main trading partners, especially the United States and the EFTA countries, placed the topic on the political agenda by voicing concerns over the effects that the completion of the internal market would have on them, arguably for fear of trade diversion. In the framework of the GATT Uruguay Round negotiations, the Commission promised that 'the Community will seek a greater liberalisation of international trade: the 1992 Europe will not be a fortress Europe but a partnership Europe' (European Commission, 1988, p. 1).

During the 1990–1991 intergovernmental conference leading to the Maastricht Treaty, the Commission advocated an upgrade of the common commercial policy into an external economic policy under the same heading as the new Common Foreign and Security Policy, including services, capital, intellectual property rights, investment, establishment and competition policy (Maresceau, 1993, pp. 6–11). However, no such Treaty reform was agreed by the member states at the time. Only many years later, with the Lisbon Treaty, did the common commercial policy become exclusive Union competence in a manner that comes closer to the external economic policy of states by encompassing all aspects of trade (in addition to development cooperation, monetary policy and other means by which a government advances and protects its economic interests in the world).

Nevertheless, the effort to complete the internal market by 1993 led to a more uniform common commercial policy, abolishing remaining national quotas for imports of certain products, such as textiles, bananas, steel or Japanese cars. Overall, the SEA marked the beginning of a more liberal and harmonized approach (Elsig, 2002, p. 30). Imported products entitled to free circulation within the internal market are assimilated to products originating in the member states. That is, the provisions for the liberalization of intra-EU trade apply in the same way to products from member states and from third countries (Art. 28 TFEU). Moreover, the internal market programme reinforced the Community's stance in the GATT where it supported – with some notable exceptions, like agriculture – liberalization in the new trade areas of services and intellectual property rights. The completion of the internal market also triggered a series of preferential EU agreements with third countries (see Chapter 7). The EU negotiated the EEA with the EFTA countries, Euro-Mediterranean association agreements with the Southern Mediterranean countries and a customs union agreement with Turkey, while the collapse of the 'Iron Curtain' was followed by the Europe Agreements with the Central and Eastern European countries and by Partnership and Cooperation Agreements (PCAs) with the republics of the Commonwealth of Independent States.

The Maastricht Treaty left the articles on the common commercial policy substantively unchanged. The need for reform resurfaced in 1994, when the Uruguay Round was to be concluded, and the subsequent Treaty revisions brought about gradual legal adaptations of the common commercial policy.

The Treaties of Amsterdam and Nice: patchwork adaptations

In its *Opinion 1/94*, the Court of Justice had effectively ruled that WTO matters were a joint competence of both the EU institutions and the member states, thus 'recognizing a political reality which had been clearly demonstrated during the Maastricht negotiations': the sensitivity of the member states with respect to the movement of persons (Cremona, 2000, p. 11). The free movement of persons, an area of shared competence, was intended to support the development of an EU labour market and is underpinned by the principle of protection against discrimination on the grounds of nationality with regard to employment, remuneration and other conditions of work. Immigration in general is a politically sensitive topic linked to many economic, social and cultural issues.

In the aftermath of the Court's opinion, the Commission and the member states engaged in negotiating a code of conduct for the exercise of the respective competences of the EC and the member states. These negotiations were overtaken by the intergovernmental conference drafting the Treaty of Amsterdam, which began in 1995. The Commission proposed to have the provisions on the common commercial policy modified so that they would cover all WTO matters. However, there was still no agreement among the member states when the Treaty was signed in 1997. The only amendment resulting from a compromise was a new paragraph, an 'enabling clause', added to Art. 133 TEC (ex-Art. 113), according to which

> [t]he Council, acting unanimously on a proposal from the Commission and after consulting the European Parliament, may extend the application of paragraphs 1 to 4 [on the procedures in trade policy] to international negotiations and agreements on services and intellectual property insofar as they are not covered by these paragraphs.

Although not mentioning the WTO, this addition was intended to cover WTO negotiations, but the article did not speak of *trade in* services or *commercial aspects of* intellectual property rights. The provision enabled the Council to extend the Community's competences without having to amend the Treaty, a process that would require an intergovernmental conference and ratification by all the member states. This enabling clause in the Amsterdam Treaty was never used, since the trade provisions became the subject of renegotiation again.

The Amsterdam Treaty, which entered into force in May 1999, failed to enact the institutional reforms deemed necessary in view of the EU's imminent Eastern enlargement and the risk of blocking decision-making processes in a larger and more heterogeneous Union. In addition, the Community still needed a stronger capacity to act on the international scene and particularly in the WTO. The discussion was also situated within the general debate on the extension of qualified majority voting.

Hence, a new intergovernmental conference had already been launched in 2000 to address some of the unresolved issues. The resulting Treaty of Nice was signed in February 2001 and entered into force two years later. The draft treaty presented to the Nice summit contained a Protocol on the participation of the Community and its member states in the WTO, aiming to improve their respective roles in areas of shared competence. However, this text was not included in the final version (Cremona, 2002b, pp. 65–68). The result of this Treaty reform was a more complex wording that replaced the paragraph cited above (see Box 2.5).

These new provisions came closer to the scope of the common commercial policy that the Court of Justice had defined with regard to the WTO agreements (see Box 2.4 above). Art. 133 TEC now entrusted the Community with the competence to negotiate and conclude agreements concerning all GATS modes of supply of services. However, the Nice Treaty also introduced a sectoral approach: Community competence

---

Box 2.5   Nice Treaty amendment of Art. 133 TEC

Art. 133 TEC (Nice)

5. Paragraphs 1 to 4 shall also apply to the negotiation and conclusion of agreements in the fields of trade in services and the commercial aspects of intellectual property, in so far as those agreements are not covered by the said paragraphs and without prejudice to paragraph 6.

    By way of derogation from paragraph 4, the Council shall act unanimously when negotiating and concluding an agreement in one of the fields referred to in the first subparagraph, where that agreement includes provisions for which unanimity is required for the adoption of internal rules or where it relates to a field in which the Community has not yet exercised the powers conferred upon it by this Treaty by adopting internal rules.

    The Council shall act unanimously with respect to the negotiation and conclusion of a horizontal agreement insofar as it also concerns the preceding subparagraph or the second subparagraph of paragraph 6.

    This paragraph shall not affect the right of the Member States to maintain and conclude agreements with third countries or international organisations in so far as such agreements comply with Community law and other relevant international agreements.

6. An agreement may not be concluded by the Council if it includes provisions which would go beyond the Community's internal powers,

---

was excluded for the politically sensitive areas of trade in cultural and audio-visual services, educational services and social and human health services. These areas required mixed agreements that were concluded jointly by the Community and the member states. The explicit reference to international agreements in paragraph 6 seemed to exclude the adoption of autonomous measures in these areas.

By introducing paragraphs 5 to 7, the Nice Treaty recognized that two hallmarks of the traditional common commercial policy – the principle of exclusivity and qualified majority voting – would not be extended to certain types of trade agreements. Moreover, a sentence added to Art. 133:3 underlined the principle of parallelism and helped dispel fears that the Community would negotiate in sensitive internal policy sectors ('The Council and the Commission shall be responsible for ensuring that the

→

in particular by leading to harmonisation of the laws or regulations of the Member States in an area for which this Treaty rules out such harmonisation.

In this regard, by way of derogation from the first subparagraph of paragraph 5, agreements relating to trade in cultural and audiovisual services, educational services, and social and human health services, shall fall within the shared competence of the Community and its Member States. Consequently, in addition to a Community decision taken in accordance with the relevant provisions of Article 300, the negotiation of such agreements shall require the common accord of the Member States. Agreements thus negotiated shall be concluded jointly by the Community and the Member States.

The negotiation and conclusion of international agreements in the field of transport shall continue to be governed by the provisions of Title V and Article 300.

7. Without prejudice to the first subparagraph of paragraph 6, the Council, acting unanimously on a proposal from the Commission and after consulting the European Parliament, may extend the application of paragraphs 1 to 4 to international negotiations and agreements on intellectual property in so far as they are not covered by paragraph 5.

Source: Treaty establishing the European Community, Nice version.

agreements negotiated are compatible with internal Community policies and rules.'). In most EU member states, cultural, audio-visual, educational, social and human health services are often in the hands of (semi-)public authorities. Many member states consider them part of the provision of public services (such as health, education, social security or cultural heritage) and support them by subsidies and other forms of protection. In the Uruguay Round, especially France had argued for a 'cultural exception' that would exclude culture-related services from WTO rules. While not providing for a clear exception, the GATS is a framework treaty that sets out how WTO members should proceed, if they wish to liberalize certain services, leaving the decision on how and to what extent to liberalize to each and every member, and thus leaving policy space to use, for instance, local content quotas for film, radio and television.

Transport services continued to fall under shared competence. Paragraph 7 contained a new 'enabling clause' that would allow the Council to broaden the scope to intellectual property agreements, which do not deal with the commercial aspects of intellectual property. Although the Commission proposed to include FDI in the scope of EU trade policy, this was not taken up in the Nice Treaty, despite the fact that the topic was on the WTO agenda at that time.

After decades of no substantial changes, the legal provisions on the common commercial policy thus evolved substantially towards an extension of exclusive competences to more areas of international trade within a few years. Yet at the same time, the EU and the member states kept sharing some competences. This patchwork changed with the Treaty of Lisbon, a treaty that resulted largely from the ill-fated Constitutional Treaty. The Treaty establishing a Constitution for Europe, which was for the first time elaborated in a convention instead of an intergovernmental conference and signed in 2004, remained unratified after the negative referenda in France and the Netherlands.

Lisbon Treaty: towards a common external economic policy

Against the background of EU enlargement and the ongoing WTO Doha Round, the Lisbon Treaty signed in 2007 kept the text of the 2004 Constitutional Treaty regarding trade largely intact. With the Treaty's entry into force in December 2009, the EU replaced and succeeded the EC. The WTO-related aspects of trade policy finally became explicitly an exclusive competence of the Union (Art. 3:1 TFEU), its scope was further clarified, and FDI was added to the common commercial policy. This means that there is no longer a need to conclude agreements encompassing these fields as mixed agreements. At the same time, the European Parliament acquired new powers in the implementation of trade policy and in the conclusion of international trade agreements (see Chapter 3). By contrast, transport remained a shared competence with separate Treaty provisions (Art. 90–100 TFEU).

Whereas the Council usually acts by qualified majority voting regarding the negotiation and conclusion of trade agreements, unanimity is required for agreements that include provisions for which unanimity applies internally and under certain conditions for trade in politically sensitive services: for trade in cultural and audio-visual services, where these agreements 'risk prejudicing the Union's cultural and linguistic diversity', and in the field of trade in social, education and health services, where these agreements 'risk seriously disturbing the national organisation of such services and prejudicing the responsibility of Member States to deliver them' (Art. 207:4 TFEU).

The Lisbon Treaty enables the EU to adopt autonomous measures with regard to all aspects of trade policy. It also codifies the case law on implied external powers (Art. 3:2 and 216:1 TFEU): the Union may conclude agreements where the Treaties so provide, where it is necessary in order to achieve a Treaty objective or to exercise its internal competence and where it is provided for in a legally binding Union act or is likely to affect common rules or alter their scope.

The Lisbon Treaty thus clarified the reach of the common commercial policy and to some extent further codified existing practice. The policy's scope now covers all current WTO matters (although the 'enabling clause' on intellectual property of ex-Art. 133:7 TEC was dropped). With the Lisbon Treaty, 'the Common Commercial Policy seems to be departing from its "traditional" trade core and is becoming the basic tool not only for serving the external needs of the internal market but also for building an [...] EU external economic policy' (Dimopoulos, 2008, p. 109).

The transfer of competences for FDI intended to strengthen the EU as an actor in bilateral or multilateral negotiations on investment policy. The Lisbon Treaty does not specify whether the new competence includes only investment liberalization (that is, market access) or also investment protection (e.g. safeguards against unlawful expropriation), nor whether it is restricted to (long-term) FDI as opposed to (short-term) portfolio investment (Bungenberg, 2010). *Opinion 2/15* of the CJEU clarified these questions (see above): investment protection falls within the common commercial policy insofar as it relates to FDI, but portfolio investment and investor-to-state dispute settlement are shared competences.

The Commission had outlined a comprehensive future international investment policy, which integrates investment liberalization and protection (European Commission, 2010d). Bilateral investment treaties concluded by the member states with third countries may, subject to review by the Commission, remain in force until replaced by an investment agreement between the EU and the state in question. The Commission may also authorize member states to negotiate and conclude new bilateral treaties.

Member states continue to be competent in the area of export promotion; they may organize trade fairs, promote national exports and inward investments through high-profile and image-enhancing missions abroad or provide advice on importing and exporting to or from their country. Such export promotion activities are often supported by national export credit agencies (e.g. Euler Hermes Kreditversicherungs-AG, Export Credits Guarantee Department or Compagnie Française d'Assurance pour le Commerce Extérieur) which provide government-backed loans, guarantees and insurance to make it cheaper and less risky for domestic corporations to export or invest abroad.

Overall, the Treaty of Lisbon consecrated the extension of EU exclusive competences in trade policy matters in line with the broadening of the trade agenda in general, both in WTO matters and in the new generation of bilateral trade and investment treaties that states have increasingly been negotiating. Simultaneously, the Treaty of Lisbon for the first time put the European Parliament firmly on the map as the third EU institution with a say in the conduct of trade policy.

Box 2.6 summarizes the main steps in the development of the common commercial policy over time.

Box 2.6   Timeline of events relevant for the development of the common commercial policy

Year	Event	Relevance for EU trade policy
1951	ECSC Paris Treaty signed (six member states), in force 1952	Customs union for coal, iron and steel
1956	GATT Geneva Round	Tariff reductions (ECSC)
1957	Rome Treaty signed (six member states), creating the EEC, in force 1958	Customs union for all goods and creation of a common commercial policy
1960–1961	GATT Dillon Round	Tariff reductions (ECSC and EEC)
1964–1967	GATT Kennedy Round	Tariff reductions and anti-dumping rules (EEC and ECSC)
1965	Merger Treaty signed, in force 1967	Establishing a single Council and a single Commission of the European Communities

→

→

Year	Event	Relevance for EU trade policy
1968	Completion of customs union	Common External Tariff, first EEC anti-dumping regulation
1971	CJEU ERTA ruling	Doctrine of implied powers (*in foro interno, in foro externo*)
1973	First Northern enlargement: UK, Ireland and Denmark (nine member states)	Accession of three member states generally regarded as more liberal-oriented
1973–79	GATT Tokyo Round	Tariff reductions and NTB codes of conduct Partly signed as mixed agreements
1975	CJEU Opinion 1/75	Principle of exclusivity
1979	CJEU Cassis de Dijon ruling	Principle of mutual recognition
1981	First Southern enlargement: Greece (10 member states)	Marginal impact
1986	SEA signed, in force 1987	Completion of the internal market, eliminating NTBs in the EC market, eliminating Art.115 national protective measures
	Second Southern enlargement: Spain and Portugal (12 member states)	Marginal impact, two countries with relatively protected sectors, such as textiles
1986–1994	GATT Uruguay Round	Tariff reductions (incl. agriculture), widening trade agenda including trade in services, intellectual property rights, investment, creation of WTO with strengthened dispute settlement Partly signed as mixed agreements →

→

Year	Event	Relevance for EU trade policy
1992	Treaty of Maastricht signed, in force 1993	EU created
1993	Completion of SEA internal market	More EU market power
1994	CJEU Opinion 1/94	EC exclusive competence for trade in goods, but not for trade in services (except cross-border services not involving movement of persons) or trade-related intellectual property rights (except circulation of counterfeit goods)
1995	Second Northern enlargement: Austria, Finland and Sweden (15 member states)	
	WTO established	EU and member states join
1997	Treaty of Amsterdam signed, in force 1999	Enabling clause to allow for future extension of competence to agreements on services and intellectual property rights
2001	Treaty of Nice signed, in force 2003	EC exclusive competence for trade in services (except trade in cultural, audio-visual, educational, social and human health services as well as transport)
2001–	WTO Doha Round	Tariff reductions (incl. agriculture), trade in services, intellectual property rights, rules, environment, developing countries
2004	First Eastern enlargement: Czech Republic, Cyprus, Estonia, Hungary, Latvia, Lithuania, Malta, Poland, Slovakia, Slovenia (25 member states)	Creating new demand for more extensive use of exclusive competence decision-making procedures

→

→		
Year	*Event*	*Relevance for EU trade policy*
2007	Second Eastern enlargement: Bulgaria and Romania (27 member states)	
	Treaty of Lisbon signed, in force 2009	Common external action goals, exclusive competence (incl. FDI), full trade policy competencies for European Parliament
2013	South-Eastern enlargement: Croatia (28 member states)	Marginal impact
2017	UK triggers Art. 50 TEU to start withdrawal from the EU	Less EU market power after 2019
	CJEU Opinion 2/15	EU exclusive competence for (incl. FDI, transport services, sustainable development provisions), except for portfolio investment and investor-to-state dispute settlement

Conclusion

This chapter has traced the incremental extension of EU competences in the common commercial policy. From the beginning, trade stood at the heart of the EU's external action. The creation of a customs union entailed a common commercial policy, which was largely characterized by liberal goals. The essentially instrumentalist view of the internal market's external dimension based on its needs and domestic objectives has over time shifted to a perception of the internal market as having 'distinctively external interests and objectives', such as the EU's international competitiveness and market access (Cremona, 2002a, p. 353).

Both internal and external factors have shaped EU trade policy. On the one hand, the changing nature of trade relations such as the rise of NTBs; the shift from industry-based to service-based economies and the changing global value chains; the outcomes of GATT/WTO rounds and disputes; the EU's responses to third country policies; non-trade concerns; or political events have all impacted on its commercial policy. On the other hand, domestic politics have played a role, with sectoral interests lobbying their governments or EU bodies which care about their chances of re-election or re-appointment. Member states have sometimes positioned themselves as veto players or deal breakers, and the EU institutions have acted as political entrepreneurs in the decision-making process. Treaty revisions have led to changes in competences and to the empowerment of new actors; the Court of Justice has handed down landmark rulings and opinions; and enlargements have hanged the overall constellation of trade interests in the Union.

The next chapter will take a closer look at the actors and decision-making processes in trade policy under the Lisbon Treaty.

Further reading

De Bièvre, D. and A. Poletti (2013) 'The EU in EU Trade Policy: From Regime Shaper to Status Quo Power', in G. Falkner and P. Müller (eds), *EU Policies in a Global Perspective* (London: Routledge), 20–37.

Eeckhout, P. (2011) *EU External Relations Law*, 2nd edn (Oxford: Oxford University Press), 11–69, 439–466.

Meunier, S. (2017) 'Integration by Stealth: How the European Union Gained Competence over Foreign Direct Investment', *Journal of Common Market Studies*, 55(3), 593–610.

Pelkmans, J. (2006) *European Integration: Methods and Economic Analysis*, 3rd edn (Harlow: Pearson Education), 2–35, 80–99.

Chapter 3

Actors and Processes in EU Trade Policy

Who makes the trade policy of the European Union (EU)? To answer this question, this chapter introduces the actors, the decision-making procedures and the trade policy instruments which the European Union has at its disposal. The most important actors in EU trade policy are on the one hand the EU institutions and on the other hand business and societal stakeholders, as well as governments of third countries. These actors interact in three types of processes: when the EU negotiates bilateral, regional or multilateral trade agreements; when it implements the common commercial policy; and when it applies unilateral trade policy measures, such as anti-dumping and market access investigations or pursues complaints at the World Trade Organization (WTO) about other countries' trade policy measures.

Actors in EU trade policy

This section provides an overview of the relevant public and private actors in the field of EU trade policy. The public actors examined are limited to the relevant EU bodies, keeping in mind that third countries lobby them, negotiate with them or are their targets for unilateral trade measures.

Directorate-General Trade of the European Commission

As set out in Chapter 2, the common commercial policy is an exclusive competence of the EU, and the European Commission has the sole right of initiative, with some minor exceptions. This exclusive EU competence generally comprises trade in goods, trade in services (except for transport), commercial aspects of intellectual property rights and foreign direct investment. The Commission proposes positions to take in relations with third countries or in international organizations, and it negotiates trade agreements on behalf of the EU member states. The Commission also proposes the legal acts to implement the common commercial policy, and it issues decisions when applying EU trade policy instruments. These trade measures include anti-dumping, anti-subsidy and safeguard investigations and measures, and the conduct of market access initiatives – for instance, under the procedure set out in the Trade Barriers Regulation (TBR) or through the filing of WTO dispute settlement cases.

The Directorate-General (DG) for Trade and the Trade Commissioner have the principal responsibility for setting out the EU's policy in matters of international trade, except for trade in agricultural products and fisheries. The proposals mostly take the form of communications, informal positions or proposals for regulations or decisions. They set out the legal framework within which the Commission exerts its different administrative functions, the concrete unilateral measures it proposes and the negotiation or the implementation of international trade agreements. Moreover, most actions take the form of positions that the Commission proposes on particular issues in bilateral relations with third countries or in multilateral organizations. DG Trade drafts the proposals and sounds out the interests of the economic sectors concerned and of the member states. For matters concerning trade in agricultural goods and fisheries, DG Agriculture and Rural Development and DG Maritime Affairs and Fisheries are the lead DGs. In many areas, DG Trade staff members coordinate with other DGs within the European Commission – such as DG Internal Market, Industry, Entrepreneurship and Small and Medium-Sized Enterprises; DG Health and Food Safety; DG Environment; DG Energy; DG Climate Action; DG European Neighbourhood Policy and Enlargement Negotiations; DG International Cooperation and Development – or with the European External Action Service (EEAS). DG Trade is currently subdivided into eight directorates (see Table 3.1). It has a staff of around 550 members, making it one of the larger DGs in the Commission services (see De Bièvre, 2015).

Both for international negotiations and for unilateral trade policy instruments, the Commission sets the agenda and submits proposals to the Foreign Affairs Council (FAC) and to the European Parliament. The Commission tries to anticipate whether it can muster consensus support or the required decision threshold for its proposals from the member states in the Council, as well as from the majority of Members of the European Parliament (MEPs). It can set up expert groups composed of national experts. Examples include the expert groups on

TABLE 3.1 *Directorates of DG Trade of the European Commission (2017)*

A.	Resources, Information and Policy Coordination
B.	Services and Investment; Intellectual Property and Public Procurement
C.	Asia and Latin America (including Australia, New Zealand)
D.	Sustainable Development (including Generalized System of Preferences); Economic Partnership Agreements - African, Caribbean and Pacific; Agri-food and Fisheries
E.	Neighbouring Countries; USA and Canada
F.	WTO Affairs, Legal Affairs and Trade in Goods
G.	Trade Strategy and Market Access
H.	Trade Defence

Source: DG Trade website.

the Generalized System of Preferences (GSP), on trade and investment relations with China, on tariffs, on trade facilitation, on trade and competition, on steel or on the control of the export of goods for dual use (that is, goods that can be used for civilian as well as military purposes). The Commission can invite the European Parliament to participate in such expert groups. In the FAC most trade matters are decided by consensus under the shadow of qualified majority voting. Decisions thus result from an organized interplay between the three main EU institutions, a process in which the European Commission proposes and the Council of Ministers and the European Parliament decide.

The Council's Trade Policy Committee and Working Parties on Trade

Apart from DG Trade and the Commissioner for Trade and his/her cabinet within the European Commission, there are two important types of Council committees on trade policy: the Trade Policy Committee (TPC), which assists and guides the Commission in the negotiation of trade agreements and advises on the common commercial policy, and the Working Parties on Trade, which deal with the implementing legislation and the application of the EU's trade policy instruments.

The Trade Policy Committee (formerly known as the 'Art. 133 Committee'), consists of representatives of the member states and the European Commission and is chaired by the Council Presidency. In practice, the TPC is the central decision location on international trade negotiations since the Foreign Affairs Council itself rarely actively engages with them. If discussions on negotiations take place at ministerial level, the FAC may also meet in the composition of the Ministers for Trade, a Council formation convening more frequently again since 2010 (Devuyst, 2013, p. 274).

The TPC convenes at three levels: the full members, the deputies and the experts. The full members (often called 'titulaires') are senior officials from national ministries responsible for external trade, meeting on a monthly basis with the Director General of DG Trade. The deputies are lower ranking, Brussels-based officials meeting on a weekly basis, and they deal with trade policy matters in a more detailed and in-depth manner. At the level of experts, the TPC convenes in constellations of experts on, for instance, services and investments, mutual recognition or steel, textiles and other industrial sectors (called 'STIS'). It advises on trade negotiations with third countries, WTO issues and the preparation of new EU legislation in the area of trade policy. The TPC sometimes meets outside of Brussels – for instance, at the margins of a WTO Ministerial Conference – and every rotating Presidency typically hosts an informal TPC meeting during its term. The TPC functions by consensus, yet members are aware that they take decisions under the shadow of a qualified majority vote in the Committee of Permanent Representatives (COREPER), which in turn prepares the documents to be rubber-stamped in the Foreign Affairs Council. It is therefore crucial for the Commission to garner the necessary support in the TPC.

Next to the TPC, which is a committee established by the Treaty, the Council created various Working Parties composed of the Trade Counsellors in the Permanent Representations of the member states to the EU in Brussels. These Working Parties deal with internal trade legislation and the follow-up of the EU's trade policy instruments, meaning their exact remit can change over time, ranging from distinct geographical areas to particular topics (Devuyst, 2013, p. 276). Perhaps the most important and also most stable and active among these, is the Working Party on Trade Questions, which covers anti-dumping and anti-subsidy measures as well as safeguard mechanisms.

The TPC and the Working Parties report to the Committee of Permanent Representatives Part II, commonly referred to as COREPER II, composed of the member states' permanent representatives (Nugent, 2017, pp. 163–181). The work of the Council in the area of agriculture is partly prepared by the Special Committee on Agriculture (SCA), instead of COREPER. The Council and thus implicitly also the TPC and the Working Parties may normally decide by qualified majority voting, although the chair generally endeavours to obtain a consensus (Devuyst, 2013, pp. 277–278). All these Council committees report to the Foreign Affairs Council, which convenes in a trade formation a couple of times per semester.

The International Trade Committee of the European Parliament

Preparations for decision-making on trade policy in the European Parliament take place largely in its International Trade (INTA) Committee, established in 2004. Compared to the Council's Trade Policy Committee, not only does the INTA Committee have much less experience in trade policy, but it is also not as well staffed.

Prior to the Lisbon Treaty, the Parliament was largely sidelined in the trade policymaking process, but now it participates on a formally almost equal footing to the Council (Van den Putte et al., 2015). When the Commission proposes to initiate negotiations on an international trade agreement, the Council alone authorizes it to do so, while the Parliament is only informed of the negotiating directives and can comment on them. This prerogative is thus retained by the Commission, which proposes, and by the Council, which adopts the negotiation 'mandate'. However, the Parliament has the right to be immediately and fully informed at all stages of the negotiation and conclusion of trade agreements, and the Commission must regularly report to it on the progress of negotiations. In addition, the INTA Committee, on behalf of the Parliament, has various other means to voice its preferences and preconditions for its final consent, including the use of non-binding parliamentary resolutions, hearings, opinions and questions to the Commission. Moreover, both the Council and the Parliament have to ratify the negotiated agreements. Given this ratification requirement, the Commission has a strong interest to ensure the Parliament's support from the very beginning. Finally, in recent years the Parliament has increasingly tried to influence the early stages of a negotiation, for instance by adopting resolutions before the Council decides on the authorization of negotiation, as well as by negotiating a Framework Agreement with the Commission, in which the Commission commits to sending the negotiating directives simultaneously to the Council and the Parliament (European Commission and European Parliament, 2010).

The INTA Committee also holds the key position in the Parliament for the shaping of the framework legislation necessary to implement the common commercial policy. It only presents the final legislative proposal to the plenary for adoption through simple majority voting. The Parliament co-decides with the Council on the Commission's proposals for regulations under the ordinary legislative procedure, and it co-monitors the implementation of delegated and implementing acts by the Commission (see below). Hence, parliamentary powers to block the legislation necessary for the domestic implementation of trade agreements provide some additional political clout in the bargaining process.

The role of societal actors

Apart from the public decision-making bodies with legal authority to decide, private interests and civil society organizations participate in the trade policymaking process. Business, labour and representatives of non-governmental organizations (NGOs) monitor the EU's trade policy, support or criticize existing policies and seek influence over future trade policy decisions or international trade agreements. Organized interests and non-state actors play a key role in providing information and expertise to EU institutions, as these stakeholders frame information as being either of technical or political relevance to a wider audience.

The landscape of interest groups in EU trade policy differs with regard to the intensity with which they monitor and influence policymaking (Greenwood, 2017). On the one hand, producers and traders dispose of a dense network of comprehensive business and employer associations (e.g. BusinessEurope), sector-wide peak associations (e.g. the European Chemical Industry Council, CEFIC), and branch-specific trade associations (e.g. the European Association of Metals, Eurometaux). These often have very specific demands to policymakers and maintain close contacts with relevant Commission officials, members of the INTA Committee and member state representatives. On the other hand, NGOs are relatively new among the interest groups following trade policy, with broader and more indirect concerns. They can devote less of their time and resources to following trade policy in detail and dispose of looser networks with public decision makers in the EU institutions and the member states. Most of these lobby organizations and NGOs are included in the so-called Transparency Register set up by the EU (http://europa.eu/transparency-register). Since registration is not mandatory, some organizations may not be included, or the information provided may not be comparable to each other because firms, associations or NGOs may be using different ways of indicating their staff numbers or their lobbying expenditure (Greenwood and Dreger, 2013).

Interest groups' participation also varies to a significant extent according to the type of trade negotiation or policy instrument used. The institutional setup of EU trade policy provides informal as well as formal channels for organized interests to voice their demands. Formally, influence may be exerted through committees and other forums. First, the European Economic and Social Committee (EESC) plays a consultative role, and its opinions are forwarded to the Council, the Commission and the European Parliament. The EESC represents employer and employee organizations, yet its importance in trade policy is at best marginal. Second, in the so-called Civil Society Dialogue, introduced in the late 1990s, DG Trade holds regular, structured meetings on trade policy issues of interest to a wider audience in order to inform, listen to and exchange views with civil society organizations (Dür and De Bièvre, 2007). Third, producers have the right to petition specialized services within DG Trade to request the imposition of anti-dumping measures or the opening of market access investigations in third countries (see below). Fourth, some regulations set up advisory committees for specific tasks, and the Commission itself may also establish expert groups to provide advice and expertise. Some of these committees have permanent status, others are temporary and some may be formal while others are informal.

Informally, private or societal actors with a stake in EU trade policy mobilize on the national and/or European level. Interest representatives approach in particular DG Trade within the European Commission, the cabinet of the Commissioner for Trade, as well as the members of the TPC and of the INTA Committee (Woll, 2009). On the national level, private interests and NGOs lobby their own member state's permanent representatives in Brussels who sit in the COREPER meetings, their members of the Trade Policy Committee, their MEPs or the responsible Ministry in their home capital.

Several factors contribute to different mixes of national and European strategies for monitoring and influencing EU trade policymaking. Interest groups and NGOs follow and try to influence Commission proposals early on in the policymaking process, in close contact with the agenda setter. At the same time, interest representatives may opt for briefing their national representatives and MEPs about their preferences so that the latter transmit these concerns to the Commission, either directly or by expressing concerns to the Commission in the meetings of the Trade Policy Committee. Consulting various actors allows DG Trade to anticipate the elements in its proposal that are likely to obtain the necessary support in the Council and the European Parliament. The quorum required to approve a decision varies from unanimity to qualified majority or a simple majority of member states, depending on the subject matter and the type of policy instrument or trade negotiation (see below). In practice, however, Council representatives usually decide by consensus.

The practice of consensus can foster national lobbying strategies, especially for constituencies which have defensive interests at stake. For instance, national agricultural associations often voice their opposition through their member state representative or MEPs. Nevertheless, an important economic sector in one member state opposing a particular decision runs the risk of isolation and thus mostly engages in coalition building through the European-level associations. This in turn increases the chances that more member states express reservations on the topic.

The next sections set out the different decision-making procedures in more detail, starting with the conclusion of trade agreements between the EU and third countries.

Negotiating international trade agreements

The decision-making process for the negotiation and conclusion of bilateral, regional or multilateral trade agreements is based on Art. 207 and Art. 218 Treaty on the Functioning of the EU (TFEU) (see Boxes 3.2 and 3.4). The trade agreements with other countries concluded under these decision rules can take various forms (see Chapter 7). Prominent recent examples are the EU negotiations on free trade agreements (FTAs) with South Korea, Canada, Singapore, Japan, Vietnam and India.

At the outset of a discussion about launching trade negotiations, the European Commission normally starts an informal dialogue with the country concerned on the content of future negotiations, known as the 'scoping exercise'. This is important to assess whether a deal can be considered feasible. Prior to the launch of negotiations, the Commission also conducts an Impact Assessment pursuant to its internal 'better' or 'smart regulation' rules under the supervision of the Secretariat-General. This assessment includes a public consultation with interested parties. For major negotiations, the Commission since 1999 also asks for a

Sustainability Impact Assessment (SIA) to be conducted by external consultants, with the aim of providing an independent study of the likely economic, social and environmental implications of a trade agreement. After implementation of the agreement, the Commission regularly conducts ex post evaluations in order to investigate the envisaged as well as the unintended effects of a particular agreement.

Three types of trade-related agreements can be distinguished: trade, cooperation and association agreements. In comparison to regular trade agreements, cooperation and association agreements have a broader coverage and usually include a 'political' or 'foreign policy' dimension, however vague those terms might be. Association and cooperation agreements are more likely to fall within the category of so-called mixed agreements. These are agreements between the EU and third countries which concern issues of Union and member state competence. They need to be signed, concluded and ratified by both the EU and member states. In the case of Belgium, the legislatures which are constitutionally required to vote on these competences include also a set of regional parliaments (see Chapter 8).

Yet regular trade agreements have also ended up being mixed in the past when they contained, for example, elements of transport policy or the criminal enforcement of intellectual property rights or because member states preferred to make them mixed agreements. A trade agreement which partly falls within exclusive EU competence and partly within member state competence has to be a mixed agreement. In EU jargon, this has long been referred to as the 'pastis principle': like a single drop of pastis makes a glass of water cloudy, an agreement including just one provision of national competence can no longer be ratified only by the EU. By contrast, mixity is optional if an agreement covers shared competences (whether or not exclusive competences are concerned as well). In such a case, the choice of an EU-only or a mixed agreement is a political decision of the Council (Van der Loo and Wessel, 2017, pp. 736–737). Member states have been inclined to consider even regular trade agreements as mixed agreements, because they have often provided the Commission with a very broad mandate to negotiate also on regulatory issues where they have legislative competences and because national parliamentary ratification gives them a veto right.

As pointed out in Chapter 2, the Court of Justice of the EU (CJEU) clarified in its recent *Opinion 2/15* that insofar as an agreement's objective is trade liberalization, the EU holds exclusive competences in the fields of market access for goods and services (including transport services), public procurement, intellectual property rights, competition rules, the protection of FDI, dispute settlement other than non-direct FDI and sustainable development, including the social protection of workers and environmental protection. Such matters are thus normally subject to a qualified majority decision in the Council (with exceptions such as those referred to in Art. 204:4 and 218:8 TFEU) and a simple majority in the European Parliament. By contrast, agreements which include portfolio investment and dispute settlement between investors and states are subject to a simple majority in the European Parliament *and* ratification by the legislatures of all EU member states that are constitutionally required to vote, and thus de facto to consensus in the Council. It makes more political sense in the Council to seek a common accord for the decisions on the signature and conclusion of mixed agreements. In fact, the steady expansion of the trade agenda into regulatory fields during the last 30 years has consistently outpaced the speed of Treaty revisions (see Chapter 2). Just like member states demanded the right to ratify the 1994 Uruguay Round GATT/WTO agreements, they have more recently demanded national parliamentary approval for agreements like the EU's FTAs with Singapore or Canada.

Regular trade agreements

The Commission's DG Trade drafts a mandate for new negotiations and enters into inter-service consultation with the other DGs before forwarding the proposal to the College of Commissioners. The Commission then presents these draft negotiating guidelines to the Council and the European Parliament. In practice, they go directly to the Trade Policy Committee, whose establishment is mentioned in Art. 207:3 TFEU (see Box 3.1). The TPC may seek to amend the proposed mandate before handing it to COREPER. As mentioned earlier, this committee plays a crucial role in the preparation of decisions that then mostly figure on the Foreign Affairs Council agenda as issues that do not need further discussion. Finally, the FAC adopts the mandate for the Commission, in principle by qualified majority vote, but usually by consensus. It does so in the form of a Council Decision authorizing the opening of negotiations which contains the negotiating directives in an annex. This Council Decision is widely referred to as a mandate although it should be kept in mind that these guidelines are not binding. For mixed agreements, a Decision of the Council and of the representatives of the governments of the member states, meeting within the Council, is necessary.

Only for association agreements and agreements which cover provisions for which unanimity is required for the adoption of internal rules does the Foreign Affairs Council need to decide by unanimity (see below). Negotiating guidelines, if the Council chooses to issue such, have long been confidential documents, yet in 2015 the Commission pledged to

---

Box 3.1 Trade-specific decision-making process

Art. 207 TFEU

3. Where agreements with one or more third countries or international organisations need to be negotiated and concluded, Article 218 shall apply, subject to the special provisions of this Article. The Commission shall make recommendations to the Council, which shall authorise it to open the necessary negotiations. [...]

   The Commission shall conduct these negotiations in consultation with a special committee appointed by the Council to assist the Commission in this task and within the framework of such directives as the Council may issue to it. The Commission shall report regularly to the special committee and to the European Parliament on the progress of negotiations.

4. For the negotiation and conclusion of the agreements referred to in paragraph 3, the Council shall act by a qualified majority.

   For the negotiation and conclusion of agreements in the fields of trade in services and the commercial aspects of intellectual property, as well as foreign direct investment, the Council shall act unanimously where such agreements include provisions for which unanimity include provisions for which unanimity is required for the adoption of internal rules.

   The Council shall also act unanimously for the negotiation and conclusion of agreements:

   (a) in the field of trade in cultural and audiovisual services, where these agreements risk prejudicing the Union's cultural and linguistic diversity;

   (b) in the field of trade in social, education and health services, where these agreements risk seriously disturbing the national organization of such services and prejudicing the responsibility of Member States do deliver them.

Source: Treaty on the Functioning of the European Union, Lisbon version.

publish them in an effort to increase transparency (see Chapter 7). They are not legally constraining, but the Commission knows that the Council must ultimately ratify a negotiated agreement. The European Parliament needs to be informed about the mandate and can comment on it, but does not formally need to approve it. Whereas the Foreign Affairs Council is normally chaired by the High Representative, in trade matters the rotating Council Presidency chairs the FAC. The Presidency also continues to chair the Council's preparatory bodies, like the TPC and the Working Parties.

The Commission initiates trade negotiations and has to report regularly to both the TPC and the European Parliament's Committee on International Trade on the progress of international trade negotiations. Yet, the Treaty specifically provides for the TPC to be consulted by the Commission and to assist it in the negotiations, whereas the European Parliament votes by simple majority on the basis of a recommendation from the INTA Committee. In order to influence negotiations, the Parliament can resort to the adoption of resolutions that signal the conditions under which it would be willing to give its consent at the end of the policy process. This is what the European Parliament did, for instance, in the case of the EU–Korea free trade agreement (see Chapter 4). The European Commission and the European Parliament (2010) have signed a Framework Agreement that specifies their interinstitutional relations, including with regard to the negotiation and conclusion of international agreements. The Commission shall immediately and fully inform the Parliament at all stages, including the definition of negotiating directives. Also, where the Commission represents the Union in international conferences, it may, at the Parliament's request, grant observer status to MEPs and include them in the EU delegation. This is the case, for example, in the EU delegations to WTO Ministerial Conferences.

When the Commission submits the negotiated agreement for approval, the Parliament cannot make any amendments but votes in favour or against the entire agreement. This form of parliamentary approval is usual for international treaties because it limits the risk of involuntary defection for the negotiators from the executive. The Foreign Affairs Council concludes the agreement in the form of a Decision, usually by consensus but formally by qualified majority (except for association agreements and agreements which cover provisions for which unanimity is required for the adoption of internal rules).

The flowchart in Box 3.2 summarizes the decision-making process with regard to the negotiation of trade agreements. The procedure for

Box 3.2 Flowchart of EU decision-making in trade negotiations

1. **European Commission** *proposes* negotiations.

↓

2. **EU Council of Ministers**
Commission *consults* the Trade Policy Committee, COREPER can *direct* the Commission, Foreign Affairs Council *authorizes* negotiations.

↓

3. **European Commission** *negotiates* the agreement, *consults* theTrade Policy Committee and *reports* to the INTA Committee.

↓

4. **European Parliament** gives its *consent* (by simple majority).

↓

5. **Foreign Affairs Council** *decides* to authorize the signing of the agreement and possibly its provisional application.

Source: Based on Art. 207 and 218 TFEU.

the initiation, negotiation and conclusion of association agreements or mixed agreements follows to a large extent the same decision-making path as for regular trade agreements. However, there are some noteworthy differences mentioned below.

Art. 218 TFEU specifies in greater detail how the EU negotiates international agreements in general (see Box 3.3).

Art. 218:7 and 218:9 TFEU foresee a simplified procedure for modifications to an agreement or for Union positions to be adopted in a body set up by an agreement. In such cases the European Parliament is only informed. The Parliament is not involved in the suspension of an international agreement, for example based on a human rights clause (see Chapter 7). The Council decides on a suspension on the basis of the same voting rules as for the conclusion of the agreement. Moreover, a member state, the European Parliament, the Council or the Commission may ask for the opinion of the Court of Justice whether an agreement envisaged

Box 3.3   Negotiation of international agreements in general

Art. 218 TFEU

1. Without prejudice to the specific provisions laid down in Article 207, agreements between the Union and third countries or international organisations shall be negotiated and concluded in accordance with the following procedure.

2. The Council shall authorise the opening of negotiations, adopt negotiating directives, authorise the signing of agreements and conclude them.

3. The Commission [...] shall submit recommendations to the Council, which shall adopt a decision authorising the opening of negotiations and, depending on the subject of the agreement envisaged, nominating the Union negotiator or the head of the Union's negotiating team.

4. The Council may address directives to the negotiator and designate a special committee in consultation with which the negotiations must be conducted.

5. The Council, on a proposal by the negotiator, shall adopt a decision authorising the signing of the agreement and, if necessary, its provisional application before entry into force.

6. The Council, on a proposal by the negotiator, shall adopt a decision concluding the agreement. [...]

    (a) after obtaining the consent of the European Parliament in the following cases:
    (i) association agreements; [...]
    (v) agreements covering fields to which either the ordinary legislative procedure applies, or the special legislative

is compatible with the Treaties (Art. 218:11 TFEU). In case of a negative opinion of the Court, the agreement does not enter into force.

Cooperation and association agreements

Cooperation agreements go beyond regular trade agreements and thus need, depending on their precise nature, another legal basis in addition to Art. 207 TFEU. If the agreement includes a part on development cooperation, for example, then Art. 209 TFEU would be added (see Chapter 6). Other provisions could relate to cooperation in fields such

→

procedure where consent by the European Parliament is required. [...]

7. When concluding an agreement, the Council may, by way of derogation from paragraphs 5, 6 and 9, authorise the negotiator to approve on the Union's behalf modifications to the agreement where it provides for them to be adopted by a simplified procedure or by a body set up by the agreement. The Council may attach specific conditions to such authorisation.

8. The Council shall act by a qualified majority throughout the procedure. However, it shall act unanimously when the agreement covers a field for which unanimity is required for the adoption of a Union act as well as for association agreements [...]

9. The Council, on a proposal from the Commission or the High Representative of the Union for Foreign Affairs and Security Policy, shall adopt a decision suspending application of an agreement and establishing the positions to be adopted on the Union's behalf in a body set up by an agreement, when that body is called upon to adopt acts having legal effects, with the exception of acts supplementing or amending the institutional framework of the agreement.

10. The European Parliament shall be immediately and fully informed at all stages of the procedure. [...]

11. A Member State, the European Parliament, the Council or the Commission may obtain the opinion of the Court of Justice as to whether an agreement envisaged is compatible with the Treaties. Where the opinion of the Court is adverse, the agreement envisaged may not enter into force unless it is amended or the Treaties are revised.

Source: Treaty on the Functioning of the European Union, Lisbon version.

as environmental or social policies, justice and home affairs or political cooperation.

Association agreements are based on Art. 217 TFEU, which stipulates that

[t]he Union may conclude with one or more third countries or international organisations agreements establishing an association involving reciprocal rights and obligations, common action and special procedure.

They typically include preferential market access or free trade, as well as various types of economic, financial or technical cooperation and a political dialogue. Such associations imply a much more elaborate institutional setup than trade or cooperation agreements. An Association Council, organized at ministerial level, takes decisions and makes recommendations to attain the agreed objectives, while an Association Committee at the level of senior officials manages the agreement and settles differences regarding its application and interpretation. Besides an arbitration mechanism, some associations also include a joint parliamentary body or a joint consultative committee for economic and social representatives.

Moreover, the Lisbon Treaty introduced a provision that calls upon the EU to develop a special relationship with neighbouring countries in the framework of which it may conclude specific agreements which 'may contain reciprocal rights and obligations as well as the possibility of undertaking activities jointly' (Art. 8 Treaty on European Union, TEU). This wording comes close to that of association agreements. In fact, the EU has in the past often concluded association agreements with neighbouring countries. Some of these agreements included the prospect of the associated country eventually becoming a member of the EU. In the European Neighbourhood Policy, most Mediterranean neighbours already have association agreements with the EU, while the Partnership and Cooperation Agreements with the Eastern partners are being replaced by more ambitious association agreements (Gstöhl, 2015). They establish stronger political relations and closer cooperation in many sectors and aim for closer alignment of the neighbours' legislation with that of the EU to facilitate the establishment of deep and comprehensive free trade areas.

The negotiation, conclusion and implementation of mixed agreements raise complex legal questions. The Treaties contain no specific provisions or explicit references to mixed agreements. The choice of the proper legal basis of an agreement is often controversial because some parts might fall within exclusive Union competence, while others fall within shared competence and sometimes even within exclusive national competence. Although the Treaty of Lisbon and the CJEU's *Opinion 2/15* have expanded the scope of the common commercial policy, for cooperation and association agreements and for deep and comprehensive FTAs, 'mixity' is likely to remain (see Chapters 2 and 7).

In order to establish which legal form the agreements will take, the examination of the objectives and contents of an agreement is crucial. In its *Opinion 2/00* on the Cartagena Protocol on Biosafety, the Court of Justice of the EU (2001) had found that an agreement fell within the scope of the common commercial policy if trade was its main or predominant purpose. With regard to the division of competences between the Union and the member states, the Court applied the so-called absorption doctrine, according to which the dominant or essential objective of an agreement 'absorbs' the possible other substantive legal bases which are pursuing objectives of a subsidiary or ancillary nature (Maresceau, 2010, p. 15). Hence, in principle, if the essential objective of an agreement is trade and the aspects of shared competence are merely secondary, a mixed agreement is not needed. However, if there is political consensus among the member states that an agreement should be mixed, they can for instance add provisions on a political dialogue which, as a national prerogative, would turn it into a mixed agreement (ibid., p. 16). Since both the Union and its member states are contracting parties, ratification of a mixed agreement can take a long time. To handle this impractical complication, the EU has often concluded a separate 'interim agreement on trade and trade-related matters', which could enter into force without ratification by the national parliaments of the member states and the European Parliament. Alternatively, the Council can decide a provisional application of those parts of the agreement covered by exclusive EU competence. In the post-Lisbon era it normally does so only after the European Parliament has given its consent. In recent years, the trend seems to consist in the conclusion of a framework, cooperation or strategic partnership agreement in parallel to an FTA.

Association agreements are usually mixed agreements, as was the case for the Cotonou Agreement with the African, Caribbean and Pacific countries, the Euro-Mediterranean association agreements, the Stabilization and Association Agreements with the countries of the Western Balkans, the European Economic Area or the association agreement with Chile (see Chapter 7). The EU has also concluded mixed cooperation agreements of a general or sectoral nature – for example, the Partnership and Cooperation Agreements with former Soviet states; the trade, development and cooperation agreements with South Africa and Mexico; or certain bilateral sector agreements with Switzerland (Maresceau, 2010, pp. 17–29).

Association agreements thus require formal unanimity instead of a qualified majority in the Council for the adoption of the mandate and the conclusion of the agreement, as well as the consent of the European Parliament. Depending on their contents and legal basis, cooperation agreements often entail unanimity in the Council as well, since they usually cover areas for which unanimity is required for the adoption of internal rules.

The next section deals with the implementation of the EU's trade policy, which concerns especially autonomous measures but sometimes also trade agreements (e.g. in case a regulation is needed to implement a part of the trade agreement).

Framework legislation for implementing the common commercial policy

The decision-making process for the implementation of the EU's trade policy is laid down in Art. 207:2 TFEU:

> The European Parliament and the Council, acting by means of regulations in accordance with the ordinary legislative procedure, shall adopt the measures defining the framework for implementing the common commercial policy.

This article provides the basis for the Parliament's co-decision powers in the implementation of trade policy, next to creating, in combination with Art. 218:6(a)(v) TFEU, the requirement that it has to give its consent to all trade agreements. The Parliament and the Council share powers to adopt EU legislation on trade instruments such as anti-dumping, countervailing duties, safeguards and the TBR; on autonomous trade measures such as the GSP for developing countries; on the regulation of foreign direct investment; or on implementing international trade agreements that the Union has concluded.

The ordinary legislative procedure involves up to three readings. Generally, the European Parliament and the Council agree on the content of most legislation before the third stage is reached (Nugent, 2017, pp. 337–341). In a simplified version, the main steps of the ordinary legislative procedure are as follows: the European Commission formally presents a legislative proposal, drafted by DG Trade after broad consultation within the Commission services as well as with expert groups and stakeholders. The Commission's text is simultaneously examined by the relevant committees of the European Parliament, by the Trade Policy Committee and the Council Working Parties, and by COREPER.

In its first reading, the Commission proposal is considered by the parliamentary committee(s) responsible, associated committees and opinion-giving committees. The Parliament adopts in plenary session a position by a simple majority with or without amendments. If the Council approves the Parliament's wording, it adopts the new legislative act by qualified majority. If not, it adopts its own position and sends it back to the Parliament with explanations. The Commission also informs the Parliament of its position on the matter.

In the second reading, the act is adopted if the Parliament approves (by a simple majority) the Council's text or if the Parliament fails to take a decision. The Parliament may reject the Council's position by an absolute majority, leading to a failure of the draft law, or it may propose amendments to the Council's text. The Commission delivers its opinion on those amendments. The Council, in its second reading, can approve the Parliament's proposal by a qualified majority. However, when the Commission has delivered a negative opinion on those amendments, the Council must act unanimously on them. If the Council does not approve the Parliament's proposal, a conciliation committee is convened, composed of an equal number of representatives of the Council (one per member state) and MEPs, with the Commission attempting to mediate. Conciliation thus consists of direct negotiations between the two co-legislators.

In order to expedite the formal procedure and in order to resolve outstanding contentious issues, it has become common practice that the Commission, the Council and the Parliament organize so-called informal trilogue meetings with the aim of preparing the way for an overall agreement. They may be held at all stages of the procedure. In these trilogue negotiations, the Council is represented by the member state holding the rotating EU Presidency, the Commission by high-ranking officials of DG Trade and the Parliament by a delegation that includes the rapporteur(s) responsible for the dossier.

Each delegation to the conciliation committee must approve the joint text in accordance with its own voting rules. If the committee fails to agree on a common text, the act has failed. If it succeeds, then the third and final phase starts. The aim of the third reading is the adoption of the act by the two institutions in line with the joint text, with the European Parliament acting by a simple majority of the votes cast, and the Council by a qualified majority. No amendments to the joint text are allowed at this stage. The entire procedure has to respect various time limits. Box 3.4 summarizes this process in a highly simplified flowchart.

Box 3.4   Flowchart of EU decision-making for trade policy regulations (ordinary legislative procedure)

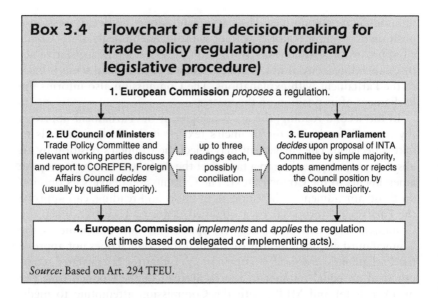

1. European Commission *proposes* a regulation.

2. EU Council of Ministers
Trade Policy Committee and relevant working parties discuss and report to COREPER, Foreign Affairs Council *decides* (usually by qualified majority).

up to three readings each, possibly conciliation

3. European Parliament
decides upon proposal of INTA Committee by simple majority, adopts amendments or rejects the Council position by absolute majority.

4. European Commission *implements* and *applies* the regulation (at times based on delegated or implementing acts).

Source: Based on Art. 294 TFEU.

Delegation and implementing powers of the European Commission

Trade-related regulations of the type just discussed above often specify how the European Commission should proceed in implementing concrete measures. Following the overhaul of the general decision-making rules in the Lisbon Treaty reforms, the EU also reformed the decision-making rules with regard to the implementation powers of the European Commission in general and in trade policy matters in particular. This is called comitology and refers to the system of oversight of implementing powers which the legislators have delegated to the Commission. These reformed rules on delegation and comitology were established in 2011 (European Parliament and Council of the European Union, 2011). They put the European Parliament and Council on equal footing when it comes to the conferral of both delegated and implementing powers to the Commission. By deciding on the type of act, they set the level of control.

In the case of delegated acts, the Commission has, under specified conditions, the power to adopt non-legislative acts of general application in order to supplement or amend certain non-essential elements of the legislative act (Art. 290 TFEU). In order to do so, the Commission may use forums, such as by convening expert groups for discussions. An example of a delegated act in the field of trade are the rules set out by the Commission for granting countries the special incentive arrangement for sustainable development and good governance under the GSP regulation (see Chapter 6). The delegated act enters into force if no objection has been expressed by the European Parliament or the Council within a period set by the legislative act. They may also decide to revoke the delegation.

In the case of implementing acts, the Commission acquires the necessary implementing powers in instances where uniform conditions for implementing legally binding Union acts are needed (Art. 291 TFEU). The member states control the Commission's exercise of these implementing powers through the so-called comitology committees (e.g. the TBR Committee, the Generalized Preferences Committee, the Committee on Trade Retaliation or the Committee for Investment Agreements).

For implementing acts in the framework of the common commercial policy, the examination procedure applies (see Box 3.5). An examination

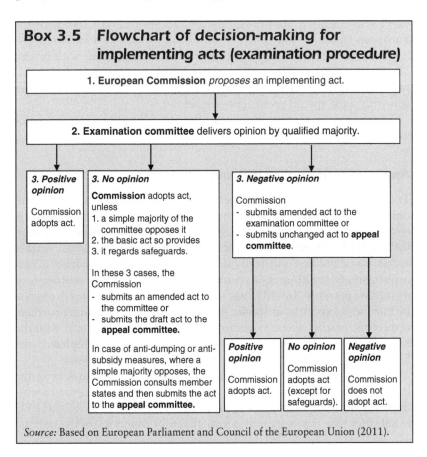

Box 3.5 Flowchart of decision-making for implementing acts (examination procedure)

1. **European Commission** *proposes* an implementing act.

2. **Examination committee** delivers opinion by qualified majority.

3. Positive opinion

Commission adopts act.

3. No opinion

Commission adopts act, unless
1. a simple majority of the committee opposes it
2. the basic act so provides
3. it regards safeguards.

In these 3 cases, the Commission
- submits an amended act to the committee or
- submits the draft act to the **appeal committee.**

In case of anti-dumping or anti-subsidy measures, where a simple majority opposes, the Commission consults member states and then submits the act to the **appeal committee.**

3. Negative opinion

Commission
- submits amended act to the examination committee or
- submits unchanged act to **appeal committee**.

Positive opinion	*No opinion*	*Negative opinion*
Commission adopts act.	Commission adopts act (except for safeguards).	Commission does not adopt act.

Source: Based on European Parliament and Council of the European Union (2011).

committee is composed of member state representatives and chaired by a representative of the Commission, who does not take part in the vote. The committee decides by the same rules of weighted voting as the Council. In case of a positive opinion, the Commission adopts the implementing act. If the committee delivers a negative opinion, the Commission may either submit an amended version to the examination committee or submit the act to the appeal committee for further deliberation. In case the examination committee has no opinion, the Commission may adopt the draft act unless a simple majority opposes it, in which case the Commission may either submit an amended version to the same committee or submit the act to the appeal committee. Only if the appeal committee votes no by qualified majority may the Commission not adopt the implementing act. The preexisting framework legislation on EU trade policy had to be brought in conformity with these new rules on the Commission's implementing powers (European Parliament and Council of the European Union, 2014a).

While the trade defence measures were in the past dealt with in separate regulations, different from the rules of comitology of other EU policies, they now have been integrated into the comitology rules, yet still with some special provisions (see below).

The following section examines how the EU applies trade defence measures and enforces international trade rules.

Applying trade policy instruments

Trade policy instruments implemented by the European Commission are unilaterally decided trade policy measures, mostly applied at the request of a group of producers or service providers following an investigation by DG Trade. There are two types of trade policy instruments: market access investigations and trade defence measures. With market access investigations, the EU seeks to enforce the market access commitments of its trading partners. The EU does so by investigating, often upon request by European exporters or service providers, whether the trading partners respect the market access commitments they have entered into with the EU in WTO or bilateral trade agreements. In cases of noncompliance, the EU can seek to induce compliance by imposing trade sanctions.

With trade defence measures, the EU imposes trade barriers in the form of anti-dumping duties, countervailing duties or safeguard measures. The most important type of trade defence measures used by the EU is anti-dumping duties against goods allegedly 'dumped' on the internal market. The European Commission receives far more industry requests for anti-dumping measures than for countervailing duties or safeguards. Countervailing duties or anti-subsidy measures are meant to offset subsidies to foreign exporters, whereas safeguards are rather blunt measures in the form of higher import duties or quotas against a sudden surge of imports (see Vermulst et al., 2004).

Trade defence measures

Trade defence measures constitute exceptions to the general rule not to raise customs tariffs above a certain level. All members of the WTO, including the EU, have committed to so-called bound tariffs. In detailed lists, each WTO member enumerates the tariff rates which its customs authorities will levy on goods imported into its territory. They have promised all other WTO members not to raise the tariffs above the bound tariff rates (see Chapter 5). In practice, applied rates often differ from bound rates. Applied rates are the tariff rates that members currently charge, which can be lower than the bound rates. As a member of the EU customs union, the United Kingdom (UK) applies the common external tariff, but after its withdrawal, it will have to adopt its own tariff rates, renegotiate its tariff-rate quotas and restructure the trade defence measures currently in place.

Yet, WTO members may raise trade barriers if a trading partner is found to be dumping, subsidizing or causing severe harm to domestic production, in which cases they can apply anti-dumping duties, countervailing duties or safeguard measures. They can do so only after an investigation into whether dumping by foreign producers or subsidization by foreign governments was actually found to be taking place or when there is a sudden upsurge in imports, whether this really caused injury to domestic producers and whether it is in the Union's interest to take defensive measures (see below). This assessment must respect the rules of the respective WTO agreements on each of these three instruments. Table 3.2 sets out the three trade defence instruments at the EU's disposal. By far the most important and most frequently used instrument is anti-dumping, while countervailing duties are not used often, and the EU hardly ever resorts to the safeguards. Whereas anti-dumping and anti-subsidy measures target individual producers from one single foreign country, safeguards protect an entire sector regardless of the exporters' origins, causing larger trade-distorting effects. The following sections thus focus on anti-dumping procedures.

TABLE 3.2   *EU Trade Defence Instruments*

Instrument	Targeted imports	Criteria for imposing a measure
Anti-dumping measures	'Unfair' (dumped) country-specific imports	1. Dumping 2. (Threat of) injury to EU producers of like product 3. Causality link 4. Union interest to act
Anti-subsidy measures	'Unfair' country-specific imports (prohibited subsidy)	1. Subsidy 2. (Threat of) injury to EU producers of like product 3. Causality link 4. Union interest to act
Safeguard measures	'Fair' imports from all countries ('safety valve' against sudden and massive surge of imports)	1. Import surge 2. Serious injury to EU producers of like (or directly competing) product 3. Causality link 4. Union interest to act

Source: Based on DG Trade website.

The EU can impose duties on imports if it comes to the conclusion that these have been 'dumped'. Dumping occurs when producers from a third country sell goods in the EU below the sales price in their domestic market or below their cost of production (or, based on a more legal definition, below the so-called normal value of goods). The exact definition and the exact method for the calculation of what is a 'normal value' is far from self-evident and often subject to controversy, although the WTO members tried to delineate this concept in the Anti-dumping Agreement. Dumping itself is allowed under WTO rules, but WTO members have the right to conduct investigations and impose anti-dumping duties if they find that dumping has taken place. During these investigations they have to respect the rules of due process contained in a WTO agreement on the implementation of anti-dumping policy.

Like in other countries, an anti-dumping case in the EU goes through a multi-step process (European Parliament and Council of the European Union, 2016a). As a first step, a firm or interest association initiates the case on behalf of a section of the producers of a particular product. WTO members, like the EU, have agreed that they will start anti-dumping investigations only if the minimum threshold of support by producers representing 25 per cent of domestic production is fulfilled. If at least a quarter of the EU producers of a particular product allege that foreign producers are dumping their products on the EU market, the Directorate of Trade Defence in DG Trade of the European Commission is obliged to investigate their request if the complainant produces sufficient apparent evidence of dumping and injury. Since 2016 the Directorate for Trade Defence of the Commission can also self-initiate an investigation in order to ensure that EU firms potentially benefiting from the imposition of anti-dumping duties are not exposed to the risk of harassment or retaliation by the foreign trading partner.

The producers themselves define the size of the industry on behalf of which they file a complaint by providing a list of all known EU producers of the 'like product'. This makes the actual use of the trade policy instrument of anti-dumping by the European Commission almost entirely dependent on collective action by firms. It also means that firms outsourcing parts of their production may be (and usually are) excluded when defining that 25 per cent proportion of EU industry. The threshold for complainant firms is thus quite low and privileges sectors with a low number of firms or a few very large producers over highly fragmented sectors.

In a second step, the Commission informs the Trade Defence Instruments Committee (TDI Committee) about the case and launches a formal investigation. The sessions of this committee, a committee which consists of member state representatives, are chaired by the Commission, like those of the countervailing duties and safeguard committees.

During the third stage of the procedure, the Commission establishes whether dumping is taking place. It makes an estimation of the level of injury to domestic European firms, establishes whether dumping was the cause of injury to the industry and decides whether the imposition of anti-dumping duties would be in the 'Union interest'. In order to do so, the Commission selects the sample of firms in the foreign country that it will investigate more closely, sends out questionnaires to those firms and conducts verification visits with them.

In order to assess whether it would be in the Union interest to impose anti-dumping duties against the foreign firms in question, the

Commission is obliged to take into account the interests of four groups: (1) the complaining EU producer firms; (2) the EU retailers and their associations; (3) the EU users processing the imported product that is alleged to be dumped on the EU market and their representative associations; and (4) the consumers in the EU. In many cases, once dumping and injury are proven and measures are expected to give relief to the complainant industry, it is presumed almost automatically that these measures are in the 'Union interest'.

As a fourth step, the Commission again consults with the TDI Committee and decides whether to impose provisional duties. The imposition of provisional anti-dumping (as well as countervailing) measures is thus only subject to the advisory procedure. The Committee's opinion is delivered by simple majority and not binding on the Commission. These provisional duties are levied at the latest nine months after the notice of initiation of the anti-dumping procedure. The European Commission can impose anti-dumping duties only if at least 50 per cent of the EU producers of this product are injured, raising the threshold of 25 per cent of European domestic industry for the acceptability of the complaint to half of the European producers for the actual increase in customs duties at the EU's external borders. One month before the expiry of the provisional duties, the Commission issues a proposal for definitive anti-dumping measures.

In the fifth phase, the Commission thus suggests definitive duties for a maximum of five years to the TDI Committee, which decides according to the examination procedure and qualified majority. In the wake of the Lisbon Treaty reforms and the new regulation on the Commission's implementing powers, the decision threshold in the Council has thus effectively been lowered to a 'qualified minority' of member state representatives. This rule by which decisions are taken gives wide discretion to the European Commission to impose duties even in the face of indifference or outright opposition from member states without producers of the good in question or with industrial consumers or traders of the good. Over time, EU member states have gradually reduced the decision threshold in the Council to approve Commission proposals to impose definitive duties: from a qualified to a simple majority vote in 1994; from abstentions not counting to abstentions counting as votes in favour in 2004; and from a simple majority to a 'qualified minority' in 2014, according to the weighted voting rules of the Lisbon Treaty (Scharf, 2015). The Commission's power to adopt trade defence measures has thus significantly increased, giving more priority 'to technical instead of political evaluation' as member states have often been subject to strong lobbying and retaliation threats from the countries targeted by the trade defence measures (Dordi and Forganni, 2013, p. 366).

Finally, as a sixth step, if the complainant firm or interest association wants an extension of the duties, it can file a request for an expiry review with the Directorate of Trade Defence three months before the end of the initial duties. If 25 per cent of the industry supports this request for prolongation and provides evidence that dumping and injury are still taking place (or would return if duties were lifted), the Commission is obliged to start reviewing the anti-dumping measures. The request needs to be endorsed by the TDI Committee, acting according to the advisory procedure. As soon as the old measures expire, the Commission starts an investigation, lasting approximately 15 months while the higher tariffs remain in place. After the investigation, the Commission presents its proposal to the TDI Committee for approval, which again can reject it only by qualified majority.

The European Commission thus takes all the decisions. However, for the most important decisions, such as the imposition, amendment or termination of definitive measures, the Commission must consult the TDI Committee, which can block the adoption by a qualified majority.

Box 3.6 provides an overview of the steps in EU anti-dumping investigations. Anti-subsidy investigations follow the same decision-making procedure, while the imposition of safeguard measures follows a similar yet less legally formalized procedure.

As is evident from this overview, the anti-dumping procedure requires a high degree of legal, procedural and economic expertise on the part of the trade associations that file the complaints, as well as on the part of the European Commission. At the same time, the procedure is clearly geared to defend the interests of domestic producers, at the expense of firms processing or importing those products. This led to increased opposition from firms that had outsourced parts of their production, from processing industries and from importers and retailers. The then–Commissioner for Trade Mandelson was sympathetic to these demands and in 2008 initiated a reform. In the face of consistent and better-coordinated lobbying on the part of those producers that are users of the anti-dumping instrument, however, the reform process failed (De Bièvre and Eckhardt, 2011). Only some minor changes were introduced, increasing to some extent the transparency and reliability of the procedure, for instance through the introduction of a so-called hearing officer in DG Trade. The post-Lisbon comitology reforms finally brought about some more substantial changes. The most important modification was the fact that the Council of Ministers would no longer

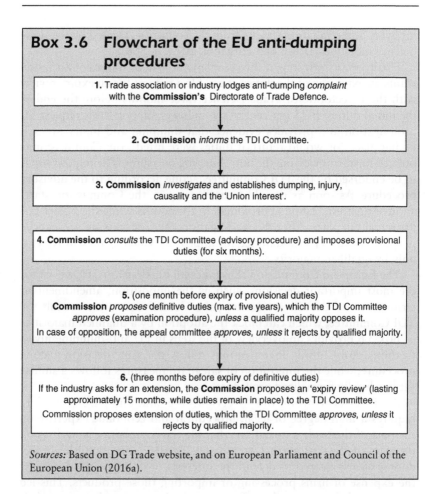

Box 3.6   Flowchart of the EU anti-dumping procedures

1. Trade association or industry lodges anti-dumping *complaint* with the **Commission's** Directorate of Trade Defence.

2. Commission *informs* the TDI Committee.

3. Commission *investigates* and establishes dumping, injury, causality and the 'Union interest'.

4. Commission *consults* the TDI Committee (advisory procedure) and imposes provisional duties (for six months).

5. (one month before expiry of provisional duties) **Commission** *proposes* definitive duties (max. five years), which the TDI Committee *approves* (examination procedure), *unless* a qualified majority opposes it.
In case of opposition, the appeal committee *approves*, *unless* it rejects by qualified majority.

6. (three months before expiry of definitive duties)
If the industry asks for an extension, the **Commission** proposes an 'expiry review' (lasting approximately 15 months, while duties remain in place) to the TDI Committee.
Commission proposes extension of duties, which the TDI Committee *approves*, *unless* it rejects by qualified majority.

Sources: Based on DG Trade website, and on European Parliament and Council of the European Union (2016a).

decide on anti-dumping by simple majority, but that the Commission proposal for anti-dumping duties takes effect *unless* a qualified majority in the appeal TDI Committee opposes it (Hoffmeister, 2015b; Scharf, 2015). Apart from this important change from Council to comitology decision-making, the Commission facilitated access to non-confidential information on the proceedings, especially for smaller companies. It also obtained the Council's approval for a further reform of the anti-dumping Regulation.

These reforms were introduced in response to a dramatic rise in Chinese and thus world-wide production over-capacity in the steel sector, and had, as before, pitted EU member states with steel production capacity against those with only very little or no domestic production capacity. In the latter member states, industries using steel products as inputs (like car manufacturers) benefited from the collapse of world steel prices and saw no reason to raise trade barriers against these cheap Chinese inflows. The United Kingdom took the lead of those countries with little or no domestic production and for a long time blocked a compromise between industries producing or using steel in the EU (see also Bollen et al., 2016). Next to having imposed a series of anti-dumping measures against Chinese steel products upon the request of European steel makers, in June 2017 the opposition to anti-subsidy measures against subsidized Chinese steel product exports subsided, and the EU imposed definitive countervailing duties of up to 35.9 per cent on hot-rolled steel from China (European Commission, 2017c). The increased awareness about Chinese preferential lending, tax rebates and other financial injections, together with the loss of credibility for the UK to be the advocate of an unconditional open-door policy towards China, thus contributed to a change of track in what is certainly one of the most important bilateral relationships in the EU's current trade policy.

Apart from the concrete decisions in individual TDI cases brought to the fore by European industry, EU institutions are currently also structurally amending the trade defence instruments regulation of the EU on the following topics (Council of the European Union, 2016). First, the imposition of provisional duties will be applied more transparently and more predictably by publishing them four weeks before applying them. Second, the Commission will be able to initiate investigations without an official request from the industry, in the event of a threat of retaliation by a third country. Third, the investigation period will be shortened. Fourth, the EU will be able to deviate from its so-called lesser duty rule. This rule stipulates that duties must not be higher than what is necessary to prevent injury for an EU industry (a practice that is not obligatory under WTO anti-dumping rules). Already now, the Commission is able to impose higher duties on raw material and energy products under specific circumstances. And finally, when anti-dumping duties are no longer maintained, duties collected during an expiry review can be reimbursed to the importers of such products. At the time of writing, the proposed changes are subject to interinstitutional negotiations between the European Parliament, the Council and the Commission.

In parallel to these changes to its anti-dumping policy, the EU has also decided it will from December 2016 onwards assess case by case whether distortions affect domestic prices or costs, abandoning its previous policy of generally treating the Republic of China as a 'non-market economy' (Bridges, 2016). The further codification of this practice into EU law is currently subject to a trilogue discussion between the Commission, the Council and the Parliament (Council of the European Union, 2017). When the Directorate for Trade Defence classifies a country as a non-market economy, it employs what is known as an 'analogue' method, whereby a good's 'normal value' is determined by using a price or constructed value from a market economy country. The issue was subject to considerable controversy in EU–China relations, as well as internally in the EU. China consistently defended the view that the EU (like other WTO members) was obliged to grant it market economy status after a 15-year transition period following its accession to the WTO in 2001. China has requested WTO dispute settlement consultations regarding these EU measures related to price comparison methodologies (WTO, 2016).

Box 3.7 showcases the example of a concluded anti-dumping case against Vietnamese bicycle producers.

Box 3.7   Case study: EU anti-dumping measures against bicycles from Vietnam

On 15 March 2004, the European Bicycles Manufacturers Association (EBMA) lodged a complaint alleging that imports of bicycles from Vietnam are being dumped and are thereby causing material injury to their members. The EBMA is an association representing the three big producer groups in EU bicycle manufacturing, totalling about 35 per cent of EU bicycle production. The European Commission published the notice of initiation of an anti-dumping proceeding in the *Official Journal of the European Union* on 29 April 2004. In this notice, the Commission indicates that the EBMA proposes the 'normal value' of a bicycle to be the price that is charged in Mexico, as this country is regarded as a similar market economy third country (the 'analogue' country to Vietnam). Put in non-legal terms, a country is regarded to have a market economy if firms in it compete with each other and the state does not systematically subsidize them. The criteria for such treatment are set out in the basic EU Regulation on anti-dumping.

The Commission further asked firms and associations in the sector to provide information by responding to a questionnaire. The

→

Commission in particular asked for information from bicycle-export-ing firms in Vietnam, from firms importing these bicycles into the EU, from domestic EU producers of bicycles, as well as from others with an interest in this matter, such as processing industries and consumer organizations. Furthermore, the notice contained the precise time limits (between 10 and 40 days) within which these actors had to provide this information in order to be included in the Commission's assessment of whether there was dumping and whether this injured EU industry. On the basis of the information obtained, the Directorate of Trade Defence launched its investigation, which had to be concluded within 15 months.

On 14 July 2005, the Council published the findings of the Commis-sion's investigation and its decision to impose anti-dumping duties of 15.8 per cent on bicycles from one particular Vietnamese bicycle producer and 34.5 per cent on bicycles coming from all other Vietnamese bicycle pro-ducers. This Regulation contains the Directorate of Trade Defence's report on which firms responded to the questionnaire, which firms Commission officials visited on site (both in the EU and in Vietnam); its chosen cal-culation of 'normal value'; the choice of the 'analogue' country, Mexico; and the Commission's decision of granting 'market economy treatment' to only one of the six Vietnamese firms that asked for such treatment. Since the EBMA had not requested an expiry review, the Commission published a notice of the impending expiry of anti-dumping measures against bicycles from Vietnam on 19 March 2010 and a notice of the actual expiry on 13 July 2010.

This anti-dumping case was thus handled by the European Com-mission, the former anti-dumping advisory committee in the Council, and subjected to a simple majority vote in COREPER. Under the new post-Lisbon rules, the case would have been handled more exclusively by the Commission Directorate of Trade Defence, with the Trade Defence Instruments Committee rather than the Council approving of the meas-ures. Only if the issue at stake had been more controversial might a simple majority of the anti-dumping committee have referred the proposal to the appeal committee. Even in such a case, however, the committee would most likely have approved the measure since reaching the qualified majority required to reject the Commission proposal is a rather hypo-thetical scenario.

Source: Based on WTO website and relevant Commission documents.

Enforcing market access commitments and international dispute settlement

Whereas anti-dumping policy protects the EU domestic market against allegedly dumped imports, the Commission also investigates and takes action to enforce market access for European exporters outside the EU. A marked difference between defensive and offensive trade policy instruments is that the former can be called upon only by producers of goods, whereas both the goods and the services sectors can turn to the Commission for help to lower trade barriers in foreign markets that are in breach of international trade agreements.

Offensive trade policy instruments take several forms. The Commission can conduct bilateral consultations with the country in question about the trade barriers; it can initiate a formal market access investigation under the EU Trade Barriers Regulation; or it can file a complaint with the WTO Dispute Settlement Body. The Market Access Unit within DG Trade is one of the venues through which the European Commission channels information from EU exporters and operators abroad on market conditions and trade and investment impediments in third countries. The Market Access Database (http://madb.europa.eu) contains information stemming from European producers and services industries; their trade associations; embassies of the member states; EU Delegations; and Market Access Teams. Market Access Teams are organized by the EU Delegations in important third countries and gather local expertise from the Delegation, member state embassies and business organizations to identify and tackle domestic trade barriers.

Under the Trade Barriers Regulation, individual firms and trade associations can submit formal complaints to the Commission, which is then obliged to start an investigation into whether trading partners are indeed upholding trade barriers incompatible with their international, especially WTO, commitments (European Parliament and Council of the European Union, 2015). Formally, EU member states can also file a TBR complaint, but none has ever used this route since its establishment in 1994. The forerunner of the TBR procedure, the New Commercial Policy Instrument of 1984, had largely remained a paper tiger because it was accessible only for associations representing a major proportion of the relevant Community industry. A TBR complaint can be considered an antechamber to a full-fledged WTO dispute settlement complaint and offers private parties indirect access to WTO dispute settlement procedures (see Chapter 5). Industries or operators confronted with foreign trade barriers not in accordance with international obligations can thus ask the Commission services to conduct in-depth investigations on excess customs duties, the violation of international rules on intellectual property protection or other impediments not in accordance with international and WTO law.

In the first instance, the Commission seeks to address these issues in bilateral consultations with the country in question. The Commission is assisted by the Trade Barriers Committee, composed of member state representatives and chaired by the Commission, which serves as examination committee. Moreover, the Trade Policy Committee is informed. Complainant industries hereby have an insurance that the Commission will not quietly dispose of their complaint in the course of the investigation if political or bureaucratic expediency would entice it to do so. Box 3.8 provides an overview of the steps in the TBR procedure.

In the past, TBR complaints have, for instance, come from the Scotch Whisky Association against Uruguay, from the Confédération Européenne des Producteurs de Spiritueux and the Comité Européen

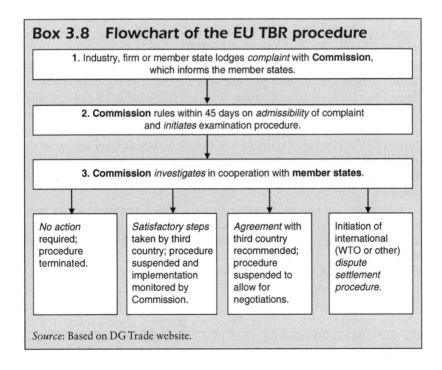

Box 3.8   Flowchart of the EU TBR procedure

1. Industry, firm or member state lodges *complaint* with **Commission**, which informs the member states.

2. **Commission** rules within 45 days on *admissibility* of complaint and *initiates* examination procedure.

3. **Commission** *investigates* in cooperation with **member states**.

| No action required; procedure terminated. | *Satisfactory steps* taken by third country; procedure suspended and implementation monitored by Commission. | *Agreement* with third country recommended; procedure suspended to allow for negotiations. | Initiation of international (WTO or other) *dispute settlement procedure*. |

Source: Based on DG Trade website.

des Entreprises Vins against India, from the Conseil Interprofessionnel du Vin de Bordeaux against Canada and from the Bureau National
Interprofessionnel du Cognac against Brazil. Other examples include
complaints from the European Federation of Pharmaceutical Industries
and Associations about the lack of intellectual property protection for
medicines in Korea, from the airplane construction firm Dornier about
WTO-incompatible subsidies to the aircraft industry in Brazil and from
the Remote Gambling Association about the discriminatory enforcement of the US Internet gambling ban.

Many firms and trade associations may prefer not to lodge a formal
TBR complaint, for fear of antagonizing business partners in a country,
even if they would have a case against them. They instead alert the Commission services and inform member state representatives about trade
barriers they are unable to overcome themselves. Also, public decision
makers may refrain from choosing the route of formal complaints –
opening a TBR investigation or filing a WTO dispute settlement – for
instance, when the country in question has very similar qualms about
EU trade policy measures. In case of countries with specialized trade policy administrations, however, the Commission, like other industrialized
members of the WTO, has had fewer reserves against using formalized
and quasi-judicial means like TBR or WTO complaints.

Most TBR investigations seem to have sufficed to clearly identify
trade barriers abroad and put pressure on the country in question to
bring its practices into conformity with international rules. Several TBR
cases also led the Commission to initiate a WTO dispute settlement
procedure in Geneva. These issues were particularly sensitive for the
targeted WTO member state, for example the Argentinean measures on
exports of hides and imports of finished leather, Brazilian measures on
textiles and clothing and Brazilian measures on trade in retreaded tyres
(see Box 3.9).

It is important to note, however, that the TBR procedure has not been
used very much by firms and has even appeared to fall into disuse since
2010. Yet, non-use should not be confused with irrelevance. Firms and
sectors may well refrain from going public by lodging a TBR complaint,
for fear of souring business relationships. They may try to get rid of
trade barriers through less conspicuous means while keeping anonymity
behind bilateral consultations conducted by the European Commission
and its representatives abroad. Yet, trade partners always interact with
the EU in the full knowledge that TBR investigations and/or WTO dispute settlement can be activated.

Box 3.9   Case study: TBR investigation and WTO complaint against Brazil

On 5 November 2003 the European Retread Manufacturers Association (BIPAVER) lodged a TBR complaint. BIPAVER complained about an import ban and financial penalties imposed by Brazil and asked to investigate whether these measures were in accordance with WTO law. The Commission duly investigated the complaint and reported to the Trade Barriers Committee that the measures contravened major WTO principles, such as non-discrimination, national treatment and prohibitions on quantitative restrictions (see Chapter 5). The Commission therefore recommended that Brazil be given until October 2004 to withdraw the measure; otherwise, the Commission would request WTO consultations. These consultations with the Brazilian authorities did not lead to a satisfactory outcome. Therefore, on 2 May 2005 the Commission adopted a decision on the existence of an obstacle to trade and on the initiation of dispute settlement proceedings at the WTO. Since the consultations in the framework of this dispute settlement case (DS 332) at the WTO did not lead to a mutually agreed solution, the EU requested the establishment of a WTO Panel. In its report on 12 June 2007, the Panel did find forms of discrimination in the Brazilian measures, but not to the extent that the EU had alleged. The EU appealed this decision. On 3 December 2007 the Appellate Body found that the ban discriminated against EU exports since it did not apply to members of Mercosur. The case even reached the ultimate and rather exceptional stage of the appointment of a WTO arbitrator at the request of the EU. At the beginning of 2009, the EU and Brazil concluded a procedural agreement on their dispute, and in September 2009 Brazil could report its full compliance with WTO obligations to the Dispute Settlement Body.

Sources: DG Trade and WTO websites.

Chapter 5 will return to the EU's enforcement of international agreements, especially its recourse to WTO dispute settlement. Suffice it to say here that the European Commission can threaten to impose, or actually impose, retaliatory measures ('suspension of concessions') to induce recalcitrant trading members to respect international agreements that they have entered into with the EU. Whereas in the past the imposition of retaliation in response to non-compliance by third countries was subject to the ordinary legislative procedure or other relevant legislative or administrative procedures, the Council and Parliament have in 2014 delegated the swift imposition of retaliation to the European Commission by adopting a trade enforcement regulation (European Parliament and Council of the European Union, 2014b).

Finally, in the specific field of market access in public procurement, the European Commission has recently put forward a proposal to enhance its leverage over its trade partners (Dawar, 2016; Bollen et al., 2016). The EU generally has a relatively open government procurement market, meaning that foreign companies can openly bid for contracts with public authorities across the Union. Some of the EU's major trading partners, like the US, Japan and China, however, have kept their own public procurement market far more closed (see also Chapter 7). As a result, the European Commission had in 2012 formally presented a proposal that would incentivize third countries to reciprocate. This proposal found wide support in the European Parliament, but not in the Council. Four years later, the European Commission (2016) formally presented an amended proposal for a so-called International Procurement Instrument (IPI). The IPI would allow the Commission to initiate public investigations in cases of alleged discrimination of EU companies in procurement markets. In case of discriminatory restrictions vis-à-vis EU goods, services and/or suppliers, the Commission could then invite the country concerned for consultations on the opening of its procurement market, possibly leading to negotiations on an international agreement. As a last resort, the Commission could consider bids from the country concerned as offering a higher price than put forward, thus providing European and non-targeted countries' goods and services a competitive advantage.

Overall, the EU has in recent years, in the context of the rise of the emerging economies and the wake of the economic crisis, started to considerably gear up its trade defence and enforcement instruments.

Conclusion

This chapter has provided an overview of the EU's trade policymaking procedures, the most important actors involved and the instruments available. There are varying processes for when the EU negotiates trade agreements, when it implements the common commercial policy and when it applies defensive or offensive trade policy measures. Consequently, the question of who makes EU trade policy requires a multifaceted answer that takes into account many legal, economic and political considerations.

The next chapter will introduce several theoretical perspectives that help explain the roots and bargaining dynamics of EU trade policy. A concrete example will illustrate the negotiation and conclusion of a free trade agreement between the EU and a third country, as well as the contributions of the different approaches to understand this process.

Further reading

Devuyst, Y. (2013) 'European Union Law and Practice in the Negotiation and Conclusion of International Trade Agreements', *Journal of International Business & Law*, 12(2), 259–316.

Hoffmeister, F. (2015) 'The European Union as an International Trade Negotiator', in J.A. Koops and G. Macaj (eds), *The European Union as a Diplomatic Actor* (Basingstoke: Palgrave), 138–154.

Woolcock, S. (2015) 'Trade Policy: Policy-making after the Treaty of Lisbon', in H. Wallace, M.A. Pollack and A. Young (eds), *Policy-Making in the European Union*, 7th edn (Oxford: Oxford University Press), 388–406.

Young, A.R. and J. Peterson (2014) *Parochial Global Europe: 21st Century Trade Politics* (Oxford: Oxford University Press), 102–129.

Chapter 4

The Political Economy of Trade Policymaking in the EU

What explains trade policy? This chapter introduces some major theoretical perspectives on the political economy of trade policymaking and its application to the trade policy of the European Union (EU). The first part investigates approaches that focus on different levels of analysis, in order to explain EU trade policy. The factors shaping the policy can mainly be located on three different levels of analysis: the international system, the society and the state. Systemic explanations view trade policymaking as a reaction to the challenges and opportunities flowing from the structure of the international system of states. Society-centred approaches start from the assumption that organized societal interests shape public decision-makers' choices in the conduct of EU trade policy, while state-centred approaches view national and European institutions as predominantly independent from the demands of interest groups and civil society. According to the state-centred view, the demand for certain policies does not necessarily translate into desired outcomes, for example when governmental actors are relatively insulated from those demands in multilevel systems or through the delegation of authority. The second part of the chapter presents tools which take into account the interaction between the levels of analysis when analysing the negotiation dynamics in EU trade policy formation. To this purpose, the chapter provides an introduction to the use of two-level game analysis and the principal–agent framework and their applications to EU trade policy. The EU–South Korea Free Trade Agreement (FTA) serves as an example to illustrate the differences between the perspectives.

Exploring the roots of EU trade policy

In international relations, the problem of selecting a level of analysis and the descriptive, explanatory and predictive implications of that choice have long been discussed (Singer, 1961). Like any policy, trade policy

84

finds its roots in societal factors, domestic institutional factors or international factors. Many explanations of foreign economic policy indeed focus on one specific level of analysis when looking for the sources of trade policy. System-centred approaches explain a country's trade policy as a function of its capabilities relative to other states; society-centred approaches view trade policy as reflecting the preferences of the dominant domestic groups; and state-centred approaches argue that domestic structures account for trade policy (Ikenberry et al., 1988). Separating the levels of analysis simply serves as a heuristic device – that is, a construct that helps increase analytical clarity when exploring the roots of trade policy. Both for analytical purposes and in trade policymaking practice, the levels tend to be closely intertwined, and understanding trade policy requires identifying actors' preferences – be they derived from systemic or domestic sources – studying how the interests at stake get organized and knowing how they are mediated through political institutions.

From a system-centred perspective, factors such as international economic structures, the prevailing distribution of power or forces of globalization and regionalization affect foreign economic policy. Trade policy is a reaction to the challenges and opportunities flowing from the international economic and security system. Countries may, for instance, engage in 'balancing' by creating their own regional blocs or networks of preferential trade agreements in response to regionalism in other areas of the world. The EU's trade policy would thus reflect the need to respond to the external challenges to Europe's relative position in the world and to promote its global competitiveness and influence as an international actor. Without unpacking the 'black box' of domestic politics, however, system-centred approaches lead to the expectation that countries facing the same international constraints pursue similar trade policies. Although certainly useful, such an explanation can work only on the macro-level, because systemic factors are likely to affect the preferences of societal actors and the decisions of governments. These actors make their decisions based on interests they have or ideas they hold. External influences of the international political economy work through these domestic actors by shaping their policy preferences. The chapter thus adopts an actor-centred perspective and focuses first on the society-centred and then on state-centred approaches.

Society-centred approaches

From a society-centred perspective, the explanation of trade policy is rooted in domestic politics. Trade policy is shaped by competing organized societal interests and reflects the preferences of the dominant groups. Government institutions essentially provide an arena for the pluralistic struggle for influence without exerting a decisive impact on the emerging policies. The objectives of trade policy are the decision-makers' responses to the demands of interest groups and civil society. Trade has domestic distributional consequences, which generate political competition as the potential winners and losers turn to the political institutions to defend their economic interests. Various theories help explain which groups organize to lobby the public authorities to adopt their preferred policies and how political actors respond.

Two common models of interest-group competition over trade policy are based either on factor incomes and class conflict or on sector incomes and industry conflict (Oatley, 2012, pp. 70–79). The factor model looks at how factors of production, in particular the competition between capital and labour, drives trade policy. When tariffs are lowered in the wake of liberalization and trade expands (or, respectively, when trade barriers are raised and trade shrinks), one factor of production will experience rising income, whereas the other will suffer an income fall as the relative prices of labour and capital change in response to demand and supply. This depends on how abundant or scarce a factor is in a society. In international trade theory, the so-called Stolper–Samuelson theorem states that, under certain assumptions (such as perfect competition and high factor mobility), a rise in the relative price of a good will lead to a rise in the return to that factor which is used most intensively in the production of the good, and conversely, to a fall in the return to the other factor. In other words, trade liberalization lowers the real wage of the scarce factor of production, and protection from trade raises it. These income effects help explain trade policy preferences and political coalition formation: scarce factors want to minimize trade and prefer protection, whereas abundant factors want to expand trade and prefer a liberal policy (Rogowski, 1989). In advanced industrialized economies such as the EU, where capital is more abundantly available relative to labour, the factor model generally suggests that capital owners (abundant factor) would support while workers (scarce factor) oppose trade liberalization.

Viewed from this perspective, one might try to interpret recent waves of anti-globalization protests and more specifically campaigns against trade agreements as the mobilization of the losers of further liberalization, especially the labour force. However, in the EU, in contrast to anti-trade sentiment in the United States, labour unions did not consistently mobilize, for instance, against the further integration of labour-abundant China into the world economy. Protests rather galvanized around bilateral trade agreements with Canada and especially with the United States (see Chapter 7). Moreover, these protests were most fierce in relatively well-off Germany and Austria (Bauer, 2016), and relatively weak in the southern EU member states plagued by high unemployment. As De Ville and Vermeiren (2016) point out, the adaptability of domestic labour market institutions in coordinated market economies like Germany actually enable them to move to types of production with more highly skilled labour input in the face of cheap labour competition.

By contrast, the sector model (or specific-factors model) follows from the so-called Ricardo-Viner theorem of international trade theory. It argues that trade policy is driven by competition between industries rather than factors of production. Since factors cannot be assumed to be highly mobile but are specific to the sector in which they are employed, trade pits workers and capitalists in one industry against the workers and capitalists in another industry. When trade barriers are lowered or raised, the wages and returns to capital in a sector both rise or both fall. In other words, the factors of production employed in a sector that relies intensively on the society's abundant factor (in line with the country's comparative advantage) both gain from trade. In advanced industrialized economies such as the EU, factors in capital-intensive and high-technology industries – usually export-oriented sectors like pharmaceuticals – benefit from trade. Conversely, labour and capital used in industries which rely heavily on the society's scarce factor – commonly referred to as import-competing sectors, such as clothing and footwear – lose from trade.

Within this literature, import competitors pushing the government for the protection of the domestic market are often treated as dominating over exporters interested in better market access abroad. For exporters, the costs of mobilization, so the reasoning goes, often outweigh the anticipated benefits due to the lack of information about opportunities abroad and due to the uncertain outcome of lobbying efforts, since foreign trade barriers are not under the control of their home government and potential benefits could in the end be reaped by other exporters (or even by exporters from other countries if trade liberalization is non-discriminatory, as required by a basic rule of the World Trade Organization (WTO)). However, unlike for the pursuit of new opportunities, exporters may lobby more when facing losses of foreign market access (Baldwin, 1997; Dür, 2010). This line of reasoning has implications for the possible explanations of both the gradual reduction of tariff levels under the General Agreement on Tariffs and Trade (GATT) and the WTO, as well as the proliferation of trade agreements in recent decades.

First, the gradual reduction of trade barriers within the multilateral trading system may be due to the empowerment of export constituencies with each successive GATT/WTO round of trade liberalization, until average tariffs reach close to zero levels, occasioning Baldwin and Robert-Nicoud (2015) to label this self-reinforcing effect of initial multilateral trade liberalization the 'juggernaut effect'. Second, the causes of regionalism may not be due to the blockage of allegedly too complex inter-state bargaining in the WTO, but rather a 'domino effect' (Baldwin, 1997). Political initiatives to deepen or widen regional integration may trigger a multiplier or domino effect that produces membership requests from third countries. Exporters excluded from the additional benefits and suffering trade diversion effects of such a deepened and/or enlarged market have a strong incentive to lobby their respective governments (Dür, 2010). This thus sets in motion a proliferation of preferential trade agreements as governments are pushed by their export sectors to enter negotiations to help them recapture foregone market shares abroad.

Hence, both the factor model and the sector model argue that trade policy preferences are determined by the income effects of trade, but they make different assumptions about factor mobility. The Stolper–Samuelson and the Ricardo-Viner theorems examine extreme cases in which factors of production are assumed to be either highly mobile or immobile. 'Allowing that factors can have varying degrees of mobility, the simple prediction is that broad class-based political coalitions are more likely where factor mobility is high, whereas narrow industry-based coalitions are more likely where mobility is low' (Hiscox, 2001, p. 4).

As the two models have shown, statements about the preferences of different groups in the economy in function of their positions can be derived from economic theory. Moreover, economic theory can also be a source of ideas in terms of beliefs about cause-and-effect relationships. The expected effects of specific government policies in the field of trade then leads to corresponding demands and lobbying efforts. Firms and governments are composed of individuals who are the bearers of ideas. The formation of trade preferences may thus not only depend on material incentives based on distributional concerns but also on exposure to economic ideas and information prevalent in the direct environment in which these actors are socially active.

Such analyses still leave open the question about how preferences are transformed into policy decisions. In order to be able to influence the policymaking process, interests must organize themselves. It cannot be taken for granted that if everyone in a group shares the same ideas and interests, they will act collectively to achieve their goals. Collective-action problems may arise from the possibility of individual actors to free ride on the efforts of others if the group is cooperating to provide public goods (Olson, 1965). Public goods are goods which are non-excludable (that is, one actor cannot reasonably prevent another from consuming the good) and non-rivalrous (that is, one actor's consumption of the good does not affect another's). Large groups face relatively high costs when attempting to organize for collective action, while small groups face relatively low costs. Furthermore, individual actors in large groups will gain less per capita in case of successful collective action, and their contribution to the common cause is very small. Hence, in the absence of specific incentives to motivate participation, large groups are less able to act in their common interest than small ones are.

The logic of collective action helps explain why it is easier for producers to dominate trade policy compared to the less organized large group of consumers and why, absent other causes, there can be a certain bias towards protectionism. Trade barriers provide large benefits to the few firms producing in the protected industry, while the costs are distributed across many other firms and consumers. For actors facing concentrated gains or losses, it is easier to overcome collective-action problems than it is for those with diffuse stakes. Once created, a trade policy coalition with well-established channels of access to public officials may defend its interests even if the stakes are not very high, whereas a more affected but unorganized group may not be able to mobilize. Moreover, governments are less willing to liberalize trade unilaterally and prefer negotiated reciprocal trade agreements, in which they can offset concessions in import-competing sectors with gains for export-oriented sectors. With regard to unilateral liberalization, politicians face protectionist pressures, whereas in case of a liberalizing trade agreement, they may be able to mobilize export-oriented sectors that would benefit from a negotiated market opening abroad. This chapter further elaborates on the negotiation dynamics of such 'games' below.

Whereas it can thus be helpful to distinguish export-oriented and import-competing firms and sectors, explanations of trade policy formation can also benefit from distinguishing more than just those two types. Especially in an era of increased economic integration, firms can come in different guises with important implications for the type of expectations and explanations available to conceive of their behaviour, the policies of public authorities and their effects on the distribution of economic and political gains and losses in society. First, intra-industry trade characterizes sectors where firms trade the same type of products yet engage in far-reaching specialization (Gilligan, 1997). Second, a whole set of firms may not be active in production itself but in processing, trading and distribution. Third, a growing number of firms are now part of so-called global value chains, whereby production, assembly and finalization may take place in different countries (Baldwin, 2014; Gereffi et al., 2005; Orefice and Rocha, 2014). This heterogeneity across firms has given rise to a set of analyses highlighting how the traditional conflict between industries against and in favour (with a lot of relative indifferent ones in the middle) has made place for a political economy of trade policymaking where distributional conflict between sectors has become relatively subdued.

For example, Eckhardt (2015) analyses how the globalization of production and the emergence of global value chains impacts on trade preferences, lobby strategies and the political influence of EU firms. Melitz (2003) has shown that only the more productive firms take the decision to enter export markets, and this increased exposure to intra-industry trade competition in turn increases their productivity. Lanz and Miroudot (2011) highlight that firms that are highly integrated into global value chains either engage in vertical foreign direct investment (FDI) – that is, create foreign subsidiaries producing for that home market – or rely on independent foreign suppliers. The political consequences of these economic changes are considerable. Not only do import-dependent firms increasingly join the ranks of those firms and sectors advocating EU FTAs with those countries with which they already have intense trading relations (Eckhardt and Poletti, 2016), but large multinational firms also turn out to gain even more than small and medium-sized firms do from FTAs (Baccini et al., 2017), since industry opposition to trade liberalization effectively breaks down in such circumstances (Osgood, 2017).

It is important to realize, however, that political institutions set the context in which competition between organized interests may unfold. The rules of political systems may filter out whether and how interests organize and how groups exert pressure on the policymaking process. In a majoritarian political system, where action is taken by voting (e.g. in a referendum), organized interests may need to show that their preferred trade policy would benefit a large share of the population and organize large movements. By contrast, in a system where decision-makers are more insulated from majoritarian pressures, small and well-organized lobbying groups with access to power may be more likely to be successful, or politicians may try to cater to a multitude of sometimes contradictory demands. Domestic political institutions may thus affect the costs of collective action because either small or large organizations might be required to be able to exert some influence. If mobile-specific factors have the possibility to secure protection, they may choose to stay in their industry as long as the costs of lobbying are lower than the adjustment costs of moving to another industry (Alt and Gilligan, 1994, pp. 177–191).

State-centred approaches

From a state-centred perspective, EU trade policy is viewed as being shaped by domestic and European political institutions and by public interventions that come about quite independently from interest-group demands. The politicians or civil servants attempt to manipulate policies in accordance with their own preferences, including economic, security or development concerns, as well as bureaucratic interests.

Important differences can be distinguished in the institutional capacities of states to shape their societies and economies within such a state-centred approach. Countries vary in the extent to which they are centralized or in the degree of autonomy that their state officials enjoy. Being situated at the intersection of the domestic and international political economies gives the state a unique position in the formulation of foreign economic policy. Policymakers may intervene in the economy to pursue objectives that are independent of the concerns of domestic interest groups. Such interventions may or may not contribute to aggregate social welfare. For example, industrial policy may use various instruments, such as subsidies, tariffs or government procurement practices, to channel resources to those industries that the state wants to promote. Strategic trade theory asserts that in many high-technology industries, often characterized by oligopolistic competition with only a few firms, government intervention can help domestic firms achieve economies of scale and economies of experience (Richardson, 1990). Economies of scale arise when the cost of production per unit falls as output increases, and economies of experience occur when efficient production requires specific skills acquired in the industry. The government's ability to intervene depends inter alia on the state strength – that is, the degree to which policymakers are insulated from domestic interests (Oatley, 2012, pp. 90–103).

In addition, ideas held by public actors, such as the predominant economic thought, may influence trade policy (Goldstein, 1988). If policymakers have incomplete information about their environment, they must rely on their beliefs about which trade policy would be best. For example, a government that believes in the concept of comparative advantage might lower tariffs, whereas a government that relies on the infant industry idea might raise tariffs. The infant industry argument states that nascent industries need to be protected until they attain similar economies of scale as their older competitors from other countries.

As so-called neoliberal economic ideas about free trade, deregulation and privatization have been on the rise in Europe and worldwide since the early 1990s, the EU's drive for trade liberalization could be attributed to these neoliberal opinions held by public decision-makers. However, liberal economists often complain that trade policy is in practice not guided (only) by liberal economic ideas. Messerlin (2001), for example, attributes this to a 'statist' bias in the EU's institutional setup, which leaves space for direct government intervention in markets (see also Winters, 2001). Moreover, according to the 'normative power' approach, the EU's trade policy is often based on a normative justification other than neoliberal economic ideas (see also Chapter 7). The EU understands itself as a community of values, and it promotes norms and ideas in its external action in line with its own identity. Manners (2009) argues that normative frames such as human and labour rights function as reference points for EU trade policy. While this, on the one hand, may well increase the legitimacy of a social dimension of trade policy in the international system, it raises the expectations about the reference point against which policymakers and policy observers (whether specialists or citizens) are likely to judge and assess the EU's performance in its actual trade policies. Drawing on a constructivist approach, Siles-Brügge (2014b) contends that the role of ideas about the EU's place in the world had an impact on the conduct of its trade relations.

Hence, differences in countries' foreign economic policies can be explained by domestic structures or by state actors with specific preferences and ideas. Combining both approaches, Hanson (1998) argues that one of the unintended consequences of the completion of the internal market was to further shield European policymakers from protectionist pressures by introducing qualified majority voting. Industries lost protection at the national level (e.g. remaining national quotas, customs procedures or product standards) and were unable to re-establish it at the European level, because small minorities could block new trade restrictions. A change in the institutional context would thus have resulted in a bias towards liberalization in EU trade policy. In a similar vein, yet from a more society-centred approach, Dür (2011) argues that greater integration in the financial services sector made the EU more open to firms from third countries.

It is worth mentioning that most legal analyses of EU trade policy can be usefully regarded as state-centred perspectives. Although legal studies do not aim to explain the outcomes of EU trade policy, most legal scholars depart from the assumption that the procedures and competencies of public actors are of primary importance and that these rules to a large degree determine both process and outcome – a view that is often logically at odds with explanations based on the distribution of preferences of economic actors, their translation into lobbying activity and their ability to weigh on the policies subsequently formulated by public decision-makers.

The following section illustrates the theoretical approaches discussed with a case study of the EU–Korea FTA, the EU's first FTA with an Asian country.

Example: EU–Korea Free Trade Agreement

The EU–Korea FTA was negotiated between 2007 and 2009 and signed in October 2010. It has been provisionally applied since July 2011 and fully ratified in October 2015. The agreement was at the time hailed the 'most ambitious trade agreement ever negotiated' by the EU, representing a new generation of FTAs (European Commission, 2010a). It aimed at eliminating 98.7 per cent of duties in trade value for both industrial and agricultural products within five years and at removing non-tariff barriers to trade (NTBs) for electronics, motor vehicles, pharmaceuticals, medical devices and chemicals. Both the EU and Korea applied already relatively low tariffs on manufactured products but maintained protection in selected areas – such as agriculture, and in the case of Korea also in textiles, clothing and footwear, as well as the automobile sector and services (Nicolas, 2009). Various studies expected the gains from the FTA to be positive for both sides, yet greater for Korea due to its higher level of protection and smaller market (e.g. European Parliament, 2010). More precisely, EU sectors such as business services, machinery, agri-foods, pharmaceuticals and chemicals were expected to gain from the agreement, while the main trade gains for Korea were seen in auto-mobiles, textiles and electronics.

From a system-centred perspective, which considers the preferences of both societal and state actors, the EU reacted to international rivalry that was inter alia caused by the US strategy to engage in 'competitive liberalization' from 2001 onwards (Evenett and Meier, 2008). In the framework of this policy, the United States indeed concluded an FTA with South Korea in April 2007. This put public and private actors in the EU under structural pressure not to be left behind in this increasingly important market in South-East Asia and to counter the expected effects of trade diversion. In view of the deadlock in the WTO Doha Round negotiations in July 2006 and the fact that the desired comprehensive agenda had been abandoned, the EU gave up the moratorium on negotiating new regional trade agreements, which it had stipulated in 1999, when a new WTO round was about to be launched. In its trade strategy 'Global Europe: Competing in the World' of October 2006, the European Commission singled out Korea as a priority because it combined high levels of protection with large market potential and was active in concluding FTAs with EU competitors (European Commission, 2006, p. 9). As the biggest trading power in the world, the EU could take advantage of its larger bargaining power vis-à-vis a middle-sized and still relatively protected economy and aim at an ambitious deal that would set a precedent for future agreements with countries like India, Singapore or Malaysia. In line with this view, the EU and others, like the United States, may have been engaging in counterbalancing the increasing geopolitical and economic standing of China, Korea's most important trading partner. As pointed out by the European Parliament (2011, p. 12), this agreement was expected to place 'the EU at an advantage compared to its most forceful competitors, such as the USA or China'.

South Korea had until 2004 exclusively relied on multilateral trade negotiations, yet as a result of the 1997 financial crisis in Asia and the problems of the WTO Doha Round, it started to actively engage in bilateral FTA negotiations. Korea had an interest in making itself less dependent on the emerging Chinese regional hegemon in South-East Asia, by siding not only with the United States but also with the EU because the EU was perceived as having less pronounced geopolitical ambitions. For Korea the main reasons for the FTA with the EU were the attractive size of the European market, the expected impact on the competitiveness of its services sector, the diversification of its trading partners and its standing as a regional power (Nicolas, 2009, pp. 37–38).

Viewed from a society-centred perspective, the fault lines of political conflict between proponents and adversaries of the EU–Korea FTA ran along sector lines. Rather than pitting labour unions against employer organizations in general, some sectors in the EU and Korea favoured the agreement, while other sectors – both employers and workers in that particular industry – voiced opposition. EU export-oriented sectors, such as services, chemicals, machinery and electronics actively lobbied to improve access to the Korean market and to offset the imminent competitive disadvantage vis-à-vis their American counterparts (Erixon and Lee, 2010). Once the negotiations were underway, other sectors that, based on impact assessment studies, were anticipated to gain from trade liberalization joined in their support. European agriculture, for example, could expect to further improve its bilateral trade surplus with Korea despite EU tariff removals. On the Korean side, the manufacturing industry had a stake in securing its access to the huge European market, since most of its activities consist of transforming intermediate goods from Japan and China into final consumer and capital products. The agreement would therefore put these sectors in a privileged position in the 'triangular trade' between China, Korea and the EU.

The sectors opposing the deal were mainly the EU car industry and Korean agriculture. In automobiles, the EU faced a considerable bilateral trade deficit because Korea successfully exported small cars for the European mass market, while European companies were hampered by Korean NTBs and mainly sold only larger and luxury cars. Moreover, Korean sales in the EU are largely concentrated on two brands, Hyundai and Kia, which already own large production plants in Europe. The European Automobile Manufacturers Association (ACEA) claimed that the FTA offered an unfair competitive advantage to Korean industries with negative consequences for employment in the car industry in Europe. As a result, the automobile companies, especially Fiat, and their workforce aligned against the agreement and even called on the EU member states not to ratify it (ACEA, 2009). In addition, when it became clear that the FTA had to be ratified by the European Parliament, since negotiations would finish only after the entry into force of the Lisbon Treaty, car manufacturers started to lobby Members of the European Parliament. In particular, the car industry opposed the fact that Korea was – for the first time in a bilateral EU FTA – granted a so-called Duty Drawback (DDB) clause. This allows Korean manufacturers to reclaim the duties on imports from low-cost neighbouring countries such as China, which are used as inputs to assemble products and then export

them to the EU. This lobbying effort was joined by the textiles industry. The European Parliament picked up this concern voiced by interest
groups in its report on the FTA:

> While the Commission considers that the impact of the DDB on the
> competitive situation of EU companies is likely to be minimal, sensi-
> tive European sectors including the European car and textile sectors
> believe that this mechanism will grant South Korea significant market
> advantages over European industries. (European Parliament, 2011,
> p. 11)

Eckhard and Poletti (2016) show that as a result of global value chains,
EU import-dependent firms had significant stakes in the liberalization of
trade with South Korea and mobilized in support of FTA negotiations.

On the Korean side, the most sensitive sector was agriculture, which
obtained transition arrangements up to 15 years, while rice – according
to the South-Korean side a 'culturally' important product for Korea –
was exempted from liberalization (Erixon and Lee, 2010, p. 3). It is also
telling that with regard to market access for services, the EU excluded the
politically sensitive medical, educational and audio-visual services sectors.

The EU–Korea FTA also contains a chapter on sustainable development, which sets up institutional structures to implement and monitor
the commitments to labour and environmental standards between the
parties, including through civil society involvement. This can be attributed either to the pressure and concerns about 'unfair' competition
from European non-governmental organizations (NGOs) and trade
unions participating inter alia in the Civil Society Dialogue of the
Directorate-General (DG) Trade and/or to the EU's aspiration as a
normative power to increasingly project the norm of sustainable development also in its external relations (Bartels, 2015).

Viewed from a state-centred perspective, the EU institutions are best
regarded as the main actors determining the process and outcome of
EU trade policymaking. When the European Commission proposed to
be granted the mandate to start negotiations with South Korea, it paid
great attention to the form that this new type of agreement would take,
so as to set a precedent for future agreements. The Council authorized
the Commission to negotiate the FTA on behalf of the EU, assisted by the
Trade Policy Committee of the Council of Ministers. The Commission
thus used its relative autonomy in setting EU trade policy to reach a far-
reaching FTA with Korea. The DDB provision stirred some controversy

in the Council and in the Parliament, which led an EU official to comment that member states faced the choice 'to give the commissioner more latitude or scrap the deal' (Financial Times, 2009), highlighting the view that EU trade policy can work properly only whenever the Commission has a substantial degree of autonomy.

Elsig and Dupont (2012) argue that the European Commission used its position strategically to pursue its own interests, without waiting for societal interests to pressure for an activist role. They see the officials 'driven by the desire to provide regulatory solutions to make sure that Europe's businesses can compete with other trading powers' (ibid., p. 499). While a majority of member states supported the negotiations, based on a broad mandate, the Korean DDB practice caused some opposition. To resist the criticism from import-competing sectors, in particular the car industry, the Commission engaged early on with interest groups and actively gathered support among actors concerned by exporter discrimination (ibid., pp. 501–504).

The EU member states initially accepted the Commission proposal for an agreement in October 2009. At a Council meeting in September 2010, the Italian government backtracked on its approval, trying to extract more concessions from the Korean side (Financial Times, 2010). However, Italy failed to garner support in the Council, and the compromise that was reached led to only a six-month delay of the entry into force of the FTA, whereas Italy had asked for 15 months. The member states simply clarified the provisions of a safeguard clause against an import surge of Korean goods in the FTA, without re-opening the negotiations with Korea.

The EU–Korea FTA was the first trade agreement which the European Parliament adopted under the Lisbon Treat, and the safeguard regulation which accompanied the FTA was its first major involvement in an ordinary legislative procedure on trade. The European Parliament had to give its consent to the FTA, but it could not amend the text. However, it seized the opportunity to flex its new muscle in the implementation of the FTA. In October 2010, the European Parliament postponed a vote on the regulation implementing the safeguard clause because of disagreement over who should be able to request the initiation of an investigation that could lead to the activation of safeguard measures (European Voice, 2010). As the EU for years now has barely used its safeguards procedure, it remains to be seen whether this clarification that the European Parliament added to the accord will activate this dormant policy instrument in the future.

Although the agreement was signed in October 2010, the Commission decided to wait on the provisional application until the European Parliament had given its consent to the FTA, which occurred in February 2011. The Korean National Assembly ratified the FTA in May 2011. Because some areas of the agreement fall under the national competence of EU member states (such as cooperation in cultural matters or provisions on the criminal enforcement of intellectual property rights), the entry into force of the full agreement also required ratification by all national parliaments. It should also be mentioned that an updated Framework Agreement between the EU and South Korea was signed in May 2010, replacing the Framework Agreement for Trade and Cooperation of 1996. It provides the overarching framework for cooperation with a legal link to the FTA, including strengthened cooperation on major political and global issues, such as human rights, non-proliferation of weapons of mass destruction, counter-terrorism and both climate change and energy security. Such a coupling of trade and political cooperation – sometimes in one agreement, sometimes in two separate agreements – can be interpreted as an expression of the EU's policy to project normative power or as a declaratory policy that tries to instil formal coherence to European foreign policy, without truly affecting the course that these discrete subfields of external European policymaking would take.

Akin to state-centred views of the EU–Korea FTA, a constructivist theoretical approach would stress the power of economic ideas in the formation of trade policy. Siles-Brügge (2011) argues that DG Trade of the European Commission deliberately constructed a discursive strategy on the imperative for liberalization which helped it overcome the opposition to the EU–Korea FTA. The agreement was portrayed as an economic necessity in the effort to find opportunities for market expansion for European exporters in exchange for giving up some remaining 'pockets of protectionism' in the EU. He thus interestingly shows how European public authorities strategically used a system-level view of the imperative to liberalize, as they pointed to the pressures of globalization, arguing that under such systemic pressures, the EU had no choice but to engage in concluding FTAs with important hubs in globalized trade.

To summarize, all theoretical approaches abstract from the complex social reality and selectively focuses on certain key aspects. Each approach has clear advantages and faces certain shortcomings. First, the level of the international system plays a role in the formation of trade policy preferences of both societal and state (or EU) actors.

Structural constraints and opportunities impact the domestic actors' assessment of the anticipated gains and losses from trade.

Second, society-centred approaches help understand the trade preferences of organized societal groups by identifying – a priori, by deducing them from theory instead of empirics – the likely winners and losers from international trade. However, they also face several shortcomings (Oatley, 2012, pp. 86–88). To explain a trade policy outcome, the relative power of the competing interest groups must be assessed: the notoriously difficult exercise of mapping preferences without inferring them from the outcome and the mediating role of decision-making structures. Moreover, political decision-makers may have preferences independent from such societal groups and thus play what is then generally called an autonomous role in trade politics. Finally, non-economic actors such as environmental, human rights or development-oriented NGOs may actively participate in trade policymaking. The perspective is thus very useful for explaining the content of the EU–Korea FTA because it incorporates the interests of both business and NGOs as well as the interests of export-oriented sectors versus import-competing sectors. However, the approach does not account for the mediating role of EU institutions, such as the Commission's capacity (1) to keep off demands of particularistic interest groups or the institutions' magnifying effects for some societal groups at the expense of others or (2) to pursue more general foreign policy objectives.

Third, while state-centred approaches can contribute towards alleviating these shortcomings, they also come with a downside. Governments do not necessarily intervene in order to enhance national welfare, nor is it always plausible that they act independently of societal interest groups. Whereas state-centred approaches highlight the consensual and multilevel decision-making process, which results in most EU trade policy outcomes being characterized by compromise, they have difficulties to explain under what conditions and how national and EU officials can act autonomously (Oatley, 2012, pp. 108–109). These approaches are good at explaining how the European Commission managed to push through a deal with Korea, even in the face of opposition. However, they have difficulties accounting for the exact content of the agreement, as the theoretical question then shifts towards where bureaucratic or ideational preferences come from.

For complex trade policy decisions or negotiations, the challenge for students of EU trade policy is to draw on insights from different approaches in order to gain more explanatory power, without sacrificing the internal consistency of such an account. This can be achieved by adopting approaches that combine different levels of analysis in one theoretical framework without a priori considering one level as more important than the other.

Explaining negotiation dynamics

Apart from analyses that focus on preference formation on the domestic side, negotiation dynamics are of course essential to an analysis of the politics of trade policy formation. This section presents two traditions that may provide useful information about negotiation dynamics. Two-level games and principal–agent approaches are closely related in that principal–agent relations take place in the context of a two-level game. The relative autonomy of public decision-makers in EU trade policy can be attributed to a principal–agent relationship between EU member states and the European Commission (e.g. Meunier, 2005; Elsig, 2007). As a result of the delegation of agenda setting and of the conduct of the negotiations to a centralised actor, the Commission enjoys quite some independence in setting EU trade policy. Specifically, this autonomy can be used in international negotiations.

Two-level games

The approach of two-level games provides a tool for the analysis of international negotiations by conceptualizing domestic–international interactions across different levels. Political leaders sitting at both the domestic and international 'game boards' try to reconcile the pressures from both arenas:

At the national level, domestic groups pursue their interests by pressuring the government to adopt favourable policies, and politicians seek power by constructing coalitions among those groups. At the international level, national governments seek to maximize their own ability to satisfy domestic pressures while minimizing the adverse consequences of foreign developments (Putnam, 1988, p. 434).

The negotiation of an agreement takes place between the chief negotiators on the international level, while the political or legal ratification process occurs on the domestic level, where each constituency discusses whether to accept the deal. The two levels affect each other since the win-set at the international level is shaped by the national level, and international pressures may 'reverberate' within domestic politics. A win-set is the set of all possible agreements that would gain the necessary support of a domestic constituency. Hence, a bilateral trade agreement becomes possible if both sides' win-sets overlap. The larger the win-sets, the greater the likelihood that win-sets will overlap. Conversely, the smaller the win-sets, the greater the risk that the negotiations will break down. The relative size of domestic win-sets is also important because it affects the distribution of the joint gains from an international agreement: the larger a perceived win-set, the more negotiators can be 'pushed around' by the other side to obtain concessions, whereas negotiators with a small domestic win-set can claim to have their 'hands tied'. Putnam's two-level game framework thus incorporates the so-called Schelling conjecture, which claims that the smaller the negotiator's autonomy, the greater its bargaining power (Schelling, 1960).

Putnam hypothesized that the size of win-sets depends on the distribution of power, preferences and coalitions at the domestic level; on the domestic political institutions, such as ratification procedures or the autonomy of a negotiator; and on the negotiators' strategies at the international level (Putnam, 1988, pp. 442–459). For example, the lower an actor's costs of 'no agreement' – that is, the weaker its preference intensity – the smaller the win-set, and the greater the autonomy of a negotiator, the larger the win-set. With regard to bargaining strategies, the negotiator may try to maximize the other side's win-set, for instance through side-payments, issue linkages, collusion, exploiting goodwill and political standing, restructuring the game or even misrepresenting the own win-set. This means that a negotiator has mixed motives: the larger the own win-set, the easier it is to conclude an international agreement, but the weaker the own bargaining position. However, in a collection of empirical studies edited by Evans et al. (1993), deliberate and intentional negotiator strategies turned out to be of minor importance, since strict domestic ratification rules constrained the negotiators' autonomy and increased bargaining power.

The two-level games logic about win-set size and both negotiator autonomy and bargaining power can be usefully applied to EU trade policy results in a three-level or double two-level game (Young, 2003, pp. 55–56; Da Conceição-Heldt, 2013). In one game, the EU is the international level at which EU member state governments representing their domestic interests seek to find a common position. In the second game, the EU is the domestic level, and the Commission negotiates at the international level. One important implication is that the EU's win-set tends to be small since it is the product of a pre-negotiation among its many member states (see Box 4.1). The requirement of a consent by the

Box 4.1   Visualization of win-sets in two- and three-level games

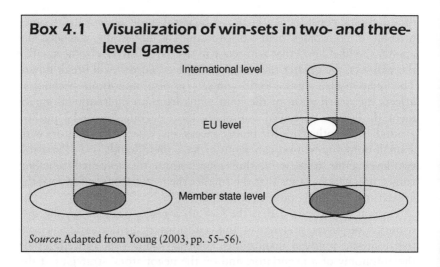

International level

EU level

Member state level

Source: Adapted from Young (2003, pp. 55–56).

European Parliament, or additional national ratification in case of mixed agreements, further constrains the EU's win-set. Because of the resulting low autonomy of the EU chief trade negotiator (personified in the Commissioner for Trade), the EU has comparatively more bargaining power or more 'leverage'. Moreover, the 'costs of no agreement' are usually lower for the EU as a big trading power than those costs are for the other side. These factors make the EU a difficult bargaining partner for third countries. On the other hand, the close coordination between the Commission and the member states in the Trade Policy Committee and the Commission's reporting to the INTA Committee reduce the risk of a ratification failure and involuntary defection and strengthen the external credibility of the EU's promised commitments.

The two- or three-level game approach is often used to merely describe various aspects of trade policymaking in the multilevel EU system (e.g. Collinson, 1999; Frennhoff Larsén, 2007). Used in its theoretical core sense, however, it helps explain why interregional agreements, such as an association agreement between the EU and Mercosur, are difficult to reach given both sides' small win-sets, how reforming the Common Agricultural Policy is linked to WTO negotiations or to what extent a negotiator's strategies have shaped bilateral trade agreements.

Two-level games conceptualize the interactions across different levels where agents try to reconcile the pressures from both the domestic level and the international level. In the following section, a second analytical toolbox – principal–agent literature – is presented, which focuses on the relationship between delegating or ratifying actors and negotiators.

Principal–agent literature

Principal–agent literature focuses on a specific aspect of two-level games: the relationship between the negotiator (or agent) and its constituency (or principal). In particular, it aims to explain why one actor delegates decision-making power to another actor and – assuming different self-interests – how it tries to keep control of the agent without jeopardizing the benefits of delegation (e.g. Pollack, 1997; Elsig, 2002; Kerremans, 2004, 2011; De Bièvre and Dür, 2005; Da Conceição, 2010; Dür and Elsig, 2011). These benefits include, for instance, lower transaction costs of policymaking, such as information and expertise or credible commitment.

If the agent and the principals have the same interests, the agent can be expected to faithfully implement the policy in line with the principals' preferences. The agent may, however, dispose of certain advantages, such as more information or more technical expertise, and may use these to pursue preferences of its own. It is often assumed that the European Commission holds generally more liberal trade preferences than the member state. Moreover, it may dispose of more information than the governments about the trade opportunities to be obtained from the EU's trading partners and may also know to a greater extent which concessions could be offset domestically through issue linkage. This, in turn, could lead to 'agency slack' – that is, an agent behaviour that is not in complete accordance with the principals' preferences. In principal–agent terminology, agency slack can take two forms: shirking takes place when the agent intentionally deviates from its mandate, whereas slippage occurs when the agent inadvertently removes itself from what the principals would want it to implement as a policy. A key source of agency slack can be diverging preferences or preference intensities between EU member states, some wanting far-reaching liberalization with a particular country and/or in a specific sector and others preferring an outcome closer to the status quo.

Because principals are aware of these risks of delegation, they develop control mechanisms. These can take the form of administrative measures, such as a careful selection of the personnel staffing the agent, the precise formulation of its mandate and the establishment of legal instruments and procedures that the agent must adhere to. Importantly, the European Commission has the sole legal right to make proposals to the member states on the parameters that will guide its negotiation behaviour. Although the European Parliament has gained powers with the Lisbon Treaty, it is still not involved in the drafting of the negotiation mandate. The principals can also install oversight mechanisms. These can consist of monitoring devices, like the establishment of a committee such as the Trade Policy Committee and the requirement to report to the INTA Committee, or the possibility of judicial review by the Court of Justice of the EU (CJEU). Oversight can also be exerted through the threat of sanctions because principals exert control over the budget or appointments, or principals can revise the mandate and hold sway over final decisions in the form of an approval of international agreements and regulations. Such controls, however, involve high decision thresholds and high costs for principals.

The principal–agent framework derives most of its usefulness from the assumption that principals and agents hold divergent preferences. Multiple principals – such as the EU member states and the European Parliament – may, however, hold diverging preferences, which in case of deep divisions may make it very difficult for the agent to craft a proposal that can find enough support. In case of less deep divisions, the agent may play out these divisions in order to broker a deal more in line with its own preference to strike a bargain with the international negotiation partner, to which the principals may then grudgingly agree for lack of a better alternative.

The principal–agent framework has also been used to explain why overt conflict between the European Commission and the EU member states is very rare. Rather than assuming that all Commission services hold more liberal trade policy preferences than member state representatives, or are swayed more by market access demands from international negotiation partners, De Bièvre and Dür (2005) start from the observation of wide-spread heterogeneity of constituency interests, some economic sectors wanting more foreign liberalization and others wanting more domestic protection. They argue that principals may well delegate specific trade policymaking powers to specialized agents, mandated with defending the interests of either import-competing sectors or export-oriented ones. EU member states thus tailor delegation to satisfy the demands of domestic constituents most mobilized in the trade policy process, resulting in a coexistence of specialized agencies.

They thus account for the high degree of bureaucratic autonomy of European Commission directorates in EU anti-dumping policy or trade in agriculture products, while conceptualizing Commission negotiators as the agents serving export-oriented interests.

The following section briefly exemplifies the theoretical approaches discussed with a case study of the EU–Korea FTA.

Example: EU–Korea Free Trade Agreement

With regard to the EU–Korea FTA, the Commission was determined to exercise leadership in trade policy by concluding a first FTA with an Asian emerging economy at an unprecedented level of liberalization. Already during the second round of negotiations, the Commission set the bar high by offering 100 per cent tariff-free market access for Korean exporters to the EU market, under the condition that Korea would make a similarly ambitious offer. As the sole negotiator on behalf of the EU, it enjoyed not only an information advantage over the member states, but it could also trade-off concessions that for some member states, such as Italy, amounted to agency slack in the form of shirking. The Commission is then viewed as having bought off Korean defensive interests, such as services, investment and agriculture, by offering concessions in the auto-mobiles and textiles sectors. However, one needs to keep in mind that the export of Korean cars to Europe may be substituted by FDI in the EU, while European car exports to Korea stand to benefit as Korea not only eliminates its respective tariffs but also significantly reduces its NTBs. Nevertheless, the inclusion of a safeguard clause is supposed to act as a potential safety valve.

The European win-set was narrowed by the opposition of certain sectors and member states, as well as by the demands of the empowered European Parliament and by the fact that the FTA was designed as a mixed agreement. This added more potential veto players. In the course of a negotiation process, domestic actors are likely to become more mobilized, which may further constrain the negotiator. With its rather small win-set, the European Commission managed to negotiate 'an agreement with emphasis on getting new market access rather than exposing domestic industries to greater competition' (Erixon and Lee, 2010, p. 2). Korea's stake in the FTA in terms of expected welfare effects – and thus its preference intensity – was higher than the EU's and therefore also larger. Despite the lobbying efforts, in particular of the European automobile industry with limited support from individual member states and the European Parliament, the Commission used its relative autonomy to negotiate a comprehensive package deal.

Elsig and Dupont (2012) argue with regard to the agent's autonomy that the European Commission was concerned about the discrimination against EU exporters on the Korean market, in particular as a result of the US–Korea FTA, and therefore actively sought support from those member states and business groups whose interests overlapped with its own. These informal coalitions also served as a buffer against criticism from import-competing interests and other principals. Finally, the lack of import competition in the EU's agricultural sector helps explain the absence of mobilization among EU farmers against the FTA.

Heron and Siles-Brügge (2012) maintain that principal–agent approaches insufficiently reflect domestic-societal and systemic pressures because they focus on the divergence of interests between principal and agent and thus potential legal–administrative strife between member state representatives and Commission negotiators. They argue that interest groups influence both the member states and the European Commission in formulating trade policy. The preferences and political mobilization of economic sectors with a stake in trade policy is determined by the wider international context in which trade diplomacy is embedded. Export-oriented sectors may favour preferential over multilateral liberalization, and they may be responsive to the trade policies of other, competing countries. With regard to the inclusion of services and investment in post-'Global Europe' agreements such as the EU–Korea FTA, export-oriented sectors may look for 'first-mover' advantages. That is, firms that are the first ones to enter a market after the elimination of regulatory restrictions may benefit from economies of scale and experience, which will help deter entry by potential rivals, especially in sectors requiring major investments. The EU's main rivals in emerging services and investment markets are still the United States and Japan, both of which were negotiating FTAs with Korea in 2006. Hence, the European Services Forum (ESF), lobbied to include the objective of far-reaching liberalization of services and investment in the 'Global Europe' strategy (ibid., pp. 256–257).

Both Korea and the EU expected benefits from concluding a comprehensive FTA for their export-dependent economies and faced rather high 'costs of no agreement' given that their strategy to seek liberalization at the multilateral level in the Doha Round was failing. In other words, they both had relatively large win-sets. Korea's win-set was comparatively bigger in view of the anticipated larger gains from trade and the fact that the ruling conservative Grand National Party, holding a majority in the National Assembly, was expected to push the ratification through. The EU successfully demanded a comprehensive agreement to exploit its bargaining leverage. Regarding the proposed chapter on sustainable development, the Commission overcame Korea's concerns, which has not yet ratified some of the core conventions of the International Labour Organization, by assuring the Korean side that none of the social commitments would actually be enforced (Bossuyt, 2009, p. 720), turning the clauses into mere declaratory politics. Korea, on the other hand, managed to present the Duty Drawback clause as a red line on which it could make no concession. The EU's constituency was more heterogeneous and the ratification procedure more constraining, given the need for a consensus in the Council and the consent of the European Parliament. The US–Korea FTA reverberated in the negotiations, as did the possibility of an 'involuntary defection' in the process of ratification: on the one hand, the US–Korea FTA became stuck in a legislative impasse in both the Korean National Assembly and the US Congress for more than four years, but it finally entered into force in 2012. On the other hand, Italy threatened a veto in the ratification process, so the European Parliament delayed its vote in order to reinforce the possibility of safeguard measures and gain more influence for itself.

The 'value added' of principal–agent theory or two-level games over purely society- or state-centred perspectives is the attempt to capture the interaction across the levels, the possible combination with other approaches and therefore the potentially increased explanatory power. Multilevel and principal–agent approaches are particularly useful for analysing the dynamics of bargaining processes, be they internal decision-making processes in the EU that may be conceived as two-level games or international negotiations between the EU and third countries. They may draw on factors stemming from different levels of analysis by focusing on the role of the negotiators without neglecting the actor's preferences or relationships. In the case of the EU–Korea FTA, the Commission's motivation to launch the negotiations can be conceived of as being driven by systemic factors such as competitive pressures from major trading partners (Hwang and Kim, 2015). Yet, it also responded, to varying degrees, to the requests of export-oriented and import-competing sectors. In the negotiations it took advantage of the small EU win-set vis-à-vis Korea and of its relative autonomy vis-à-vis the principals.

Conclusion

This chapter has introduced various theoretical perspectives that aim to explain trade policy. Approaches that focus on different levels of analysis identify different roots of trade policy, while two-level games and principal–agent theory take into account the interaction between the levels of analysis. The case of the EU–Korea FTA illustrated some strong and weak points of these approaches. Depending on the case study at hand, it can be fruitful to bring together insights from different theoretical perspectives in order to better explain an outcome. In general, a political economy approach combines both economic and political analysis: First, how actors perceive being affected by the global economy and what kind of trade policy they therefore prefer depend primarily on how they make their living. Second, how groups organize to lobby and how policies are made in a political entity depend largely on the structure of its institutions.

The next chapter will place the EU in the broader context of the multilateral trading system of the WTO, as a global forum for trade negotiations and for the enforcement of the commitments entered into.

Further reading

Da Conceição-Heldt, E. (2013) 'Two-Level Games and Trade Cooperation: What Do We Now Know?', *International Politics*, 50(4), 579–599.

Dür, A. and M. Elsig (eds) (2011) *The European Union's Foreign Economic Policies: A Principal–Agent Perspective* (London: Routledge).

Kerremans, B. and J. Orbie (2013) 'Towards Engaged Pluralism in the Study of European Trade Politics', *Journal of Contemporary European Research*, 9(4), 659–674.

Oatley, T. (2012) *International Political Economy*, 4th edn (New York: Pearson), 69–110.

Poletti, A. and D. De Bièvre (2013) 'The Political Science of European Trade Policy: A Literature Review with a Research Outlook', *Comparative European Politics*, 12(1), 101–119.

Chapter 5

The European Union in the World Trade Organization

The European Union (EU) is one of the most prominent members of the World Trade Organization (WTO). The common commercial policy has to comply with the rules of this multilateral trade organization – rules that the EU subscribes to and most of which it has actively helped crafting. This chapter provides an overview of the EU's role in the WTO. It first presents the main components of the world trade regime and the WTO in particular. The WTO is simultaneously a forum for intergovernmental trade negotiations, a set of commitments to trade liberalization that its members have entered into and an organization ensuring the enforcement of those commitments through its dispute settlement mechanism. The chapter looks at how the EU has co-shaped the multilateral trade regime and discusses the EU's role both as defendant and complainant in the WTO dispute settlement mechanism.

The global trade regime

In order to prevent a recurrence of the protectionism that prevailed during the economic depression in the interwar period, the United States and the United Kingdom pushed for the creation of rules for an open trading system. They were also the main driving forces for the establishment of the United Nations and of the Bretton Woods institutions after World War II. As a first provisional agreement on the way to an International Trade Organization (ITO), the General Agreement on Tariffs and Trade (GATT) was concluded in 1947 ('GATT 1947'). It became the principal set of rules governing international trade for almost five decades (Barton et al., 2006, pp. 27–48). The 23 countries that signed the GATT were 'contracting parties' and not members, because the GATT was not a formal treaty. The so-called Havana Charter, the Final Act of the UN Conference on Trade and Employment, was in 1948 signed by 54 states.

It provided for the establishment of the ITO, which would encompass the GATT in addition to many other topics. However, the Havana Charter never entered into force, inter alia because it was not ratified by the US Congress, which found that the Treaty foresaw too broad powers for the international organization and considered its disciplines on protectionist policies too strict.

The global trade regime under the GATT developed through trade rounds of multilateral negotiations based on certain core principles, of which liberalization, non-discrimination, and reciprocity are the most important. As a result of the eight GATT negotiating rounds, the average industrial tariffs in developed countries were lowered from nearly 40 per cent in 1947 to less than 4 per cent after the Uruguay Round (Ruggiero, 1998). In addition to substantially lower tariffs, the use of quantitative restrictions has dramatically decreased, in particular in textiles and clothing and in agriculture. Falling barriers to trade and investment, lower costs of transportation and the revolution in information technology have significantly contributed to the growth in international trade.

It was only at the end of the comprehensive GATT Uruguay Round in 1994 that the WTO was created as a formal international organization, equipped with a stronger dispute settlement mechanism and many new trade agreements. Most of these agreements were accepted as a 'single undertaking', meaning that all participants and future members of the WTO are required to adopt them (Steinberg, 2002).

Today, the WTO has achieved quasi-universal membership. By mid 2017, it counted 164 members, and several countries were in the process of accession. Thanks to its broad membership, the WTO's rules cover more than 95 per cent of world trade.

WTO institutions and decision-making rules

The highest decision-making body of the WTO is the Ministerial Conference, which normally meets every two years and provides political guidance. Such WTO Ministerial Conferences have been held in Singapore (1996), Geneva (1998), Seattle (1999), Doha (2001), Cancún (2003), Hong Kong (2005), Geneva (2009 & 2011), Bali (2013) and Nairobi (2015). The next Ministerial Conference is scheduled to take place in Buenos Aires in December 2017. In between the meetings of the Ministerial Conference, the General Council manages the day-to-day business of the organization. It consists of all members of the organization and meets in three guises at the level of Heads of Mission: the General Council, the Dispute Settlement Body (DSB) and the Trade Policy Review Body, which deals with the surveillance of members' trade policies. Within the General Council, WTO members have established three specific Councils, each of which is in charge of one of the main agreements: the Council for Trade in Goods, the Council for Trade in Services and the Council for Trade-Related Aspects of Intellectual Property Rights (TRIPs) (see Box 5.1).

Under the different Councils, members convene in various committees, working parties and working groups, for example the Committees on Market Access, on Agriculture, on Technical Barriers to Trade or on Trade in Financial Services. The General Council has also established special committees not specifically linked to the day-to-day monitoring and implementation of WTO agreements, such as the Committee on Trade and Environment, on Trade and Development or on Regional Trade Agreements. Finally, the WTO Secretariat, which has offices only in Geneva, provides technical and professional support to WTO member governments on all of the activities carried out by the organization. It is headed by a Director-General and has a regular staff of about 600, of which the majority are translators, making it a very small international

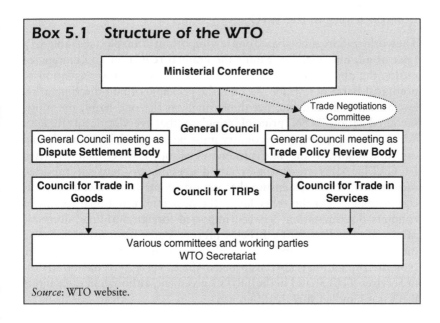

Box 5.1   Structure of the WTO

Ministerial Conference

Trade Negotiations Committee

General Council

General Council meeting as **Dispute Settlement Body**

General Council meeting as **Trade Policy Review Body**

Council for Trade in Goods

Council for TRIPs

Council for Trade in Services

Various committees and working parties
WTO Secretariat

Source: WTO website.

organization with such near-universal membership. Since decisions are taken by members, the Secretariat has no decision-making powers.

The general decision rule of the WTO is formally 'one member, one vote', but in practice, it is consensus. Consensus does not mean unanimity but is the practice of considering something decided when no delegation represented in a meeting raises any objections. The WTO Agreement nevertheless does foresee voting in some distinct instances. For example, unanimity is required for amendments of general core principles, such as non-discrimination. Interpretations of the multilateral trade agreements and waivers of a member's obligation need a three-quarters majority. Furthermore, a two-thirds majority is necessary for amendments that do not concern the organization's general principles and for admission of new members. For decisions on issues not otherwise specified, a simple majority is sufficient. When convening as Dispute Settlement Body, the General Council also decides by consensus. Yet, this is a very particular kind of consensus, namely reverse consensus. Since no WTO member can veto the adoption of a Panel report against it, the Dispute Settlement Body automatically adopts a Panel report, unless there is a consensus not to do so. In effect, this means that the Panels and the Appellate Body have the last word in WTO trade disputes and not the members themselves.

Core principles of the WTO

The world trade regime is based on a few important principles (see Table 5.1). First of all, liberalization entails the gradual reduction and binding of tariffs, the abolition of quantitative restrictions and the regulation of non-tariff barriers to trade. Second, the principle of non-discrimination has an external and internal dimension: on the one hand, the most-favoured nation (MFN) principle stipulates that every trade advantage a WTO member gives to any country must be extended, immediately and unconditionally, to the 'like' product of all other WTO members (Art. I:1 GATT). MFN treatment or non-discrimination between imported foreign products helps ensure that imports come from lowest-cost foreign suppliers. On the other hand, the principle of national treatment counters discrimination between imported foreign and 'like' domestic products (Art. III GATT). It helps prevent states from using domestic measures such as taxation or regulation against foreign competition. Non-discrimination is also enshrined in the General Agreement on Trade in Services (GATS) and in the TRIPs Agreement, although in each agreement it is handled slightly differently.

TABLE 5.1   *Major WTO Principles*

Principle	Implication
Liberalization	Reduction and binding of tariffs, no quantitative restrictions, regulation of non-tariff barriers, etc.
Non-discrimination:	
– most-favoured nation (MFN)	No discrimination between imported foreign products
– national treatment	No discrimination between imported foreign and domestic products
Reciprocity	Roughly equivalent mutual benefits in terms of trade concessions
Injury avoidance	Possibility of using anti-dumping, countervailing duties and safeguards as safety valves
Special and differential treatment (SDT) of developing countries	No reciprocity, lower level of obligations, longer transition periods, technical assistance, etc.
Peaceful dispute settlement	Rules-based system with consultations before launch of formal procedure
Transparency and predictability	Rules affecting trade must be as transparent as possible (notification, trade policy reviews, etc.)

Source: WTO website.

Third, according to reciprocity, which is not a legal principle, a contracting party benefiting from another party's trade concessions should provide roughly equivalent benefits in return. This rule helps limit free riding. It also implies that the multilateral trade negotiations reflect the interests of the major trading powers, such as the EU, since they have the largest domestic markets and the greatest reciprocal concessions to offer (Cohn, 2012, p. 178). At the same time, it is important to realize that being member of the WTO in no way obliges a contracting party to lower all tariffs or reduce other trade barriers. If other negotiating partners are willing to accept a comparatively high tariff on a good or a relative closure of a particular services industry in exchange for market access in another area, this constitutes a legitimate and normal sovereign decision of that WTO member. Japan, for instance, has deemed it necessary to keep its market for rice imports virtually closed by maintaining a 100 per cent tariff on imports of foreign rice, which Japan's trading partners have been willing to accept in exchange for other sectors in which Japan did grant them market access by lowering its trade barriers.

Liberalization, non-discrimination and reciprocity are the three core principles. In addition, some other WTO principles are sometimes mentioned, such as the avoidance of injury through anti-dumping, anti-subsidy or safeguard measures; transparency and predictability; and the peaceful settlement of trade disputes. Transparency means that all rules affecting trade must be available, either through publication, notification or trade policy reviews. Since transparency enhances the predictability of trading conditions, it in itself already contributes to the aim of upholding propitious conditions for long-term investment and trade. This is why it is a legal obligation enshrined in various provisions in the WTO agreements. On the other hand, transparency has also been used in another sense, in the form of criticism of the WTO members as largely operating behind closed doors. Meetings of the General Council and of the negotiating groups are not open to the public, but dispute settlement proceedings can be opened if the parties agree. In response to this criticism, the WTO Secretariat set up a programme for the participation of registered non-governmental organizations in the WTO's Ministerial Conferences and organizes a yearly Public Forum (Hanegraaff et al., 2015; Hannah et al., 2017).

Finally, the principle of special and differential treatment (SDT) of developing countries was introduced in the 1960s and has grown in importance over time with the political clout of the countries concerned. In fact, these special provisions are usually exceptions to the rules. It should be noted that the term 'developing countries' is not defined in the WTO, but members decide themselves whether they are developing. In 1966, a part on trade and development was inserted into the GATT, which inter alia stipulated non-reciprocity for developing countries, yet only in the form of legally non-binding 'best endeavour' clauses. In 1979 the General Council took the 'Decision on Differential and More Favourable Treatment, Reciprocity, and Fuller Participation of Developing Countries' (GATT, 1979). This 'Enabling Clause' allows derogations from MFN treatment in favour of developing countries, both for preferential tariff treatment accorded by developed members to products originating in developing countries and for preferential arrangements among developing countries themselves. For example, it serves as legal basis for the EU's Generalized System of Preferences (GSP) (see Chapter 6). Additional exceptions in favour of developing countries include specific waivers, restrictions of imports for balance-of-payment purposes or to promote or establish a particular industry (Art. XVIII GATT) and special provisions foreseen in various WTO agreements.

Other exceptions to MFN treatment concern the general exceptions related to measures for the protection of public morals; human, animal or plant life or health; measures related to products of prison labour; and the conservation of national heritage or of exhaustible national resources (Art. XX GATT). Further exceptions may be justified by essential national security interests requiring measures related to traffic in arms, times of war or national emergencies, or actions of the UN Security Council (Art. XXI GATT). A very important exception to the principle of MFN treatment is enshrined in the provisions that under certain conditions allow for the formation of bilateral or regional customs unions and free trade agreements (Art. XXIV GATT). A similar provision is found in Art. V GATS, which stipulates that members may enter into a regional agreement liberalizing trade in services, provided that such an agreement has substantial sectoral coverage and eliminates all discrimination in the sectors covered.

The WTO: a forum for trade liberalization, negotiation and enforcement

Countries participating in the GATT Uruguay Round agreed to bundle all their international trade agreements into one package. This means that joining the WTO entails acceding to all the rights and obligations created by the other agreements. The Agreement establishing the WTO sets out the structure and administrative functioning of the organization. The most important feature of the agreement, however, is that it brings into one single package a whole range of agreements in different areas of international trade regulation. All members of the WTO, whether founding members or acceding to the organization later on, subject themselves to the same set of rules and bind their liberalization commitments towards each other under these rules.

The WTO as a set of liberalization commitments

WTO members are, in principle, free to choose to what extent they open up their domestic economies to foreign trade. In its most basic form, WTO membership consists of a list of tariff levels that a member promises to all other members not to surpass. These so-called bound tariff levels constitute the cornerstone of the organization. Member countries may levy lower tariffs (the so-called applied tariffs), but they commit not to go above the levels in their bound tariff schedule. For trade in services, the same logic applies. A member state that commits to opening up specific service industries for foreign operators commits not to arbitrarily or suddenly unwind these market openings. Each WTO member state thus sets its liberalization commitments at the level of its choosing, depending on the favourable market access for its own export goods and services that it can obtain from its most important trading partners. This balance of 'concessions' between WTO members constitutes the basis for today's open trading system. Since member states bind each other, they create a stable, foreseeable trading environment which in turn constitutes the prerequisite for investment in production and the growth of trade. Since each WTO member has but one list of liberalization commitments, it commits to non-discrimination. This means that it will treat no member of the organization worse than stipulated in its bound tariff schedule or its services commitments. Moreover, WTO members commit to treat foreign goods, once they have entered their territory or services that are being delivered, the same way as they treat their domestically produced goods or domestically provided services. Through this national treatment rule, WTO members cannot impose more stringent technical, health or environmental rules for foreign products or services, but they decide how high they want to set these rules for all economic operators – the only condition being that they should not discriminate between domestic and foreign operators. The key principle of non-discrimination applies across all the organization's agreements. Table 5.2 gives an overview of the most important WTO agreements and a brief summary of their main purpose.

Whereas all WTO agreements are multilateral – that is, concluded by and binding on all WTO members – there are also a few so-called plurilateral WTO agreements. These are agreements that not all WTO members have signed and whose benefits accrue only to the signatories, yet the membership is open to those who want to join later. For example, the Agreement on Trade in Civil Aircraft first entered into force as a GATT agreement in 1980 and had 32 signatories by 2017 (including

TABLE 5.2 *Main WTO Agreements*

Agreement	Content
Umbrella agreement	
Agreement establishing the World Trade Organization (WTO Agreement)	Agreement establishing the organization with a single institutional framework
Multilateral agreements on trade in goods	
General Agreement on Tariffs and Trade 1994 (GATT 1994)	Key agreement on liberalizing trade in goods
Agreement on Agriculture	Rules on liberalization of agriculture (market access, domestic support, export subsidies)
Agreement on the Application of Sanitary and Phytosanitary Measures (SPS)	Rules on application of food safety and animal and plant health standards
Agreement on Textiles and Clothing (until 2005)	Integration of textiles and clothing into GATT (phasing out of quotas negotiated under the Multifibre Arrangement)
Agreement on Technical Barriers to Trade (TBT)	Rules on application of technical regulations and standards
Agreement on Trade-Related Investment Measures (TRIMs)	Rules on investment measures restricting trade
Anti-Dumping Agreement	Rules on the application of anti-dumping measures
Agreement on Rules of Origin	Agreement aiming at long-term harmonization of rules of origin
Agreement on Subsidies and Countervailing Measures (SCM)	Agreement defining subsidies and rules on application of anti-subsidy measures
Agreement on Safeguards	Rules on the application of safeguard measures (incl. prohibition of 'grey area' measures like voluntary expert restrictions)

→

$\rightarrow$

Agreement	Content
Other multilateral agreements	
General Agreement on Trade in Services (GATS)	Key framework agreement for liberalization of services trade
Agreement on Trade-Related Aspects of Intellectual Property Rights (TRIPs)	Rules on protecting foreign intellectual property rights
Dispute Settlement Understanding	Agreement setting out the procedure of WTO dispute settlement
Trade Policy Review Mechanism	Agreement setting out the procedure of the Trade Policy Review
Plurilateral agreements	
Agreement on Trade in Civil Aircraft	Agreement eliminating tariffs in the civil aircraft sector
Government Procurement Agreement (GPA)	General rules and obligations with regard to tendering procedures and coverage schedules per signatory member
Information Technology Agreement (ITA)	Agreement eliminating tariffs on IT products covered

Source: WTO website.

the EU). The Government Procurement Agreement (GPA) was signed at the end of the Uruguay Round; a revised version entered into force in 2014 and currently has 19 contracting parties (including the EU). The GPA does not require all government procurement to be liberalized, but rather sets out the framework within which governments, if they so wish, can set out those elements of their public procurement market that they want to open for foreign bidding.

After the establishment of the WTO, some members (including the EU) engaged in further negotiations of plurilateral agreements: an Information Technology Agreement (ITA) concluded in 1996 and expanded at the Nairobi Ministerial Conference in 2015, negotiations on a future Agreement on Environmental Goods started in 2014 and since 2013 negotiations on a future Trade in Services Agreement (TiSA). The ITA commits its signatories to keep zero tariffs on IT products, while these benefits are extended to all WTO members under MFN. Given the tremendous growth of this sector in recent decades, this agreement very much forestalled the early imposition of national trade barriers in this sector, and it contributed to the rapid growth into a global market of information technology. The Environmental Goods Agreement seeks to promote trade in a number of key environmental products, such as wind turbines and solar panels. A TiSA would be an agreement formally concluded outside the WTO, but it could subsequently be 'multilateralized'.

The WTO as a negotiation forum

The WTO is a member-driven organization. In order to launch a new round of negotiations, the Ministerial Conference needs to adopt a decision and a Trade Negotiations Committee is established, comprising all members and the Director-General of the WTO. Negotiations can take different forms: formula approaches may cut tariffs by a certain linear or non-linear percentage, whereas request-offer negotiations involve one member asking another member to make a specific concession, to which the other member responds with an offer and a request of its own.

The shift from 'at-the-border' to 'behind-the-border' measures is reflected in the agenda of the trade rounds (see Table 5.3). Until the 1960s, tariff reductions dominated the negotiations. When non-tariff barriers become more visible and more important, codes of conduct were signed on a voluntary basis for the first time at the end of the Tokyo Round. This was then much further developed in the specific agreements of the Uruguay Round.

The principle of MFN treatment plays a crucial role not only in the trade rounds but also in accession negotiations (Zimmermann, 2007). New members enjoy the trade privileges that other members give to them, and in return, they make commitments to open their markets and to abide by the organization's rules. Broadly speaking, an application goes through four stages, during which candidate countries are considered WTO observers. First, the government has to describe all aspects of its trade and economic policies that have a bearing on WTO agreements. This is submitted to the WTO working party dealing with the country's application, which is open to all WTO members. Second, parallel bilateral talks begin between the candidate and interested individual

TABLE 5.3   *GATT/WTO Trade Rounds*

Years	Round	Subjects
General Agreement on Tariffs and Trade		
1947	Geneva	Tariff reductions
1949	Annecy	Tariff reductions
1951	Torquay	Tariff reductions
1956	Geneva	Tariff reductions
1960–1961	Dillon Round	Tariff reductions
1964–1967	Kennedy Round	Tariff reductions, anti-dumping measures
1973–1979	Tokyo Round	Tariff reductions, non-tariff barrier codes of conduct
1986–1994	Uruguay Round	Creation of WTO, tariff reductions, dispute settlement and trade policy review mechanisms, services, investment, intellectual property rights, agriculture, textiles and clothing
World Trade Organization		
2001–	Doha Round	Tariff reductions, agriculture, services, intellectual property rights, trade facilitation, rules, environment, SDT for developing countries

Source: WTO website.

members. The new member's resulting commitments are to apply equally to all WTO members, even though they are negotiated bilaterally. Third, when the working party has completed its examination and the parallel bilateral market access negotiations are over, it finalizes the terms of accession in a report. Fourth, the final package, consisting of the report, protocol and lists of commitments, is presented to the WTO General Council or the Ministerial Conference for approval. Formally, this body then decides by a super-majority of three-quarters of the WTO membership. The non-discrimination rule implies that not all members need to negotiate with all other members in trade rounds or accession negotiations. If a country is satisfied with what the others have negotiated, it may choose not to ask for bilateral talks (see De Bièvre, 2006).

Among the disadvantages for small and poor countries are the many important informal procedures which characterize the WTO in addition to the formal rules of decision-making set out above. With quasi-universal membership, consensus is not always easy to reach, despite the fact that the simple rule of MFN does not require that everyone negotiates with everyone. In order to hammer out deals on contentious issues, meetings of small groups of major interested parties are often held. Since they originally took place in a green meeting room adjacent to the Director-General's office in Geneva, these gatherings are still often referred to as 'green room' meetings. They became controversial in the late 1990s as many developing countries objected to being excluded. Efforts were made in the Doha Round to make the green room process more inclusive and transparent. For example, at Ministerial Conferences specific ministers are appointed as 'facilitators' that consult and transmit discussions to all members.

Furthermore, members form many coalitions of which the EU is but one grouping. For a long time one of the most important informal groupings was the so-called Quad (the EU, the United States, Canada and Japan). However, since the start of the Doha Round, other groups of developing and emerging countries have considerably gained in importance in WTO negotiations (see below).

The WTO as an enforcement organization

The rules and liberalization commitments WTO members have entered into are not only de jure (that is, legally) binding, they are also to a very large extent de facto (in reality) binding. This is so for two reasons. First, liberalization commitments in the form of reciprocal tariff concessions or the opening up of particular service industries between two WTO members are so-called self-enforcing agreements. Second, the organization disposes of an enforcement system, enabling members to obtain independent legal rulings from Panels (and, upon appeal, from the WTO Appellate Body) in cases of non-compliance.

The self-enforcing nature of reciprocal trade liberalization commitments means that both sides to the agreement can hold each other to respect the agreement through the threat of withdrawal of concessions in case the other side does not abide by the rules. Such simple 'tit-for-tat' enforcement of trade agreements is key to the stability and predictability of today's open world trade regime. A 'tit-for-tat' strategy implies that when the other side provides an actor with the promised market access, this actor reciprocates cooperation. Since each actor knows that reneging on the agreement means the other side can revoke some of its liberalization commitments, the mere threat of incurring costs of lost market access suffices to stabilize the agreement. In other words, the threat of non-cooperation being reciprocated with non-cooperation, or retaliation, can to a large extent stabilize expectations about the strength of the promises contained in individual countries' lists of liberalization commitments.

Within the WTO, however, members have committed to more than such reciprocal, self-enforcing agreements. They have agreed to a whole range of regulatory agreements that set boundaries to government discretion with regard to trade-related measures or that sometimes even contain positive obligations. The former type are agreements limiting domestic authorities' discretion in applying anti-dumping and counter-vailing duties and safeguards or in granting subsidies. The TBT, SPS and TRIPs Agreements entail positive obligations on how WTO members should govern their respective standards. Such agreements are more difficult to monitor and enforce. The WTO can, in principle, not set standards for non-trade concerns related to public health, labour and environmental issues or intellectual property rights, but it can 'import' those of other international bodies (Gstöhl, 2010a).

The WTO disposes of sophisticated monitoring and enforcement mechanisms. With regard to monitoring, each WTO member, with the help of the WTO Secretariat, draws up a trade policy review at regular intervals. This review assesses a member's trade performance, trade policies and record of implementation of its WTO commitments. The modalities for these regular trade policy reviews are laid down in the Agreement on the Trade Policy Review Mechanism. All WTO members are regularly reviewed, but the frequency varies according to the member's relative share of world trade. The four largest members (the EU, the United States, Japan and China) are reviewed every two years, the next 16 members are reviewed every four years, and all other members are, in principle, reviewed every six years, but a longer period may be fixed for least developed countries (LDCs). The review of the EU's trade policy is based on a report presented by the WTO Secretariat, a report from the EU and written questions from members, to which the EU replies in writing.

The WTO Dispute Settlement Understanding stipulates the rules to be followed when a particular member has a complaint about alleged non-compliance by another WTO member. Only governments have the right to bring cases to Geneva. If consultations do not lead to the elimination of the trade barrier that is deemed incompatible with WTO law, the complainant member can ask for the establishment of a Panel. This Panel consists of three trade policy experts appointed ad hoc, and it rules whether and to which extent the defendant member is in breach of WTO law. Either side to the dispute can ask for a legal appreciation by the so-called Appellate Body, which consists of seven permanent members from the different continents. Each member is appointed by the Dispute Settlement Body for several years and must be a recognized authority with demonstrated expertise in international trade law. An appeal is heard by three of them. In the vast majority of cases, the defendant settles the dispute to the satisfaction of the complainant or changes its disputed measures after a Panel ruling. While the Panel reviews factual and legal issues, the Appellate Body reviews only the legal interpretations developed by the Panel. Both reports need be adopted by a negative consensus, which means that reports are adopted automatically unless there is a consensus to the contrary – an utterly unrealistic scenario. Under the old GATT rule of a so-called positive consensus, any GATT contracting party, including the losing party to a dispute, could block the adoption of a Panel Report. In cases where the defendant refuses or is unable to implement the ruling, the WTO Dispute Settlement Body can authorize the complainant to impose retaliatory trade measures. That is, the winner can act in a 'tit-for-tat' retaliatory way by raising tariffs or suspending obligations under a WTO agreement to the detriment of the defendant in the dispute. Box 5.2 provides an overview of the dispute settlement procedure.

EU membership in the WTO

Any state or customs territory having full autonomy in the conduct of its trade policies can become a member of the GATT/WTO. Although the European Community (EC) had never formally applied to become a contracting party to the GATT, it de facto acquired this status. As a result of the common commercial policy, it has acted and been treated like a contracting party since the 1960s. The WTO Agreement of 1994 (Art. XI) stipulates that all contracting parties to GATT 1947, as well as the EC, become founding members of the WTO. It should be noted that at that time the agreements of the new organization covered areas of both exclusive EU and shared competence (see Chapter 2).

Together with the United States and China, the EU is among the most important members of the WTO in terms of its relative share of world

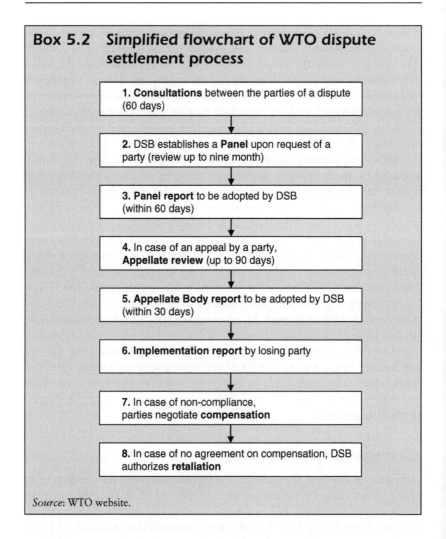

Box 5.2   Simplified flowchart of WTO dispute settlement process

1. **Consultations** between the parties of a dispute (60 days)

2. DSB establishes a **Panel** upon request of a party (review up to nine month)

3. **Panel report** to be adopted by DSB (within 60 days)

4. In case of an appeal by a party, **Appellate review** (up to 90 days)

5. **Appellate Body report** to be adopted by DSB (within 30 days)

6. **Implementation report** by losing party

7. In case of non-compliance, parties negotiate **compensation**

8. In case of no agreement on compensation, DSB authorizes **retaliation**

Source: WTO website.

trade. At the same time, the EU member states are also full members of the WTO. This does, however, not render the membership of the EU less important, because representation and negotiation is systematically done by the European Commission and the Permanent Mission of the EU to the WTO in Geneva, on behalf of the Union. After the United Kingdom withdraws from the EU, it will have to take care of its own representation at the WTO, in both negotiations and trade disputes.

Following the entry into force of the Lisbon Treaty, the Delegation of the European Commission in Geneva became the Delegation of the EU. With the creation of the European External Action Service (EEAS) in 2011, to which all EU Delegations belong, the EU split its former Commission Delegation into two separate representations: the Permanent Delegation of the EU to the United Nations Office and other international organizations in Geneva and the Permanent Mission of the EU to the WTO.

The tasks of the EU Mission to the WTO, which comprises staff from Directorate-Generate (DG) Trade as well as the EEAS, include representing the interests of the EU and its member states in the area of multilateral trade, negotiating on their behalf at the WTO and coordinating their positions. Therefore, the EU is represented by the European Commission in the WTO General Council, the Dispute Settlement Body and the Trade Policy Review Body. The same applies to the subsidiary WTO bodies, for example the Council for Trade in Goods or the Committee for Trade and the Environment. The EU Trade Commissioner represents the EU in the Ministerial Conference.

The 'double membership' of the EU and its member states in the WTO does have some peculiar consequences. First, the annual contributions to the WTO budget are calculated on the basis of a member's share of world trade. The WTO considers intra-EU trade to be part of world trade. As a result, the EU member states finance a very large part of the WTO budget, while the EU itself does not contribute. However, the EU may for example separately contribute to funds for technical assistance to developing countries, which are not part of the general budget. In 2016 the 28 EU member states financed 36.2 per cent of the total WTO budget, compared to 11.3 per cent for the United States and 8.6 per cent for China (WTO website, 2016). Since the WTO is a comparatively small multilateral organization, the absolute figures of these contributions remain modest. Unlike in all other WTO bodies, where the representatives of the European Commission (respectively of the EU Mission to the WTO) speak on behalf of the EU, in the Committee on Budget, Finance and Administration, the EU member states speak and vote.

Second, since the General Council of the WTO is composed of the entire membership, the 28 EU member state representatives as well as the Head of the Permanent Mission in Geneva attend the meetings. However, only the EU Ambassador in Geneva or the European Commission representative speaks on behalf of the EU. In semi-formal, technical or informal meetings, the EU member state representatives are usually not present.

Third, the EU holds as many votes as it has member states, while the EU Delegation itself does not have an additional vote (Art. IX WTO Agreement). The member state delegates may attend some (formal) meetings in the WTO, but the Commission speaks 'with one voice' for the EU. Given the exclusive Union competence in the common commercial policy, EU positions in the WTO are agreed upon through continued consultations in the Trade Policy Committee, and the Commission reports regularly to the Parliament's International Trade (INTA) Committee as well (see Chapter 3). The Head of the Permanent Mission to the WTO chairs meetings of Heads of Missions of EU member states, in Geneva. Compared to the Trade Policy Committee (TPC) meetings in Brussels, these short meetings take place before WTO meetings in order to share information and, if necessary, carry out last-minute coordination.

When it comes to the initiation and handling of trade disputes, the Commission – more precisely DG Trade in cooperation with the Legal Service and sometimes also other Directorates-General – takes the lead as well, with the support of the Council. Whereas DG Trade handles disputes during the consultation phase and manages implementation, the Legal Service is in charge of litigation, both for Panels and the Appellate Body. In trade disputes the Trade Policy Committee is less powerful than it is in trade negotiations (Billiet, 2005, p. 214). Only the EU files complaints against other WTO members, not the individual EU member states. By contrast, WTO members can choose whether they target the Union or individual EU member states as defendants. If an EU member state faces a complaint, the EU will respond, but member state representatives are invited to all litigations. The EU usually also requests 'third party' status in cases in which it is not directly involved, in order to monitor disputes it deems of systemic relevance.

The EU's role in the WTO

The EU – for better or for worse – has played a key role both in the creation and in the activities of the WTO. The EU has been a key co-shaper of the world trade regime from the early 1960s onwards and a key player in the crafting of the large package deal of the Uruguay Round, which created the new organization. Moreover, the EU has been a leading WTO member, demanding the launch of the Doha Round. Finally, the EU has been a frequent user of the dispute settlement system.

The EU as co-shaper of the world trade regime

Although the GATT 1947 had provided its contracting parties with a framework for conducting trade negotiations, the West European countries had difficulties convincing the United States to launch talks about substantial reciprocal tariff reductions. By 1955, when economic recovery in Western Europe fuelled demand for market access abroad, the European countries decided that regional liberalization among themselves was the faster and better path to pursue. The founding of the European Communities in the 1950s and their regular enlargement since the 1970s have exerted profound effects on the world trade regime.

As explained in Chapter 2, the enlargement of a common market generates trade creation and trade diversion. Trade diversion caused substantial fears of loss of market share for American exporters, which in turn started lobbying the US Congress and President Kennedy to engage with the EC (Dür, 2010). They sought to maintain and improve access to the growing European market. The US government subsequently asked the EC to engage in trade negotiations involving substantial tariff cuts.

At the beginning, the EC was a defensive player in the GATT, as it had just liberalized internally and completed its common external tariff of the customs union in 1968 (Mortensen, 2009, pp. 83–86). In the Kennedy Round, the EC fended off US demands for international market liberalization, in particular with regard to its Common Agricultural Policy (CAP). The achievements of the Tokyo Round also remained limited. The early GATT rounds mainly consisted of negotiations between the Europeans and the Americans whose reciprocal liberalization commitments formed the core of the world trading system. Through the principle of non-discrimination, the other contracting parties of the GATT also profited from the lower tariffs across the Atlantic.

From the mid 1980s the EC became more proactive, whether due to neoliberal ideas, the pressures of globalization, transnational business interests, the completion of the internal market or a combination of those. Based on case studies of the Kennedy Round and the Doha Round, Dür (2008) argues that the EU's negotiating positions during GATT rounds were largely in line with the demands voiced by economic interests in Europe. New issues entered the international trade agenda, and during the Uruguay Round, the United States–EU tandem began to 'co-author' the rule book of the world trading system. The trade agenda shifted from traditional 'at-the-border' measures such as tariffs or quotas to 'behind-the-border' issues that regulate competition (like the GATS,

TRIPs and TRIMs Agreements) and address market failure (such as the TBT or SPS Agreements). Within the EU the Commission and certain member states argued before the Court of Justice about the division of competences in the new fields (see Chapter 2).

Accession to the WTO was made conditional on the acceptance of all the tariff-binding commitments that individual members had been submitting during the Uruguay Round and on the substantial package of regulatory agreements. The threat of being excluded generated incentives for the emerging and developing countries to join the new organization. Even those countries that had been lukewarm to some of the liberalization commitments or the regulatory agreements deemed it best to support the Agreement establishing the WTO (Steinberg, 2002). The EU was also a crucial player in the reform of the GATT dispute settlement system, which was in particular driven forward by the Americans (Elsig and Eckhardt, 2015).

The EU as 'demandeur' of the Doha Round and its failure

Soon after the creation of the WTO, the EU for the first time assumed leadership in the promotion of a new round of multilateral trade negotiations. All previous rounds had been launched at the behest of the United States. Most importantly, the Uruguay Round Agreement on Agriculture had mandated members to start new negotiations on the further liberalization of agricultural trade and the reduction of different levels of domestic subsidization of agricultural products. This so-called in-built agenda was part of the unfinished business of the Uruguay Round. Negotiations in the field of both agriculture and services were scheduled for 2000. In particular for the Cairns Group of agricultural exporting countries, the WTO Agreement on Agriculture was not sufficiently far-reaching, while the EU had insisted on coupling the new negotiations on agriculture with trade in services (Poletti, 2010).

The EU wanted to reach a package deal in a 'comprehensive' round that would allow it to trade agricultural concessions for advantages in other areas of interest (Ahnlid, 2005). In order to further balance the negotiations, the European Commission added other items to the agenda. The envisaged package comprised both 'at-the-border' measures such as better market access in non-agricultural products and 'behind-the-border' measures such as services, the so-called Singapore issues and rules on core labour standards, environment and consumer safety (Young, 2007). The Singapore issues were already initiated at the 1996 Singapore

Ministerial Conference and comprised competition policy, investment protection, transparency in public procurement and trade facilitation. Working groups were set up to study these questions. In return for the EU's acceptance to for the first time negotiate an end to agricultural export subsidies, non-trade concerns were originally included on the Doha Development Agenda (Poletti, 2010). The EU had put forward its 'trade and ...' agenda, which included core labour standards and environmental protection besides trade and investment or competition, in response to the domestic demands of member states and civil society (Poletti and Sicurelli, 2012).

In 1999, the then–Commissioner for Trade Pascal Lamy announced the so-called Lamy doctrine, a moratorium on the conclusion of new regional and bilateral free trade agreements, in order to convey the EU's strong political support for the multilateral WTO negotiations (see Chapter 7). However, the WTO's Ministerial Conference in Seattle in 1999 failed to launch the so-called Millennium Round of trade negotiations. In the 'battle in Seattle', 'anti-globalist' activists had protested against the WTO, and members disagreed on many issues (De Bièvre, 2014).

Whereas in the past the EU had been the courted actor to whose market other members desired to gain access, the EU now found itself to be asking for better access abroad. The EU had become a mature and saturated market for many goods and services with low economic growth rates. This contrasted starkly with the emerging economies, especially in South-East Asia, where demand has been growing rapidly. The economic attractiveness of the EU's internal market had dwindled relative to other markets.

In 2001 the Ministerial Conference in Doha launched a new round in the shadow of the 9/11 attacks. At the same time, China joined the WTO. Many WTO members shared the perception that the industrialized countries had gained more from the Uruguay Round than the developing countries had, and those members sought to rectify this imbalance. In order to build confidence with developing countries, the EU supported their secure access to medicines for diseases, such as HIV/Aids, under the TRIPs rules, and stressed the importance of aid for trade and launched the 'Everything-But-Arms' (EBA) initiative, which granted duty-free and quota-free access to all imports from LDCs (see Chapter 6). The EU's agenda for the Doha Round was still broad (see Box 5.3).

The compromise of Doha was unravelled two years later, at the Ministerial Conference in Cancún (Kerremans, 2004). The majority of WTO

Box 5.3   The EU's objectives for the Doha Round

- lower tariffs on industrial goods in both developed countries and emerging economies, such as China, Brazil and India

- improve the WTO rulebook on subsidies that distort the production of industrial goods

- reform farm subsidies in developed countries (in line with the EU's 2003 reform of the CAP)

- create new market access opportunities for business and tangible benefits to consumers in services trade

- agree a package of development measures, including unlimited market access for LDCs (like the EU's 2001 EBA initiative) by as many countries as possible and a global package of aid for trade

- establish a new set of WTO rules for trade defence instruments and trade facilitation

- improve the protection of geographical indications in the field of intellectual property rights.

Source: DG Trade website.

members did not support a shift to positive regulation of non-trade concerns. The Ministerial Conference in 2003 broke up, without decision, over serious divergences on agriculture and the Singapore issues. Cancún saw the emergence of new vocal groupings of developing countries that 'marked the end of bilateral co-hegemony in multilateral trade' (Mortensen, 2009, p. 86). The G20 are developing countries pushing for ambitious reforms of agriculture in developed countries. It should not be confused with the G20 of finance ministers and central bank governors and its summit meetings at head of state level, which is a forum for international cooperation on the most important issues of the global economic and financial agenda. Furthermore, the G90 comprises the African Group, the LDCs and the group of African, Caribbean and Pacific (ACP) countries. The G33 (also called 'Friends of Special Products' in agriculture) are a coalition of developing countries pressing for flexibility for developing countries to undertake limited market opening in agriculture. The 'Cotton-4' are four West African countries seeking cuts in cotton subsidies and tariffs. By contrast, there is with the G10 also a coalition of industrialized countries (not including the EU) which are lobbying for agriculture to be treated as diverse and special because of non-trade concerns.

Although the developing countries have differing interests, they remained relatively united at Cancún in their opposition to developed countries, especially regarding agriculture and textiles, but also with regard to their problems of implementing commitments from the Uruguay Round and new proposals in the field of non-trade concerns. In particular, the G20 opposed a deal on agriculture jointly proposed by the EU and the United States.

Since then, the Doha Round negotiations had broken down several times. In July 2004 the Doha Round seemed to be back on track when the WTO General Council agreed on a framework package. It foresaw more liberalization in agriculture, including cutbacks in trade-distorting subsidies, more tariff cuts in industrial products, improved offers regarding services, a strengthening of SDT and aid for trade with a 'round for free' for LDCs and a TRIPs waiver on access to medicines for developing countries. The EU was forced to drop the Singapore issues from the negotiating agenda, with the exception of trade facilitation.

Some further progress was made at the Hong Kong Ministerial Conference in 2005. As part of a future package, it was agreed to eliminate all export subsidies in agriculture by 2013, for cotton even by the end of 2006; to offer duty-free and quota-free access for LDCs to the markets of developed countries; and to substantially step up 'aid for trade' for developing countries (e.g. the EU offered 2 billion euros as of 2010). The modalities for the negotiations on agriculture, on non-agricultural market access and on services were clarified, and the TRIPs Agreement was amended to facilitate access to cheaper medicines for poor countries.

However, already a few months later, negotiations were suspended. In July 2006 the EU, the United States, Japan, Brazil, India and Australia disagreed on agricultural tariffs, agricultural (domestic) subsidies and industrial tariffs. Their positions polarized on the extent of liberalization in agriculture (in the North) versus non-agricultural market access (in the South). Negotiations resumed in 2007, and in July 2008 a new package came close to an agreement, but a dispute over a special safeguard mechanism for developing countries to counter import surges in food halted that agreement. This time the dispute involved in particular the United States versus India and China. In addition, there were other unresolved questions.

Efforts have since then been made in various international forums to relaunch the negotiations, but progress has remained limited. The reasons for the failure of the Doha Round are manifold. First, the trade agenda has turned the Round into complex multisector negotiations. Second, WTO membership has grown in numbers and heterogeneity. Developing and emerging countries have become more assertive, leading to a shift in relative power away from the developed trading powers. Third, the rise of emerging powers did not go hand in hand with their taking on responsibility for the trade round. Moreover, the recently acceded members felt that they already opened up considerably during their accession process. At the same time, the 'old' big players, the Quad of like-minded countries, was no longer centre-stage, and in particular it did no longer suffice that the EU and the United States displayed or tried to display leadership to conclude the Round. Fourth, the principle of single undertaking negotiation ('nothing is agreed until everything is agreed') may have become too cumbersome, even though linking issues can in principle enable members to obtain benefits dear to them into the overall package. Fifth, the global economic crisis since 2008 may have made many countries more reluctant to liberalize further, even though this seems to be contradicted by members' appetite for preferential trade agreements with large coverage but restricted membership. Sixth, the relatively low level of tariffs in most sectors may well have diminished the demand for multilateral trade liberalization agreements, with matters of regulation having come to the forefront and making industries and countries turn to clubs of preferential trade agreements. Finally, the expectations for a 'development round' turned out to be simply too high for a trade organization like the WTO (Mavroidis, 2011).

The rise of China, Brazil and India in the global trading system – and in 2012 Russia joined the WTO – has significantly curtailed the ability of the EU and the United States to shape policy outcomes in the WTO to their liking. Moreover, the increased judicialization of the world trade regime caused the EU, just like any other WTO member, to be more vulnerable to legal challenges (Poletti et al., 2016). The EU found that its WTO partners were able to force substantial concessions in agricultural negotiations by threatening to resort to WTO dispute settlement against the EU's domestic support schemes. As argued by Kerremans (2004, p. 364), the WTO both complicates and facilitates EU trade policymaking: it forces the EU to deal with issues that are highly controversial among its member states, but it also provides opportunities for policy entrepreneurs to overcome internal divisions.

As a result of all these developments, the agenda of the Doha Round negotiations was trimmed down drastically. This should, however, not obscure the fact that at the Bali Ministerial Conference of 2013, WTO members reached the Trade Facilitation Agreement (TFA), committing members to considerably limit border processing costs. The Agreement entered into force in early 2017.

Depending on the expectations and normative demands vis-à-vis the WTO, one can have very different views of the TFA and the negotiation of several plurilateral agreements in the WTO. On the one hand, they appear to be proof that a single package and comprehensive regulatory negotiations have become unattainable in the multilateral trade regime. Or else, they can be interpreted as a vindication of the fact that the WTO is a member-driven organization that can enable the pragmatic easing of market access to the benefit of all its members. The protracted Doha Round negotiations have multiplied the calls for reforming the global trading system and for revisiting in particular the single under-taking practice and consensus-based decision-making (Hoekman and Mavroidis, 2015; Trebilcock, 2015).

The EU in the WTO dispute settlement system

As may have become clear from the short characterization of the WTO dispute settlement mechanism above, the most important aspect of the WTO's enforcement role is what cannot be observed empirically. That is, the mere existence of the dispute settlement system exerts pressure on members to comply with WTO commitments, meaning that – counterfactually – the world would have seen far more violations of WTO commitments in the absence of the shadow of WTO enforcement (Poletti et al., 2015). Members may therefore anticipate that they better not adopt certain trade measures incompatible with WTO rules. Moreo-ver, many disputes are resolved through bilateral consultations and peer pressure before they reach the formal stage. An early settlement before the establishment of a Panel is indeed the rule rather than the exception in the actual dispute settlement process. This aspect of the WTO dispute settlement process easily gets lost if one looks only at actual cases. The popular prism of 'trade wars', customarily used in press reports, obscures this simple fact. Of course, those disputes that turn out to be particularly difficult to solve attract attention exactly because they entail political conflict. A somewhat disproportionate amount of attention has been devoted – in the public debate and in the academic literature – to a set of high-profile dispute settlement cases. These cases have been the EU's discriminatory banana regime favouring African, Caribbean and Pacific over Latin American developing countries; the question whether the EU's regulations on hormone-treated meat as challenged by the United States were admissible under different sets of WTO rules; and whether the EU's procedures for the approval and marketing of biotech products (the so-called genetically modified organisms case) conformed with WTO rules (WTO DS 26, 27, 48, 291, 292 and 293; see WTO website).

The EU has been one of the most active participants in the dispute settlement mechanism, both as an initiator ('complainant') and as a target ('defendant'). The EU has been since the establishment of the WTO in 1995 until June 2017 a defendant in 84 cases and has acted as complainant against another WTO member in 97 disputes (see WTO website). Whereas in the past most trade disputes were of a transatlantic nature, the dispute settlement system is now increasingly used by emerging economies, most notably Brazil, China and India, whose requests for consultations often target EU policies.

A WTO dispute initiated by the EU can follow either the formalized procedure of the Trade Barriers Regulation (TBR) or the more informal, traditional procedure based on Art. 207 Treaty on the Functioning of the EU (TFEU) (Billiet, 2005). In the latter case, the initiative is taken by the European Commission and thoroughly examined by DG Trade and the Legal Service before a proposal is made to the Council. In practice, the Commission does not proceed with a WTO complaint unless it has the support of a qualified majority of the Trade Policy Committee. The European Parliament's INTA Committee is also briefed. The Art. 207 TFEU procedure is more political than the TBR route in the sense that action is likely only if there is strong backing from the Commission or influential member governments.

In the TBR case, EU companies (or member states) complain to the Commission, which is obliged to investigate. If the Commission decides to pursue a dispute settlement procedure at the WTO, which is one possible option, it must consult the member governments, represented in the advisory Trade Barriers Committee (see Chapter 3). The TPC is informed, but it has no express powers to intervene in the TBR procedure.

WTO dispute settlement cases can be of a very different nature. Many disputes merely seek to restore WTO-compatible market access to the targeted, 'defendant' member. In the example set out in Box 5.4, the EU successfully sought the elimination of a 25 per cent Chinese charge on imports of automobile parts that discriminated against foreign producers

Box 5.4   Case study: EU against Chinese auto parts measures at the WTO

In 2006 the EU requested consultations with the Republic of China regarding the latter's measures concerning the imports of automobile parts (see WTO, 2008). The Chinese authorities had introduced a 25 per cent charge on imported auto parts whenever particular thresholds were surpassed. These thresholds concerned particular combinations of automobile parts or were surpassed when the price of the imported parts attained 60 per cent or more of the vehicle. In China's bound tariff schedule, the average tariff rate on automobile parts is 10 per cent and 25 per cent on complete motor vehicles. According to the Chinese authorities, the imported auto parts were to be characterized as complete motor vehicles, for which reason they deemed it right to implement an administrative surcharge of 25 per cent on vehicles imported from abroad.

The United States and Canada also filed WTO complaints against these Chinese measures. In order to group these three complaints regarding the same issue, the Dispute Settlement Body established one single Panel to rule on the case. In their different submissions to the Panel, the three complainants submitted similar, yet not identical, reasons for why they thought China was acting against its WTO commitments. They did so by specifying the articles in different WTO agreements which they deemed China to be contravening, among which articles from the GATT 1994 agreement, China's Protocol of Accession, the TRIMs Agreement and the SCM Agreement. A number of WTO members asked to assist the legal proceedings as so-called third parties to the dispute.

The Panel issued its report in mid 2008, after which the Dispute Settlement Body formally adopted the Panel report and asked China to bring its measures into conformity with its obligations. The Panel found the Chinese measures to be incompatible with the national treatment requirement since imported automobile parts were being discriminated to the benefit of Chinese domestically produced automobile parts. China decided to file an appeal against certain legal aspects of the Panel's ruling, in response to which the Appellate Body issued its ruling at the end of 2008. It upheld most of the Panel's findings, and the Dispute Settlement Body asked China to bring its measures into conformity with WTO law. After agreeing to the decision that the reasonable period of time to implement the ruling was 7 months and 20 days, China informed the Dispute Settlement Body that its authorities had issued a decree that stopped the implementation of the surcharge on automobile parts and a repeal of the original decree.

Source: WTO website.

and thus favoured Chinese domestic production. Most cases combine this simple goal with more sophisticated, technical-legal characteristics. Since the WTO dispute settlement is a highly developed legal system, members sometimes seek rulings from it that may create some form of weak precedent, or may clarify the implications of some of its rules for concrete trade policy measures. This explains why some seemingly mundane cases are about more than just a particular product. In such disputes, WTO members seek to obtain a ruling from the WTO with implications for similar barriers to trade. In the famous EU bananas disputes, developing countries that are not members of the ACP group aimed at the abolishment of discriminatory elements of the preferential EU–ACP arrangement (see Chapter 6). In the EU sugar dispute with Brazil, the Brazilian agricultural sector and the Brazilian government wanted to show that some aspects of the subsidies in the EU's CAP were not compatible with its WTO commitments, and they thus exerted pressure on the EU to reform those aspects.

Generally, the European Commission takes on several roles in WTO dispute resolution (Young, 2006, p. 191): it is an advocate for particular economic interests, generally a champion of multilateral trade rules and a defender of the *acquis communautaire* – that is, the accumulated legal acts and Court decisions which constitute the body of EU law. Overall, the EU has been able to effectively use the WTO's dispute settlement system (ibid., p. 203).

In cases in which the defendant in a WTO dispute brought by the EU does not comply with the Dispute Settlement Body's ruling and does not bring its trade regulation in line with its previous commitments under WTO law, the EU can threaten to impose or in fact impose retaliatory measures. Formerly, such measures had to go through the normal decision-making procedures applicable to implement such measures, sometimes requiring the entire process under the ordinary legislative procedure. In 2014, the EU adopted a regulation delegating the swift imposition of such withdrawal of concessions under WTO or other international agreements to the Commission (European Parliament and Council of the European Union, 2014b).

When the EU is the defendant in a WTO dispute, DG Trade, together with the Commission's Legal Service, coordinates the EU's response to the challenges brought against its trade policies. Generally, the EU complies with WTO rulings, yet there can be considerable differences in the periods of time within which it is willing or able to do so. It often takes the EU – like other WTO members – longer to implement a WTO legal ruling when the dispute involves strongly mobilized import-competing sectors, and shorter when the dispute concerns a sector with a high degree of integration in international chains of production (see Yildirim, 2016; Yildirim et al., 2017). On the other hand, whether or not the EU brings its policies in line with the complainants' demands strongly depends on the number of veto players in the domestic implementation process (see Young, 2010; Poletti and De Bièvre, 2014). WTO law does not require its direct effect in domestic legal orders. The Court of Justice of the EU (CJEU), like many other courts, has adopted the doctrine of treaty-consistent interpretation. However, the question of direct effect of WTO law – that is, whether it should be possible to invoke a provision of WTO law in European courts in case of a conflict with national or EU law – is controversial (Van den Bossche and Zdouc, 2013, pp. 66–71). The CJEU has so far denied direct effect to WTO law. This implies that the validity of EU acts which are inconsistent with WTO obligations is protected, and economic actors who bear the burden of retaliatory measures cannot challenge it. Among the reasons for this lack of direct effect are that it would affect the EU's institutional balance and deprive the EU of its scope for manoeuvre with respect to (non)compliance compared to its main trading partners.

Conclusion

This chapter has outlined the role that the EU plays in the WTO and how it co-shaped the multilateral trade regime. The WTO is in the first place a large set of binding liberalization commitments and rules governing the regulation of international trade, but it is also an important forum for multilateral negotiations and the institutional locus for the enforcement of these rules. As one of the WTO's largest members, the EU has long been a force to be reckoned with in this organization. In line with the relative decline of the WTO as the most important venue for international trade agreements, the EU has witnessed its dwindling capacity to shape outcomes in the WTO (Young, 2011; De Bièvre and Poletti, 2013; Ahnlid and Elgström, 2014). The UK's departure from the EU is likely to weaken the EU's position, and the scepticism that the new US Administration under President Trump has displayed so far vis-à-vis the WTO further undermines any potential transatlantic leadership in this multilateral organization.

With the demise of the Doha Round, the EU did not drop its strategy of prioritizing the multilateral level, yet it ended its moratorium on the pursuit of bilateral trade agreements. With its 'Global Europe' trade strategy of 2006, it began to strategically pursue free trade agreements with emerging and developed economies, in particular in Asia and North America (see Chapter 7). The EU's change of its bilateral trade strategy in parallel to the Doha Round might have diminished the WTO's prominence as a negotiation forum for trade liberalization in the global economy. Yet, the EU's trade policies remain governed by the WTO rules, and the EU continues to seek the enforcement of those commitments.

Further reading

Dee, M. (2015) *The European Union in a Multipolar World: World Trade, Global Governance and the Case of the WTO* (London: Palgrave Macmillan).

Poletti, A. (2012) *The European Union and Multilateral Trade Governance: The Politics of the Doha Round* (London: Routledge).

Poletti, A. and D. De Bièvre (2014) 'Political Mobilization, Veto Players, and WTO Litigation: Explaining European Union Responses in Trade Disputes', *Journal of European Public Policy*, 21(8), 1181–1198.

Young, A. R. and J. Peterson (2014) *Parochial Global Europe: 21st Century Trade Politics* (Oxford: Oxford University Press), 71–101.

Chapter 6

EU Trade and Development Policy

The European Union (EU) and its member states are important trading partners and donors for developing countries. This chapter explores the relationship between the common commercial policy and European development policy, arguably the most developed, if not the most important, intersection of the EU's external policies. The first part analyses the longstanding and well-developed trade and aid relations between the EU and the African, Caribbean and Pacific (ACP) countries. It is followed by a short section on the EU's relations with developing countries in Asia and Latin America. The third part deals with the EU's Generalized System of Preferences (GSP), which is not restricted to a geographical group of countries and which in the past was often referred to as the EU's 'single most important trade tool for development' (Mandelson, 2005). Finally, the chapter presents the goals, actors and instruments of EU development policy and humanitarian assistance. Trade has become increasingly important for development cooperation since the EU considers its trade agreements to 'underpin sustainable development, human rights protection and rules-based governance' (European External Action Service, 2016, pp. 26–27). Yet only when combined with development cooperation can trade serve as 'a powerful engine of growth in developing countries' (European Commission, 2015, p. 3).

The development of EU–ACP relations

The relationship between the EU and the group of ACP countries has undergone considerable changes over time. It was built on the two pillars of trade and aid, and it has later on been complemented by political dialogue as a third pillar. This section focuses in particular on trade relations.

Association of dependent territories (1958–1963)

In the negotiations on the Rome Treaty, the question of the future status of the (former) colonies of some member states of the European Community (EC) was one of the last points on the negotiation agenda. French proposals, supported by Belgium, faced German-Dutch counterproposals, and in the end, the French government made its signature conditional upon an association of the overseas countries and territories. This association – negotiated without the involvement of the territories concerned – combined preferential trade relations with the newly created Community with financial aid that allowed France and Belgium in particular to share their burden with the other member states. Despite a preference for open markets and a global development policy in Germany and the Netherlands, the Franco-Belgian conception of a special relationship and managed markets for tropical products prevailed. The French and Belgian historical national preferences were extended to all EC members, and in order to comply with the requirements of the General Agreement on Tariffs and Trade (GATT), the dependent territories had to reciprocate the trade privileges (Ravenhill, 1985, pp. 48–57). In return, they became the sole beneficiaries of a new European Development Fund (EDF). For this purpose Directorate-General (DG) for Development was created within the European Commission to exclusively deal with the associated territories. This DG was largely shaped by former French colonial officials, although it underwent some transformation later on with the accession of the United Kingdom, the advent of conditionality and the reforms of the Lisbon Treaty (see Dimier, 2014).

The association between the EC and the 18 African and Malagasy States (known under the French acronym EAMA, *Etats africains et malgache associés*) officially aimed at promoting the economic and social development of the territories and at establishing close economic relations between them and the Community. The EC member states gradually reduced duties and quantitative restrictions while imposing high tariffs on certain products of interest to the associates, such as coffee, cocoa and bananas, as the new Common External Tariff vis-à-vis non-ACP countries (Bartels, 2007, pp. 721–722).

Only a few years later, most of the African territories declared independence, yet the association survived the decolonization process by taking the form of international treaties.

Yaoundé I and II Conventions (1964–1974)

Ravenhill (1985, p. 22) argues that the ACP countries pursued a strategy of 'collective clientelism': a group of weak states attempts to exploit the special ties that link them to a more powerful group of states. In other words, clientelism offers the weaker party the opportunity to ask for special treatment in order to gain resources that help reduce this dependence in the future. While the ACP countries hoped to draw on their joint bargaining power and obtain advantages not available to other developing countries, such a privileged relationship undercuts, however, the horizontal cooperation among the ACP countries themselves. The Yaoundé Convention was concluded in the form of an association agreement with preferential trade based on reciprocity, supported by the EDF. The Convention provided for a multilateral framework with joint institutions: an Association Council, an Association Committee, a Parliamentary Conference and a Court of Arbitration. The dominant perception was that only with mutual obligations could Africa negotiate as an equal with Europe. With minor exceptions, trade between the EC and its associates did not involve products that were competitive in their respective markets. This made it possible for both sides to impose high taxes on these products without harming domestic production and without infringing on the GATT principle of national treatment (Bartels, 2007, pp. 724–725). The initial obligation to liberalize trade among the associates themselves was abandoned, specifically to allow for regional integration among some of them.

With the United Kingdom joining the EC in 1973, the Commonwealth countries faced possible discrimination in their traditional British export market if they did not join the Lomé Convention. Yet not all of them were interested. In 1964 the UN Conference on Trade and Development (UNCTAD) had been born out of frustration with the GATT system's perceived inability to respond to development concerns. Developing countries used UNCTAD as the international venue through which they pushed for better market access for them, commodity stabilization agreements, compensatory financing and support for regional arrangements. The deteriorating terms of trade between the primary products exported by developing countries and the manufactured goods imported from industrialized countries negatively affected their purchasing power. In light of the debate about a 'New International Economic Order', the unsatisfactory trade results of the Yaoundé Convention and the addition of a part on trade and development to GATT that encouraged non-reciprocity, the African Commonwealth took the view that any new comprehensive agreement with the EC would have to be based on non-reciprocal trade (Ravenhill, 1985, pp. 72–97). The United Kingdom had demanded that the EC's association be made available for Commonwealth Africa, the Caribbean and Pacific islands but conceded that this status was not necessary for the economically more advanced Commonwealth Asia. In fact, India preferred to conclude in 1973 a trade cooperation agreement with the EC.

The EC responded to the increasing criticism of a 'neo-colonial association' and of dividing Africa by abandoning the principle of reciprocity in relations with the ACP countries; by establishing a lesser, generalized system of non-reciprocal trade preferences for all developing countries (see below); and by concluding bilateral preferential trade agreements with its Mediterranean neighbours, supplemented by financial protocols. In the late 1960s the Community began to engage in food aid as a first form of external aid without any geographical links. In the mid 1970s the EC also started to earmark financial assistance for the developing countries of Asia and Latin America.

Lomé I-III Conventions (1975–1990)

Lomé I (1975–1980) was widely perceived as a model for North–South relations (Holland and Doidge, 2012, pp. 54–57). It was negotiated between the then nine EC member states and the newly established group of 46 ACP states that was created by the Georgetown Agreement in 1975. Nevertheless, each ACP country signed the Convention individually.

The Lomé Convention removed the reciprocity of trade preferences and expanded the scope of cooperation to the industrial field and the stabilization of export earnings from agricultural commodities. Although this led to discrimination between ACP and non-ACP developing countries, for a long time no objections were raised in GATT. The ACP countries enjoyed almost full duty-free access for all their exports. Only their products that directly competed with products under the Common Agricultural Policy (CAP) were excluded, but these still enjoyed more favourable treatment than they would have enjoyed under most-favoured nation (MFN) terms. The ACP countries were under no obligation to offer reciprocal market access, but in case of similar agreements with other non-developing countries, they would have to offer the EC countries no less favourable treatment. Yet, the rules of origin with which ACP products had to comply in order to benefit from duty-free access were still quite restrictive despite allowing for cumulation across ACP countries. Rules of origin are the regulations and practices used to identify the country of origin of internationally traded goods. Cumulation refers to the fact that under certain conditions, inputs (materials and/or processes) originating in another country within a preferential trade area are counted as coming from the exporting country itself, thus contributing to satisfy the rules of origin.

Foreign aid was based on contractual relations and, at that time, was free from interference in domestic politics. Financial assistance was thus contractually secure and not subject to changes in politics. Another key principle was the joint management – that is, EDF spending had to be signed off jointly by the Commission representative and the national authorizing officer of the country concerned – a first instance of what years later would become the principle of joint ownership. Another innovation was special support schemes for commodity exports suffering from price fluctuations. A financing scheme called STABEX (Stabilization of Export Earnings) was introduced to compensate for the shortfall in export earnings and stabilize ACP revenue from certain agricultural exports. STABEX was the first scheme by a group of industrialized countries for the stabilization of commodity export earnings of a group of developing trading partners. It did not include mineral products or products included in the CAP.

A few special commodity protocols were added to the Lomé Convention. Of these, sugar, rum and bananas proved to be problematic because they conflicted with domestic interests in some EC member states either with producers of competitive substitutes or with importers using other sources of supply (Ravenhill, 1985, pp. 219–251). The protocols offered ACP producers, up to certain quotas, preferential access to the Community market, which was attractive for them because EC prices were generally higher than those of world markets.

When in the 1980s Africa was increasingly coping with debt problems and a growing marginalization in the world economy, Lomé II (1980–85) introduced an additional compensatory financing scheme called SYSMIN (System of Stabilization of Export Earnings from Mining Products). This scheme provided aid to ACP mining industries for their export of minerals to the European market.

The successor convention, Lomé III (1985–1990), continued to be overshadowed by the debt crisis in many ACP countries. With Greece having joined the EC in 1981 and Spain and Portugal in 1986, the then 12 member states faced a group that had already increased to 66 ACP countries. No important changes marked the contents of the revised convention, though, while its implementation coincided with the GATT Uruguay Round negotiations.

Lomé IV Convention (1990–2000)

With the collapse of the Soviet Union came a new development priority for the EC: Central and Eastern Europe. The end of the Cold War witnessed worldwide movements in favour of democratization and transition to a market economy, as well as open regionalism. Building on the Lomé Conventions, the Maastricht Treaty provided the first legal basis for EU development policy, aiming not only at fighting poverty and enhancing development but also at the integration of developing countries into the world economy and the promotion of democracy and respect for human rights. At the same time, the Common Foreign and Security Policy (CFSP) came into being, contributing to the end of 'political neutrality' in trade and development policy.

The Lomé IV Convention introduced a human rights clause as a 'fundamental part' of cooperation. This did not allow for the suspension of the agreement in case of serious violations. With the 1995 revision of the 'Lomé IV' Convention, the human rights clause was turned into an 'essential element' of the agreement, making suspension legally possible. This marked the beginning of the EU's policy of political conditionality (see Chapter 7). It was not until the Cotonou Agreement, however, that a political dialogue was added as a third pillar that clarified the procedure to follow for the suspension and resumption of relations.

Furthermore, the completion of the EU's internal market, the conclusion of the Uruguay Round, the erosion of ACP preferences compared to other countries' access to the EU market and a series of banana disputes at the GATT (see Box 6.1) increased the pressure for reciprocity in trade with the ACP countries. It was only over the course of these disputes that the EU finally asked for and obtained in 1994 a first waiver for the Lomé IV Convention (although it was not a complete waiver, because challenges to the Banana Protocol would be allowed). The establishment of the World Trade Organization (WTO) one year later abolished the veto in the dispute settlement system.

Overall, Lomé was early on considered a disappointment: it failed to preserve the ACP countries' share of the European market as well as their tariff advantages relative to others, and it did not initiate a truly equal and jointly managed partnership (Ravenhill, 1985, p. 309). Although the EU unilaterally granted free market access for specific tropical goods included in the Lomé Conventions, these concessions could always be limited through quantitative restrictions. The resulting perpetuation of unilateral dependence of ACP countries on the benevolence of the Community contributed to a lack of economic diversification and long-term investment in processing and distribution capacity in these ACP clientele countries. The EU thus effectively used its bargaining power to unilaterally close its market whenever its own domestic producers would start facing competition (De Bièvre and Poletti, 2013). The perceived 'Lomé failure', the lack of WTO compatibility and the phenomenal economic growth that South-East Asia experienced led to a renewed debate on the future of the EU–ACP partnership in the late 1990s. On the one hand, years of privileged trade and aid relations still left many ACP states economically marginalized, impoverished and uncompetitive (see European Commission, 1996). On the other hand, the international discussion leading up to the Millennium Development Goals (MDGs) of the United Nations called for new efforts to reduce extreme poverty and set out a series of targets to be reached by 2015.

Cotonou Agreement and the Economic Partnership Agreements (2000–2020)

In 2000 the Cotonou Agreement was signed for a period of 20 years by 77 members of the ACP group except for Cuba. Timor Leste became an ACP member in 2003, shortly after its independence, and South Sudan is on the way to join, which would bring the number of ACP countries to 80.

The Cotonou Agreement added a comprehensive political dimension to aid and trade, thus aiming at a more global partnership. It embraced the concept of participatory development, involving civil society and local authorities, as well as private sector development, and it introduced a reform of financial cooperation (in particular by adding performance criteria) and a new framework for trade. At the same time, the Cotonou Agreement put an end to the price-stabilization mechanisms STABEX and SYSMIN. The suspension clause was extended to include good governance, but as a mere 'fundamental' and not an 'essential' element of the agreement – except for serious cases of corruption. In the 2005 revision of the Cotonou Agreement, cooperation on the non-proliferation of weapons of mass destruction was added as an 'essential' element, and the parties were and are encouraged to join the Rome Statute of the International Criminal Court.

The most radical innovation in the trade pillar was the introduction of the principles of differentiation and regionalization (Faber and Orbie, 2009). With the expiry of the WTO waiver at the end of 2007, the trade chapter of the Cotonou Agreement was to be replaced by so-called EPAs

Box 6.1   Brief chronology of the banana disputes

The EU is the largest market for bananas, and it produces only around 20 per cent of its own consumption. US firms like Chiquita, Dole and Del Monte account for two-thirds of the international trade in bananas. The production costs for European and ACP bananas are higher than those of the Latin American 'dollar bananas'. The EU faced conflicting interests: the protection of EU producers, the support to ACP producers, the support to EU distributors, the consumer interest in cheap bananas and the reconciliation of its international obligations vis-à-vis GATT/WTO members and those towards ACP countries. Before the completion of the internal market in 1993, the member states still maintained different national import regimes. Some members imposed quotas; others charged a 20 per cent tariff across the board; and Germany had negotiated duty-free access for bananas in the Rome Treaty.

In 1992, the EU Council of Ministers adopted a controversial 'Common Organization of the Market in Bananas' by qualified majority voting. It entailed tariff-free quotas for ACP bananas and 20 per cent tariff quotas for 'dollar bananas' with prohibitive tariffs for imports beyond those quotas. The Commission issued import licences to all banana distributors. In 1993 Costa Rica, Colombia, Guatemala, Nicaragua and Venezuela requested a Panel ('Banana I') to rule on the GATT compatibility of the national European regimes. They won the case, but the EU vetoed the adoption of the Panel report. The same countries requested a Panel ('Banana II') on the new EU regime and won it too. Again, the EU used its veto. In 1994, before the entry into force of the WTO, the EU negotiated a Framework Agreement on Bananas between with Colombia, Costa Rica, Nicaragua and Venezuela which granted them national quotas for the EU market in return for suspending the complaint.

with several regional groupings of ACP countries. The EPAs provide for a phased establishment of WTO-compatible free trade areas based on asymmetrical reciprocity, and regional integration is expected to boost local trade and attract investment. They would, within a reasonable transition period, comply with the requirement of Art. XXIV GATT to cover 'substantially all trade'. The EU's standard request was that the ACP countries liberalize 80 per cent of their trade in goods for that

→

During 1995–1996 the United States, Guatemala, Honduras, Mexico and Ecuador launched a complaint ('Banana III') at the WTO. The Panel considered the EU regime incompatible with certain WTO commitments. The EU appealed, but the Appellate Body confirmed the ruling. In 1999, the EU introduced a new licensing system that still used quotas. This was again challenged by the United States and Ecuador, and the WTO authorized trade sanctions for the United States and Ecuador against EU products. In 2001 the EU agreed to a new tariff-only import regime as of 2006. After several rounds of WTO-led arbitration, the new regime foresaw a tariff of €176/tonne for Latin American bananas and for ACP bananas duty-free access up to an annual quota of 775,000 tonnes (based on a waiver until the end of 2005). Several Latin American countries subsequently demanded consultations with the EU. In 2007 a Panel requested by Ecuador, followed by the United States, found that the EU had failed to implement the previous ruling. The Appellate Body upheld the Panels' findings.

During 2007–2008 at the request of some of the parties, WTO Director-General Pascal Lamy helped broker a new agreement. As of 2008, the EU offered the ACP countries duty-free, quota-free access as part of Economic Partnership Agreements (EPAs) (see below), while it continued to negotiate on bananas with the Latin Americans and the United States in the context of the Doha Round. In 2009 the Geneva Agreement on Trade in Bananas was reached as an 'early outcome agreement' of the Doha Round. It stipulated a gradual reduction of tariffs for non-ACP bananas to €114/tonne by 2017 in exchange for the settlement of all WTO disputes. It entered into force in 2012 and thereby ended the longest-running series of disputes in the history of the multilateral trading system. In addition, some Latin American countries afterwards negotiated bilateral free trade agreements with the EU that included lower tariffs for bananas.

Sources: Based on WTO website and Guth (2012).

purpose. A full or comprehensive EPA covers not only trade in goods, as the Lomé and Cotonou Agreement did, but also trade in services and a host of other trade-related areas, such as investment, competition policy, government procurement, intellectual property rights and labour and environmental standards. Hence, the proposed scope of the new agreements was broader than required by WTO rules. Heron (2014) argues that the EU used WTO compatibility strategically in order to persuade

ACP countries of the merits of reciprocal free trade. At the same time, the decision to grant all least developed countries (LDCs) duty-free and quota-free access under the 'Everything But Arms' initiative at the beginning of the Doha Round undermined the EU's bargaining leverage in the EPA negotiations.

Several regional groupings were formed to negotiate the new agreements as of 2002. The 78 ACP countries were free to choose which group to join, and some of them switched in the course of the negotiations (see Table 6.1). Yet the regions are not entirely identical regarding existing integration schemes, leading to difficulties and tensions during the negotiations. For example, the Southern African Development Community (SADC) negotiating with the EU as a group actually comprised only seven of its members, while the other six members have been negotiating as part of the Central African group or the group of Eastern and Southern Africa (ESA). Botswana, Lesotho, Namibia, Swaziland and South Africa form the Southern Africa Customs Union (SACU), and trade between the EU and South Africa is, in addition, governed by the bilateral Trade, Development and Cooperation Agreement (TDCA). The East African Community (EAC) and the Economic Community of West African States (ECOWAS) are also customs unions whose members are mainly, yet not only, LDCs.

For the first time, the ACP countries negotiated with DG Trade instead of DG Development, which has been interpreted as leading to a shift from the promotion of social development to the promotion of deep free trade (Elgström and Frennhoff Larsén, 2010, p. 214). The negotiations soon turned out to be highly controversial, resulting in increased mobilization by civil society organizations and growing criticism of the Commission from the ACP countries and some EU member states. Although the EPAs aimed to promote trade and development, regionalization and poverty reduction, many feared that they would rather undermine the long-term sustainable development of ACP countries and their regional integration processes. The controversial issues included in particular the prospect of significant tariff revenue losses due to the required market opening, reduced policy space for governments, threats to local industries unable to compete, job losses, trade diversion and the disruption of existing or planned regional customs unions (see European Parliament, 2014). A number of ACP countries only agreed to interim EPAs focused on trade in goods and development aid, which contain a 'rendezvous clause' for further negotiations towards more comprehensive agreements.

In 2007 the Commission, under pressure for demonstrating a more development-friendly approach and to meet the deadline set by the WTO waiver, offered 100 per cent tariff- and quota-free market access (with transition periods for rice and sugar); an asymmetric, gradual market opening of ACP markets for EU exports (with protection for sensitive products); and more development aid. The aid concerned the EDF, aid for trade and additional assistance to adjust to the EPAs, for instance compensating for the loss of tariff revenue and increased competition. The goal was to sign interim EPAs focusing on trade, while the open issues would be negotiated later. Based on a new Market Access Regulation, the 35 ACP countries that had concluded negotiations and at least initialled an interim agreement by the end of 2007 obtained temporarily duty- and quota-free access to the EU market as of 2008 (Council of the European Union, 2007a). Four years later, however, only half of these countries had taken the necessary steps towards ratification of the initialled agreements. The Commission announced that those countries lagging behind would no longer benefit from this unilateral market access arrangement as of January (then October) 2014. This additional pressure led to the conclusion of some EPA negotiations.

The potential withdrawal of market access posed a problem for, in particular, those African countries that depend on the EU market for their (often narrow range of) exports and for countries in regional customs unions. The alternatives to an EPA were either the GSP (see below) or the less attractive MFN treatment as WTO member. The expiry of the Market Access Regulation coincided with the GSP reform (see below), and thus increased the pressure on those ACP countries that would in 2014 fall out of the new GSP. Thereafter, the EU granted another two-year extension for the ratification of signed EPAs until 1 October 2016, and the Market Access Regulation was replaced by another regulation which provisionally applies the EPAs to countries that have concluded an interim EPA (European Parliament and Council of the European Union, 2016b).

For the LDCs, the alternative to an EPA was mainly the continued reliance on the 'Everything-But-Arms' initiative in place since 2001 (see below). It grants duty-free and quota-free access without reciprocity. In fact, 40 (plus future ACP member South Sudan) of the world's 48 LDCs, as defined by the UN, are ACP countries, most of them in Africa (see Table 6.1).

After 15 years of negotiations, the results were rather disappointing. By mid 2017, the members of Cariforum – the Caribbean ACP countries except for Cuba – were the only group that had concluded the

TABLE 6.1   *Regional Groups for EPA Negotiations and LDCs*

EPA group	Members (LDCs in italics)
Caribbean (Cariforum)	**Antigua and Barbuda, Bahamas, Barbados, Belize, Dominica, Dominican Republic, Grenada, Guyana,** *Haiti,* **Jamaica, St Kitts and Nevis, St Lucia, St Vincent and the Grenadines, Surinam, Trinidad and Tobago**
Central Africa	**Cameroon,** *Central African Republic, Chad,* **Congo,** *Democratic Republic of Congo, Equatorial Guinea,* **Gabon,** *São Tomé and Príncipe*
East African Community	*Burundi,* **Kenya,** *Rwanda, Uganda, Tanzania*
Eastern and Southern Africa	*Comoros, Djibouti, Eritrea, Ethiopia, Madagascar, Malawi,* **Mauritius, Seychelles,** *Somalia, Sudan, Zambia,* **Zimbabwe**
Pacific (Pacific Islands Forum except Australia and New Zealand)	**Cook Islands,** *Timor Leste,* **Federated States of Micronesia, Fiji,** *Kiribati,* **Marshall Islands, Nauru, Niue, Palau, Papua New Guinea,** *Samoa, Solomon Islands,* **Tonga,** *Tuvalu, Vanuatu*
SADC (partial)	*Angola,* **Botswana,** *Lesotho, Mozambique,* **Namibia, South Africa, Swaziland**
West Africa (ECOWAS and Mauritania)	*Benin, Burkina Faso,* **Cape Verde, Ivory Coast,** *Gambia,* **Ghana,** *Guinea, Guinea Bissau, Liberia, Mali, Mauritania, Niger,* **Nigeria,** *Senegal, Sierra Leone, Togo*

Source: DG Trade website.

negotiations by the initial deadline of December 2007 (with Haiti's ratification pending). Other regional EPAs were finally concluded a few years later with the EAC (all five countries, but so far only Kenya and Rwanda signed) and with West Africa (covering all 16 countries, of which so far only Ivory Coast and Ghana signed and provisionally apply a 'stepping stone' EPA). Only the Caribbean countries and the SADC group (except for Angola – and those SADC members in different negotiating groups) have so far signed a full and comprehensive EPA. In Central Africa, only

TABLE 6.2 *ACP Countries' Current Trade Relations with the EU (June 2017)*

EPA group	Members and their trade status
Caribbean (Cariforum)	Full EPA, except for Haiti (EBA, EPA pending)
Central Africa	EBA, except for Cameroon (EPA), Congo (GSP) and Gabon (MFN)
East African Community	EBA (signatures of EPA pending), except for Kenya (EPA)
Eastern and Southern Africa	EBA, except for Madagascar, Mauritius, Seychelles and Zimbabwe (EPA)
Pacific (Pacific Islands Forum except Australia and New Zealand)	EPA for Papua New Guinea and Fiji, EBA for LDCs, and GSP for the others
SADC (partial)	Full EPA, except for Mozambique (pending ratification in EBA) and South Africa (TDCA)
West Africa (ECOWAS and Mauritania)	EBA, except for Cape Verde (GSP+), Ivory Coast and Ghana (EPA) and Nigeria (GSP)

Source: DG Trade website.

Cameroon signed and ratified the EPA, and in ESA Madagascar, Mauritius, Seychelles and Zimbabwe. In the Pacific region Papua New Guinea and Fiji ratified the EPA. Hence, after a long and protracted process, a majority of ACP countries concluded EPAs with the EU, yet in many cases implementation is still pending or questionable. Table 6.2 summarizes the state of play, keeping in mind that for many ACP countries which committed to an EPA, the provisional application still needs to be followed up by ratification.

Compared to the other developing countries, the ACP countries have for historical reasons enjoyed privileged relations with the EU. However, in recent years they have been facing a kind of 'privilege erosion'. Their trade preferences have very much been 'streamlined' with the GSP and the EU's preferential agreements with other countries, and there is no reference to the ACP group anymore in the Lisbon Treaty. Nevertheless, the ACP countries continue to be organized in a highly institutionalized relationship with the EU, and they are still the biggest recipients of European development aid. The relevance of the EU in many ACP countries has been challenged not only by the lack of success of the EPAs but also by the rise of the BRIC (Brazil, Russia, India and China) countries, which for some developing countries represent an alternative source of (unconditional) aid and trade and potential allies in international forums. The EU and the ACP countries are therefore rethinking their future partnership for the post-2020 era, when the Cotonou Agreement will expire. The EU has proposed three distinct regional partnerships with the ACP countries that would pursue tailored priorities in line with the United Nations's Sustainable Development Goals (SDGs), adopted in 2015 (European Commission and High Representative, 2016). These regional partnerships would be placed under a common ACP umbrella and also reach out beyond ACP. For trade the EPAs would remain the key instruments. The post-Cotonou discussion is thus underway, and the impact of Brexit on the EU–ACP relations adds further uncertainty.

The EU's relations with Asian and Latin American countries

Unlike the ACP countries, the Asian and Latin American countries have not been subject to a single, overarching EU approach, nor profited from special trade privileges or a specific own fund (Holland and Doidge, 2012, pp. 134–158). Their trade relations with the EU have been governed mainly by the GSP and since the 1990s increasingly by free trade agreements (FTAs). European aid to these regions began to be delivered in the mid 1970s but remained low compared to the funds transferred to the ACP countries, because most LDCs are on the African continent (Holden, 2009, pp. 146–169).

Regarding trade relations, the EU turned rather late to Latin America. One of the reasons might be the predominance of the United States in this region. In 1995 the EU concluded a framework cooperation agreement with Mercosur. Five years later, negotiations for an ambitious association agreement including free trade were launched. These bi-regional negotiations have been fraught with many difficulties (Doctor, 2007). They were suspended in 2004 and relaunched in 2010, and they are still continuing. In 1997 the EU concluded trade agreements with Mexico and in 2002 with Chile (Dür, 2007), both of which are currently undergoing modernization negotiations, and in 2010 with Central America (Arantza Gomez, 2015). In 2012 – after negotiations for an association agreement with the Andean Community failed – the EU concluded an FTA with Colombia and Peru, which Ecuador joined in 2014 (García, 2015).

In comparison, the development of Asia was given very little attention despite some shared colonial history. Asia was 'geographically remote, generally poor, comparatively diverse, and regarded as a less reliable supplier of the raw materials' that Europe needed during the Cold War besides the fact that the United Kingdom's influence in the region was considerable (Holland and Doidge, 2012, pp. 159–160). In 1980 the EC concluded a cooperation agreement with the Association of Southeast Asian Nations (ASEAN). However, trade persisted largely on the GSP level, and European aid remained modest.

Since 2006 Asian countries have become important trading partners for the EU, and trade agreements have proliferated (see Chapter 7). The EU and ASEAN launched negotiations in 2007 for a free trade agreement that were suspended after two years (Meissner, 2016b). Instead, the EU pursued bilateral negotiations with individual countries. The first comprehensive FTA with an Asian partner was concluded with South Korea in 2010, followed two years later by Singapore as the first ASEAN country. FTA negotiations with other Asian countries followed and are ongoing, including India and Japan. The EU's negotiations with Japan have been progressing, pushed in 2017 by the US withdrawal from the Trans-Pacific Partnership and by Brexit, but those with India have been much more protracted (Khorana and García, 2013).

In spite of these differences in the EU's approach to the three world regions, all developing countries could since 1971 benefit from the GSP.

The EU's Generalized System of Preferences

In addition to FTAs, the EU derogates from the Common External Tariff rates and from the WTO's principle of MFN treatment through unilateral non-reciprocal trade preferences for developing or transition countries. Examples include the autonomous preferences which the EU granted to the countries of the Western Balkans in 2000 in the context of the Stabilization and Association Process and to Moldova in 2008 until they were replaced by bilateral trade agreements. The largest, oldest and most important scheme is the GSP. Although the GSP was initially thought to be only a temporary measure, the EC has since the 1970s regularly renewed the system, thereby broadening its coverage of products and countries and increasing the level of differentiation as well as the degree of political conditionality. Besides the EU, a dozen developed countries currently have various GSP schemes in place.

The origins of the Generalized System of Preferences

The GSP goes back to a recommendation of the second United Nations Conference on Trade and Development in 1968, calling on the industrialized countries to grant non-reciprocal trade preferences to all developing countries, including special measures for the LDCs (UNCTAD, 1968). The underlying expectation was that a generalized non-reciprocal, non-discriminatory system of preferences in favour of developing countries would increase their export earnings and promote their industrialization. This also explains the focus at the time on preferences for manufactures and semi-manufactures instead of primary products. In 1971, the Contracting Parties to the GATT agreed to a general waiver to the MFN principle to allow for discriminatory treatment between developed and developing countries for ten years. In 1979, this exception was perpetuated by the so-called Enabling Clause negotiated in the Tokyo Round (see Chapter 5). According to the principle of self-election, countries can designate themselves as 'developing countries' and thus potential beneficiaries, but the developed countries had reserved the right to exclude countries from their tariff concessions and to use graduation mechanisms which would phase out non-reciprocal preferential market access for countries which made progress. The United Nations only provides a definition of LDCs only based on per capita gross national income, human assets and economic vulnerability to external shocks. The European Community ((EC) was the first actor to create a GSP in 1971, which has since undergone many reforms (see Gstöhl, 2014, pp. 52–62).

The increasing differentiation of the EU's GSP

Several phases can be distinguished in the development of the EU's GSP. The first phase ran from 1971 to 1980 and was renewed until 1990. In the framework of the ten-year cycles, the GSP was implemented through different regulations and decisions. Generally, 'non-sensitive' goods received duty-free access within the fixed quantities, while 'sensitive' goods were granted a reduction on the MFN tariff only. The policy thus distinguished several degrees of product sensitivity, depending on the extent to which imported goods competed with goods produced in the EC. The Commission's initial list of products to be covered was heavily cut back by the Council, virtually eliminating all processed agricultural goods which a member state (and particularly France and Italy) considered sensitive (Tullock, 1975, p. 61). The Community imposed tariff quotas and ceilings, and within these maximum limits there were restrictions at the national level of either the importing member state or the exporting developing country in order to 'spread' the burden or benefit, respectively. During this phase, the EC GSP was reviewed each year, leading to changes in product coverage, quotas, ceilings and their administration, beneficiaries and depth of tariff cuts for agricultural products.

The second phase began with a new system that entered into force in 1995 for the next decade. The reform due for 1991 was postponed in order to await the results of the Uruguay Round, which ended in 1994 and led to the creation of the WTO. The main innovations were the replacement of tariff quotas and ceilings by a tariff modulation (i.e. tariff rates classified according to different categories of product sensitivity), the introduction of a graduation system and the creation of 'special incentive arrangements' alongside the general arrangement. The system of graduation by country and sector combined criteria of a development index and a specialization index and aimed to transfer preferential margins gradually from advanced to less-developed countries. Preferential tariffs are either suspended or re-established when a country's performance on the EU market exceeds or falls below a set threshold. The special schemes attempted to induce developing countries to pursue particular political goals in order to obtain additional trade preferences as a reward.

Five arrangements were available for beneficiary countries under the GSP in this phase: the general arrangement and separate special incentive arrangements for the protection of labour rights, for the protection of the environment, for the LDCs, and the special arrangement to combat drug production and trafficking. The 'labour arrangement' encouraged beneficiary countries to introduce effective policies for the protection of workers' rights, more precisely according to the Conventions of the International Labour Organization (ILO) concerning the freedom of association, the right to bargain collectively and the minimum age for employment. The 'environmental arrangement' rewarded the sustainable management of tropical forests in conformity with the International Tropical Timber Organization (ITTO), at the time the only internationally recognized environmental standards. Interested countries had to apply for these two special incentive arrangements, but the response was very limited (Orbie and Tortell, 2009, pp. 669–670). By contrast, the EU decided whom to grant additional preferences under the 'drugs regime'. This special arrangement was already established in 1991 for the Andean countries (Bolivia, Colombia, Ecuador and Peru), which received exemptions from quotas and ceilings as well as duty-free access to certain industrial and agricultural products in order to combat the production and trafficking of cocaine. It was subsequently extended to some other Latin American countries.

At the Singapore Ministerial Conference in 1996, WTO members pledged to improve access to their markets for LDCs. In 1998 the EU offered the LDCs not party to the Lomé Convention preferences equivalent to those enjoyed by the ACP countries. In 2001, in view of the launch of the Doha Round negotiations, the EU adopted the 'Everything-but Arms' initiative, which grants the LDCs duty-free and quota-free market access for all products, except for arms and ammunitions (and with short transitional periods for sugar, rice and bananas). Unlike the other arrangements, the EBA is not subject to periodic renewal, and the graduation mechanism does not apply. A country is withdrawn from the list of beneficiaries soon after the United Nations removes it from its list of LDCs. The EBA initiative helped the EU gain the developing countries' support for a new WTO round, while it differentiated – if not split – the ACP group (Orbie, 2007).

The GSP was challenged in the WTO when the EU added Pakistan to the list of beneficiaries of the 'drugs arrangement' in order to help stabilize the country in the aftermath of the terrorist attacks of September 2001 in the United States and the subsequent United States–led invasion of Afghanistan. The Indian government successfully contested the scheme's WTO compatibility. The Panel found that the 'GSP drugs' was indeed inconsistent with the MFN principle and not justified under the Enabling Clause. In 2004 the Appellate Body confirmed this finding and added that preference-granting countries are required, by virtue of the term 'non-discriminatory', to ensure that identical treatment is available to all similarly situated GSP beneficiaries – that is, to all GSP beneficiaries that have the same 'development, financial and trade needs' (WTO, 2004, para 165). This need must meet an objective standard, for instance through broad recognition by international organizations, and it should be such that it can be effectively addressed through tariff preferences. However, the 'GSP drugs' operated through a 'closed list' that precluded an assessment of potential beneficiaries and the same treatment of countries in the same situation.

Growing political conditionality in the EU's GSP

The third phase began with a new GSP in 2006 and lasted until 2013. Partly in response to the WTO ruling, the EU replaced the labour, environmental and drugs arrangements with an integrated special incentive arrangement for sustainable development and good governance ('GSP+'). The new system was thus composed of three arrangements only. First, the general arrangement granted duty-free access for non-sensitive products and tariff reductions for sensitive products (mainly agriculture and textiles) to 176 beneficiary countries and territories. Second, the 'GSP+' provided duty-free access to all the products covered by the GSP's general arrangement (plus a few more), without distinction in terms of their sensitivity. Third, the EBA continued offering duty-free and quota-free access to all products from LDCs.

Beneficiaries were expected to abide by 16 UN/ILO conventions. In case of serious and systematic violations of the core human rights and labour rights laid down in these international conventions, any arrangement could temporarily be withdrawn (see Chapter 7). Following a Commission investigation into forced labour in Myanmar, the Council had suspended the country's GSP benefits in 1997. In view of the political reforms in that country, they were reinstated in July 2013. Belarus had its trade preferences withdrawn in 2007 due to the non-respect of the freedom of association for workers. This became obsolete with the GSP reform, which removed the upper-middle income country in 2014.

Countries wishing to benefit from the extended preferences of 'GSP+' had to apply, qualify as 'vulnerable' economies and commit to ratify and implement a list of 11 additional international conventions in the fields of human rights, labour standards, sustainable development and good governance. A 'vulnerable' country was defined in terms of three cumulative conditions: it is not classified by the World Bank as a high-income country, its exports are poorly diversified (i.e. its five largest sections represent more than 75 per cent of its GSP-covered exports to the EU), and its EU share of GSP-covered imports is lower than 1 per cent. Hence, the 'GSP+' beneficiaries faced more political conditionality and risked losing the additional preferences if they did not effectively implement the international conventions. The 15 beneficiary countries that had qualified for the first round of 'GSP+' in 2005 were all countries that had already participated in the earlier 'drugs' or 'labour' arrangements, except for Pakistan.

The negotiation of a new system was accelerated by the entry into force of the Lisbon Treaty before the ten-year cycle between 2006 and 2015 was over. In 2014 the revised GSP entered its fourth phase, starting another ten-year cycle. For the first time the European Parliament participated in the drafting of the regulation in the framework of the ordinary legislative procedure. The main changes in the GSP regulation concern the coverage of countries, the criteria for graduation and vulnerability, and political conditionality (European Parliament and Council of the European Union, 2012).

The EU's current GSP and the EPAs

The main objective of the GSP reform was to focus on the countries 'most in need', in view of the increasing preference erosion as a result of the GATT/WTO rounds and the EU's active pursuit of FTAs. The product coverage remained largely the same, and the three arrangements (GSP, 'GSP+' and EBA) continue to exist. Countries which the World Bank classifies as either high-income or – new – upper-middle income were no longer eligible, and beneficiaries covered by other trade arrangements were removed. This halved the number of countries and territories covered to around 90 in 2014. In mid 2017 fewer than 30 countries were in the standard GSP, 9 in the 'GSP+' (including Sri Lanka, which was readmitted after a period of sanctions) and 49 in the EBA (48 official LDCs, plus Samoa being phased out). The post-Lisbon Treaty scheme is more dynamic because it can be directly amended by the European Commission via delegated acts (e.g. the list of eligible countries) or implementing acts (e.g. the withdrawal or reinstatement of preferences).

In order to further strengthen the conditionality in the 'GSP+', the 'burden of proof' for compliance was put on the beneficiary and no longer on the EU side. The vulnerability criteria have been loosened (by increasing the maximum threshold of GSP-covered imports to 2 per cent and the number of the largest sections to 7 per cent), and the graduation mechanism was abolished. Instead of fixed deadlines, applications for the 'GSP+' can be launched at any point in time. There are now 15 international conventions relevant for all GSP schemes and 12 additional international conventions for the 'GSP+' (see Table 6.3). The UN Framework Convention on Climate Change has been added to the list of conventions (the Kyoto Protocol was already included), while the International Convention on the Suppression and Punishment of the Crime of Apartheid was removed. Effective implementation of the ratified conventions requires that the relevant monitoring bodies do not identify a serious failure.

In addition to the application of political conditionality, the GSP allows the temporary withdrawal of trade preferences in case of export of goods made by prison labour, insufficient control of drug trade, money laundering, serious and systematic unfair trading practices or infringement of the objectives of regional fishery organizations. Moreover, countries can

TABLE 6.3 *International Conventions to be Respected by GSP Beneficiaries*

Withdrawal of preferences in case of serious and systematic violation of principles laid down in these conventions (for all arrangements):

1. Convention on the Prevention and Punishment of the Crime of Genocide
2. International Convention on the Elimination of All Forms of Racial Discrimination
3. International Covenant on Civil and Political Rights
4. International Covenant on Economic Social and Cultural Rights
5. Convention on the Elimination of All Forms of Discrimination Against Women
6. Convention Against Torture and other Cruel, Inhuman or Degrading Treatment or Punishment
7. Convention on the Rights of the Child
8. ILO Convention concerning Forced or Compulsory Labour
9. ILO Convention concerning Freedom of Association and Protection of the Right to Organise
10. ILO Convention concerning the Application of the Principles of the Right to Organise and to Bargain Collectively
11. ILO Convention concerning Equal Remuneration of Men and Women Workers for Work of Equal Value
12. ILO Convention concerning the Abolition of Forced Labour
13. ILO Convention concerning Discrimination in Respect of Employment and Occupation
14. ILO Convention concerning Minimum Age for Admission to Employment
15. ILO Convention concerning the Prohibition and Immediate Action for the Elimination of the Worst Forms of Child Labour

Additional conventions to be ratified and effectively implemented for the 'GSP+':

16. Convention on International Trade in Endangered Species of Wild Fauna and Flora
17. Montreal Protocol on Substances that Deplete the Ozone Layer

$\rightarrow$

Additional conventions to be ratified and effectively implemented for the 'GSP+':
18. Basel Convention on the Control of Transboundary Movements of Hazardous Wastes and their Disposal
19. Convention on Biological Diversity
20. UN Framework Convention on Climate Change
21. Cartagena Protocol on Biosafety
22. Stockholm Convention on Persistent Organic Pollutants
23. Kyoto Protocol to the UN Framework Convention on Climate Change
24. UN Single Convention on Narcotic Drugs
25. UN Convention on Psychotropic Substances
26. UN Convention against Illicit Traffic in Narcotic Drugs and Psychotropic Substances
27. UN Convention against Corruption

Source: European Parliament and Council of the European Union (2012, Annex VIII).

cease to benefit partially or totally from the EU's GSP because they are classified as diversified, high-income or upper-middle-income countries, because they graduated, because of a safeguard clause or because they obtained at least equivalent treatment under a preferential trade agreement concluded with the EU. Table 6.4 summarizes the main steps in the development of the EU's GSP. Also, the United Kingdom's withdrawal from the EU raises the question whether the British government will establish an own scheme of autonomous trade preferences for developing countries.

The GSP has become closely intertwined with the EU's negotiations with the ACP countries: the GSP was the 'fall back option' for those unwilling to conclude an EPA. By excluding upper-middle-income countries from the GSP as of 2014, the EU regained some bargaining power vis-à-vis the non-LDCs. Moreover, the EU considered ACP countries Cape Verde, the Republic of Congo and Nigeria as eligible to apply for 'GSP+'. Siles-Brügge (2014a) argues that the GSP reform – as part of an effort to refocus trade preferences on the 'neediest' – was in fact

TABLE 6.4 *Main Changes in the EU's GSP over Time*

	Phase 1: 1971–1994	Phase 2: 1995–2005	Phase 3: 2006–2013	Phase 4: 2014–2023
Type of preferences	tariff quotas and tariff ceilings	tariff modulation: duty-free access and reduced tariff rates according to sensitivity of products and scope arrangement		
Different arrangements	general arrangement	general arrangement; special arrangement to combat drugs; special arrangement for LDCs; special incentive for protection of labour rights; special incentive for protection of environment	general arrangement; special incentive for sustainable development and good governance ('GSP+'); special arrangement for LDCs ('EBA initiative')	
Coverage	no high-income countries; no graduation mechanism	no high-income countries; graduation mechanism (except for LDCs)	no high- or upper-middle-income countries; graduation only for general GSP	
Political conditionality	none	forced labour, in 2002 extended to core labour standards	core human and labour rights for all arrangements, plus environmental and good governance standards for 'GSP+'; reverse burden of proof	

Source: Based on GSP regulations.

part of a broader 'reciprocity agenda' in the EU's pursuit of free trade negotiations, aimed in particular at recapturing leverage with emerging economies. In a paradoxical way, the EU has placed greater emphasis on trade as a tool for development, while the general thrust of its trade policy at the same time eroded the value of preferential market access (Young and Peterson, 2013). Among the major remaining challenges to the GSP besides the increasing preference erosion is the under-utilization of preferences due to the need to comply with EU product standards and rules of origin. Effectiveness has thus been mixed, also due to the EU's inconsistent application of conditionality (see Chapter 7). Although the GSP improved market access for developing countries, there is little evidence that it led to a diversification of their exports. Especially preference programmes that do not cover all products may encourage beneficiaries to produce the goods with preferential market access and not contribute to export diversification. Many developing countries therefore still require European support based on development cooperation.

EU development policy: goals, actors and instruments

Initially focused on the former colonies of certain member states, EU aid to third countries has expanded globally, although sub-Saharan Africa has remained the major recipient of EU funds. For many years the EU and its member states have together represented the world's largest donor of both official development assistance (ODA) and humanitarian aid. In 2016, only Luxembourg, Sweden, Denmark, Germany and the United Kingdom individually reached the United Nations' ODA target of 0.7 per cent of gross national income (GNI), whereas the average of EU countries reached 0.51 per cent of their combined GNI (European Commission, 2017a). The EU and its member states thus failed to reach the 0.7 per cent target by 2015 in the framework of the MDGs, a target that has been reaffirmed for the timeframe until 2030.

Carbone (2008, pp. 31–37) distinguishes four phases of development cooperation. The first phase, which started with the Treaty of Rome and ended in the mid 1980s, was characterized by a controversy among 'regionalists' composed mainly of France, Belgium and the southern member states versus the 'globalists' in the North. Whereas the regionalists emphasized the strategic links with their former colonies, the globalists stressed poverty eradication worldwide. The regionalists dominated the debate and the European Commission services, but the influence of the globalists grew over time. The European development approach thus started out with a very narrow focus on francophone Africa, which began to broaden slowly in the 1970s with the GSP and the British accession to the EC. The second phase from the late 1980s to the late 1990s was significantly affected by the end of the Cold War. The EU transferred considerable funds to Central and Eastern Europe while the so-called Washington Consensus prevailed on the global level, focusing on macroeconomic stability and export-led growth. In addition, the EU increasingly introduced and reinforced political conditionality in its trade agreements and the GSP. While the Southern enlargements of the EU in the 1980s added a focus on Latin America and the Southern Mediterranean, the Northern enlargement in 1995 widened the scope of development cooperation by new themes, such as gender equality, sustainable development and conflict prevention and resolution. The third phase, in the 2000s, was characterized by a stronger focus on the development-security nexus and an emphasis on complementarity, coordination and coherence. The so-called post–Washington Consensus shifted to a more poverty-focused approach that prioritizes sustainable development, the involvement of civil society, good governance and policy coherence. The EU and its member states were major players in the global debate on the MDGs and SDGs. Finally, the EU's Eastern enlargement in 2004 and 2007 helped trigger the European Neighbourhood Policy, which encompasses 16 countries to the East and South of the EU (see Gstöhl, 2008).

Legal basis and goals of EU development policy

Unlike the common commercial policy, development policy is a shared parallel competence. Therefore, in this area the EU has competence to carry out activities and to conduct a common policy, without preventing the member states from exercising competence as well.

The European Community has de facto conducted a development policy since the Rome Treaty, yet only the Maastricht Treaty established a legal basis, in 1993 (Art. 177–181 Treaty establishing the EC, TEC, at the time; see Box 6.2). The objectives set out in Art. 177 TEC reflected the wave of democratization and transition to a market economy at the end of the East–West conflict. Furthermore, the legal provisions encapsulate the '3 Cs' in the development discourse: complementarity between the development policies of the member states and of the EU; coordination between the member states and the EU on all levels; and coherence of all EU policies. One might add consistency in all EU external action as a fourth challenge.

Box 6.2 Maastricht Treaty provisions on development policy

Art. 177 TEC (Maastricht)

1. Community policy in the sphere of development cooperation, which shall be complementary to the policies pursued by the Member States, shall foster:
   - the sustainable economic and social development of the developing countries, and more particularly the most disadvantaged among them;
   - the smooth and gradual integration of the developing countries into the world economy;
   - the campaign against poverty in the developing countries.

2. Community policy in this area shall contribute to the general objective of developing and consolidating democracy and the rule of law, and to that of respecting human rights and fundamental freedoms.

3. The Community and the Member States shall comply with the commitments and take account of the objectives they have approved in the context of the United Nations and other competent international organizations.

Art. 178 TEC

The Community shall take account of the objectives referred to in Article 177 in the policies that it implements which are likely to affect developing countries.

Art. 179

[...] 3. The provisions of this Article shall not affect cooperation with the African, Caribbean and Pacific countries in the framework of the ACP–EC Convention.

Source: Treaty establishing the European Community, Maastricht version.

Art. 180 TEC requested the Community and the member states to coordinate their policies and consult each other on their development policies, and Art. 181 TEC required them to cooperate with third countries and with competent international organizations.

In 2009 the Lisbon Treaty placed development policy, like trade policy, under the external action chapter of the Treaty on the Functioning of the European Union (TFEU), to which the overall goals of Art. 21 Treaty on European Union (TEU) apply. At the same time, it made the eradication of poverty the primary objective of EU development cooperation (Art. 208 TFEU; see Box 6.3) and strengthened the consistency of

---

Box 6.3   Lisbon Treaty provisions on development policy

Art. 208 TFEU (Lisbon)

1. Union policy in the field of development cooperation shall be conducted within the framework of the principles and objectives of the Union's external action. The Union's development cooperation policy and that of the Member States complement and reinforce each other.

   Union development cooperation policy shall have as its primary objective the reduction and, in the long term, the eradication of poverty. The Union shall take account of the objectives of development cooperation in the policies that it implements which are likely to affect developing countries.

2. The Union and the Member States shall comply with the commitments and take account of the objectives they have approved in the context of the United Nations and other competent international organisations.

Art. 210 TFEU

1. In order to promote the complementarity and efficiency of their action, the Union and the Member States shall coordinate their policies on development cooperation and shall consult each other on their aid programmes, including in international organisations and during international conferences. They may undertake joint action. Member States shall contribute if necessary to the implementation of Union aid programmes.

2. The Commission may take any useful initiative to promote the coordination referred to in paragraph 1.

Source: Treaty on the Functioning of the European Union, Lisbon version.

external action. Art. 21(d) TEU equally states the goal of fostering 'the sustainable economic, social and environmental development of developing countries, with the primary aim of eradicating poverty'. The creation of the European External Action Service (EEAS) had far-reaching consequences for the decision-making processes in this field (see below).

Art. 209 TFEU foresees the ordinary legislative procedure for the measures necessary to implement development policy (e.g. financial instruments and cooperation programmes). Without prejudice to the member states' competence in this field, the EU may also conclude agreements with third countries and international organizations in order to achieve the objectives of development cooperation. The procedure to negotiate international agreements follows Art. 218 TFEU.

In the new millennium, a new array of UN documents placed development policy firmly on the international agenda. The EU and its member states committed themselves to the MDGs in 2000, followed by the Monterrey Consensus on Financing for Development two years later and the Paris Declaration on Aid Effectiveness in 2005. In this context, the European Consensus on Development Policy was in December 2005 signed by the Presidents of the Commission, the Parliament and the Council. It defined a framework of common principles within which the EU and its member states implement their development policies in a spirit of complementarity (European Parliament, Council and Commission, 2006). They reaffirmed their commitment to poverty eradication, delivering more and better aid and promoting policy coherence for development. Policy coherence for development means 'ensuring that the EU shall take account of the objectives of development cooperation in all policies that it implements which are likely to affect developing countries and that these policies support development objectives' (ibid., para 9). Two years later the EU adopted the Code of Conduct on Complementarity and Division of Labour in Development Policy (Council of the European Union, 2007b). In this Code, member states commit to 'in-country complementarity' in order to ensure balanced funding between all the sectors, independent of their political interest. Each member state concentrates on no more than three sectors per country and in each sector a lead donor is in charge of coordination. Member states also commit to 'cross-country complementarity', aiming to balance resources between 'aid orphans' and 'aid darlings', as they are called, and ensuring that the EU has a more regular presence in all the developing countries. In 2017 the European Consensus on Development Policy was revised, calling for more coherence and coordination between the EU and its member states and for a more tailored and inclusive approach (European Parliament, Council and Commission, 2017).

In recent years, the EU has tried to reprioritize and differentiate its delivery of aid to developing countries to ensure maximum impact on poverty reduction and to enhance synergies between trade and development policies. As Carbone (2008) points out, promoting policy coherence for development risks being a 'mission impossible' due to the interplay of various commitments and interests and the EU's institutional framework. For instance, the CAP is often referred to as a prime example of policy incoherence with development objectives, even if over the years successive CAP reforms have addressed some of the problems (Matthews, 2008). Improving policy coherence for development is one of the most crucial areas for further improvement, and since 2007 the EU has reported every two years on the achievements in this field. Yet, trade policy calls for action in line with the EU's own economic preferences, whereas development policy calls for measures in the interest of developing countries. The legal requirement of coherence enshrined in the Treaty is thus bound to remain an operational horizon to strive for and a policy dilemma, where sometimes only political decisions can seek to strike an acceptable balance between two legitimate public policy goals.

Actors in European development policy

Within the European Commission, Directorates-General other than DG International Cooperation and Development (DEVCO) have a bearing on development policy such as trade, agriculture, fisheries, environment or enlargement. The College of Commissioners brings them together. Since the creation of the EEAS, which has absorbed the former DG External Relations and parts of DG Development as well as parts of the Council Secretariat and has created single geographic desks, there is no longer a special 'ACP Directorate-General'. Before the Lisbon Treaty, DG Development was responsible for relations with the ACP countries, while DG External Relations covered relations with other developing and developed countries. They were in charge of policy formulation, while DG EuropeAid implemented the policy and external aid instruments, except for humanitarian assistance. In 2011, EuropeAid was merged with the remaining DG Development to constitute today's DG DEVCO. In the post-Lisbon structure, the EEAS participates in the preparation, programming and management of some financial instruments (see below). The EEAS is under the authority of the High Representative and

Vice-President of the Commission (HR/VP), who is also a member of the College of Commissioners and chairs the Foreign Affairs Council.

The Council decisions are prepared by COREPER II (the Committee of Permanent Representatives), which is supported by various working groups and committees. Some preparatory bodies of the Council are chaired by EEAS officials representing the HR, for instance the Africa Working Party, the Working Party on Latin America or the Asia–Oceania Working Party, while others are chaired by the rotating Council Presidency, such as the ACP Working Party, the Working Party on Development Cooperation or the Working Party on Humanitarian Aid and Food Aid. By contrast, the Committee of the European Development Fund is chaired by a Commission representative.

In the European Parliament the Development Cooperation Committee (DEVE) deals with the promotion, implementation and monitoring of the Union's development policy and matters relating to EU–ACP relations.

The EU Delegations play an important role in the formulation and implementation of development assistance. They are composed of staff from the EEAS (including diplomats seconded from EU member states) and from the Commission. Both the EEAS headquarters and DG DEVCO (respectively DG Trade) can give instructions to the Delegations, but all staff members are under the authority of the Head of Delegation. For geographic instruments the EU Delegations assess the political situation and the national development plans in a country and draft an EU response that is then reviewed at the headquarters in Brussels. The national development plan of a recipient country serves as the basis for the programming. If there is no such national development plan, the EU Delegations draft a Country (or Regional) Strategy Paper in dialogue with the partner countries. They may also, depending on the instrument in question, prepare the indicative programmes, which describe the development goals agreed and indicate financial allocations (see Furness 2012).

As of 2012, joint programming between the European Commission, the EEAS and the member states has been launched in some countries in order to help reduce duplication, inconsistencies and inefficiency. In such cases the programming documents are drafted jointly by the EU Delegation and the member state embassies in a country. In principle, EU member states have committed to joint programming, but they still have concerns about national visibility in developing countries and are often unwilling to accept more coordination by the EEAS.

Financial instruments of EU development cooperation

With the multiannual financial framework 2014–2020, the financial instruments for external cooperation can be divided into two categories, depending on their nature: geographic and thematic instruments (see Table 6.5). The EU's external relations funding also includes extra-budgetary instruments, such as the EDF for the ACP countries or the Emergency Aid Reserve, which is used to finance humanitarian, civilian crisis management and protection operations in non-EU states in unforeseen events. Moreover, the budget for the CFSP, which is part of the Union's multiannual financial framework, covers only non-military expenditures (e.g. civilian crisis management, non-proliferation and disarmament actions, conflict resolution measures and EU Special Representatives). The CFSP military operations are financed by the member states under the so-called Athena mechanism, which finances the common costs of EU operations having military or defence implications.

The 11th EDF (2014–2020) for cooperation with the ACP countries is still the main instrument for delivering EU development aid to the ACP states. Cuba is an ACP member but not yet a signatory to the Cotonou Agreement, while South Africa is a signatory but not a beneficiary of the EDF. Both countries receive bilateral support through the Development Cooperation Instrument (DCI). In addition, ACP countries also benefit from other instruments financed under the EU budget. The EDF is the financial protocol to the EU–ACP agreement and based on an intergovernmental agreement between EU member states. Every five to seven years it is replenished directly by the member states whose weighted voting rights in the EDF Committee depend on their financial contribution. It is therefore not subject to co-decision and the scrutiny of the European Parliament, which has led to calls for the Fund's 'budgetization'. However, many member states oppose an inclusion in the regular Union budget in an attempt to keep control of the aid decision-making process for the ACP countries.

The total amount of financial programming for external action – the heading 'Global Europe' – in the multiannual financial framework 2014 – 2020 is around 63 billion euros (ca. 6 per cent of the total EU budget). For the same time period, the EDF is funded by an extra approximately 30 billion euros, which corresponds more or less to the amount available to the DCI and the Instrument for Pre-accession Assistance (IPA) combined (see Table 6.5). The United Kingdom's withdrawal from the EU will reduce the financial support available for the developing countries.

TABLE 6.5   *Main EU Financial Instruments for External Cooperation (2014–2020)*

Instrument	Coverage	Share
Geographic instruments		
European Development Fund (EDF)	ACP countries (except for South Africa and Cuba)	outside EU budget
Development Co-operation Instrument (DCI)	South Africa, Asia, Latin America, Middle East; thematic programmes for all developing countries	31.2%
European Neighbourhood Instrument (ENI)	Countries of the European Neighbourhood Policy (ENP)	24.5%
Instrument for Pre-accession Assistance (IPA)	(Potential) candidates for EU membership	18.5%
Partnership Instrument (PI)	Industrialized countries and emerging economies	1.5%
Other instruments	Greenland, Turkish Cypriot community	0.7%
Thematic instruments		
Instrument for Stability (IfS)	Crisis response and conflict prevention	3.7%
European Instrument for Democracy and Human Rights (EIDHR)	Promotion of human rights and democracy	2.1%
Instrument for Nuclear Safety Cooperation (INSC)	Nuclear safety, in particular neighbouring countries	0.4%
Instrument for Humanitarian Aid (IHA)	Humanitarian assistance in third countries	10.5%
Common Foreign and Security Policy (CFSP)	Non-military CFSP expenditures	3.7%
Other instruments	Macro-financial Assistance, Civil Protection Mechanism, European Voluntary Humanitarian Aid Corps, etc.	3.2%

Source: European Commission (2013, p. 16, Heading 4 – Global Europe, based on current prices).

With respect to the responsible agencies, there are three groups of instruments. First, the three big financial instruments – the geographic part of the DCI, the EDF and the ENI – unite the bulk of EU funding, and they rely on joint programming between the European Commission and the EEAS, under the responsibility of the Commissioner for Development but with the EEAS as the lead service for the strategic steps (see Table 6.6). Both the Commissioner and the HR/VP sign the strategic documents and submit them to the College of Commissioners for adoption.

Second, there are some instruments exclusively managed by the Commission services under the responsibility of a Commissioner other than the HR/VP. This is the case of the IPA, of which the Commissioner for Enlargement and European Neighbourhood Policy is in charge, the Instrument for Humanitarian Aid under the leadership of the Commissioner for International Cooperation, Humanitarian Aid and Crisis Response (DG ECHO) and the thematic programmes under the DCI (which are dealt with by DG DEVCO).

Third, the rest of the instruments of external assistance are led by the EEAS under the responsibility of the HR/VP, in consultation with DG DEVCO. This is the case for the EIDHR and the INSC but also for the two special cases of the IfS and the PI. The IfS is split into a long-term component, for instance measures to counteract global and trans-regional threats, and a short-term component for crisis response and preparedness. While DG DEVCO implements the long-term measures under the IfS, the service for Foreign Policy Instruments (FPI) is tasked with implementing the crisis response and prevention measures financed under the IfS. The FPI is legally part of the Commission but

TABLE 6.6 *Programming Responsibility for EU Financial Instruments*

Commission	Joint programming	HR/VP and EEAS
DCI thematic	DCI geographic	EIDHR
IPA	EDF	INSC
IHA	ENI	IfS – long-term measures
		IfS – crisis response (FPI)
		PI (FPI)

Source: Based on European Commission (2012).

physically co-located with the EEAS. Under the authority of the HR/ VP, it works closely with the EEAS and EU Delegations. Due to the nature of the events with which it deals, the short-term components of the IfS are – like in the case of the IHA – not programmable. The FPI is also in charge of the EU's cooperation with industrialized countries (PI) as well as the actions under the CFSP budget for which the EEAS is responsible.

The decisions on the priorities of EU development policy are divided into several steps which, for some instruments, require close coordination between the European Commission and the EEAS. For the geographic programmes (DCI, EDF and ENI), the EEAS shares the responsibility for the first three phases of the programming cycle with the Commission. Its task is to give strategic political guidance (see Tannous, 2013).

Whereas development cooperation takes a long-term perspective, humanitarian aid generally consists of short-term interventions.

EU humanitarian assistance

Like development policy, humanitarian aid is a shared parallel competence. Although the European Communities had granted ad hoc emergency assistance since the 1960s, and despite the establishment of the European Community Humanitarian Office (ECHO) in 1992, the first specific legal basis was only introduced in the Lisbon Treaty (see Box 6.4). In 2004, ECHO became the Commission's Directorate-General for Humanitarian Aid, which in 2010 integrated civil protection for a better coordination and disaster response inside and outside Europe. A first dedicated Commissioner for International Cooperation, Humanitarian Aid and Crisis Response was appointed in 2010.

Like in the case of development policy, there is also a great need for close coordination, coherence and complementarity in the field of humanitarian aid (Orbie et al., 2014). Unlike in development policy, however, the EU attaches no political conditionality, despite the reference to the principles and objectives of the EU's external action set out in Art. 21 TEU. Humanitarian aid operations should be impartial, neutral and non-discriminatory (Art. 214:2 TFEU). This was already stipulated in the 2007 European Consensus on Humanitarian Aid, which stressed the needs-based emergency response aimed at preserving life and preventing human suffering (European Parliament, Council and Commission, 2008, para 8).

Box 6.4   Lisbon Treaty provisions on humanitarian assistance

Art. 214 TFEU (Lisbon)

1. The Union's operations in the field of humanitarian aid shall be conducted within the framework of the principles and objectives of the external action of the Union. Such operations shall be intended to provide ad hoc assistance and relief and protection for people in third countries who are victims of natural or man-made disasters, in order to meet the humanitarian needs resulting from these different situations. The Union's measures and those of the Member States shall complement and reinforce each other.

2. Humanitarian aid operations shall be conducted in compliance with the principles of international law and with the principles of impartiality, neutrality and non-discrimination.

3. The European Parliament and the Council, acting in accordance with the ordinary legislative procedure, shall establish the measures defining the framework within which the Union's humanitarian aid operations shall be implemented.

4. The Union may conclude with third countries and competent international organisations any agreement helping to achieve the objectives referred to in paragraph 1 and in Article 21 of the Treaty on European Union.

   The first subparagraph shall be without prejudice to Member States' competence to negotiate in international bodies and to conclude agreements.

5. In order to establish a framework for joint contributions from young Europeans to the humanitarian aid operations of the Union, a European Voluntary Humanitarian Aid Corps shall be set up. The European Parliament and the Council, acting by means of regulations in accordance with the ordinary legislative procedure, shall determine the rules and procedures for the operation of the Corps.

6. The Commission may take any useful initiative to promote coordination between actions of the Union and those of the Member States, in order to enhance the efficiency and complementarity of Union and national humanitarian aid measures.

7. The Union shall ensure that its humanitarian aid operations are coordinated and consistent with those of international organisations and bodies, in particular those forming part of the United Nations system.

Source: Treaty on the Functioning of the European Union, Lisbon version.

Despite this different approach, humanitarian aid and development cooperation are closely intertwined. Humanitarian assistance often addresses emergency situations in developing countries, and complex emergencies have an impact upon the development process. Humanitarian aid is provided in case of natural or man-made disasters, mainly by channelling funds from the Union budget through donor partners such as non-governmental organizations, the Red Cross or UN organizations like the UN High Commissioner for Refugees or the World Food Programme. To avoid a gap between the initial emergency phase and the subsequent reconstruction and development phase, the Commission relies on the concept of 'linkage between relief, rehabilitation and development' (LRRD). LRRD helps to phase out humanitarian assistance when the emergency is over and mobilize longer-term instruments such as the EDF or DCI to step in. In practice, this transition can be quite complex, involving many actors (Versluys, 2008). By contrast, humanitarian trade preferences – autonomous trade preferences with a humanitarian justification – are hardly ever used by the EU since emergency aid should be unconditional and not fraught with political and economic interests (Gstöhl, 2014, pp. 62–70).

Conclusion

This chapter has introduced the intersection of the EU's trade and development policies. EU trade with developing countries takes various, interwoven forms. On the multilateral level, the EU has to some extent supported special and differential treatment at the WTO and in the Doha Development Round. On the bilateral level, the EU has concluded trade and development agreements with negotiated trade preferences, first and foremost with the ACP countries. On the unilateral level, the EU adopted autonomous trade preferences such as the GSP and provides aid for trade. A major challenge thereby consists in striving for policy coherence between trade and development policy. Whereas the EU's trade policy tends to be driven mainly by commercial interests, its development policy aims to eradicate poverty in developing countries. The challenge of coherence, as stipulated in the Lisbon Treaty, is therefore bound to remain, as it ultimately comes down to political decision-making in an attempt to reconcile European economic interests with the value of worldwide development.

The next chapter discusses additional challenges for EU trade policy, such as the spread of more and deeper bilateral or inter-regional trade agreements, the intersection between trade and other external or internal EU policies, as well as new political challenges.

Further reading

Bartels, L. (2007) 'The Trade and Development Policy of the European Union', *European Journal of International Law*, 18(4), 715–756.

Carbone, M. and J. Orbie (eds) (2015) *The Trade-Development Nexus in the European Union: Differentiation, Coherence and Norms* (Abingdon: Routledge).

Holland, M. and Doidge, M. (2012) *Development Policy of the European Union* (Basingstoke: Palgrave Macmillan).

Young, A.R. and Peterson, J. (2013) '"We Care about You, but…": The Politics of EU Trade Policy and Development', *Cambridge Review of International Affairs*, 26(3), 497–518.

Chapter 7

Challenges for EU Trade Policy

This chapter discusses some of the main challenges that EU trade policy currently faces. The rise of the emerging economies and the stagnation of the negotiations in the World Trade Organization (WTO) contributed to a reorientation of EU trade policy towards more bilateral trade agreements in the form of an unprecedented proliferation of free trade agreements (FTAs) and also a reorientation of trade relations with many developing countries. Yet not only the quantity but also the quality of the FTAs has changed as they became deeper and more comprehensive, reflecting a degree of externalization of the EU's internal market. Moreover, beyond the trade-development nexus discussed in Chapter 6, trade policy has increasingly become intertwined with other external or internal EU policies, such as human rights, competition or environmental policy. As a result, it is facing new institutional and political challenges.

The EU's global network of trade agreements

WTO members trading with the EU on the basis of most-favoured nation (MFN) treatment are the exception and not the rule. In the past the EU had often concluded trade agreements for political reasons – in particular with neighbouring and developing countries (European Commission, 2006, p. 9) – but since the mid 2000s, the EU has clearly sought to further economic liberalization goals by invoking competitiveness as the main aim of its policy agenda. This section first introduces the major EU trade agreements before explaining the shift in the EU's trade strategy during the past decade.

Types of trade agreements

The EU's network of trade agreements has dramatically changed with an evolving hierarchy or 'pyramid' of preferential market access. To improve their access to the European market, third countries have since the mid

1990s increasingly sought to negotiate trade agreements with the EU (e.g. see Gstöhl, 2015). The closest association to the internal market is still the European Economic Area (EEA) of 1992 between the EU and the members of the European Free Trade Association (EFTA). Only the EFTA state Switzerland rejected EEA membership in a referendum and has instead pursued a plethora of bilateral sectoral agreements. The EEA covers the free movement of goods; services; capital and persons; competition rules as well as horizontal policies (e.g. environment, social policies, consumer protection, statistics and company law); and flanking policies (e.g. cooperation in research or education). Excluded are the EU's external relations; the common agricultural, fisheries and transport policies; budget contributions and regional policy; taxation; and economic and monetary policy. The EEA constitutes a dynamic, *acquis*-based association with an institutional setup that aims to maintain the internal market's homogeneity and that leaves EFTA without a real right of co-decision.

In 1996, pursuant to their 1963 association agreement, Turkey and the EU established a (partial) customs union that allows industrial goods and certain processed agricultural products that comply with EU norms to circulate freely. Turkey adopted the common external tariff and aligns to the relevant technical *acquis*, without having a say in policy formulation or reciprocal access to the market of the EU's free trade partners. In 1999 Turkey became a candidate for EU membership, but the accession negotiations, which were opened in 2005, have encountered many political obstacles. In 2017, a modernization of the customs union with a view to broadening it to services, public procurement and further liberalization in agricultural products was launched.

Andorra and San Marino also have customs union agreements with the EU, while Monaco continues to rely on its special relationship with France to be part of the EU's customs territory. To upgrade their access to the internal market, the three small-sized countries are negotiating association agreements with the EU.

The EU's Partnership and Cooperation Agreements (PCAs) with the transition countries to the east, which were concluded in the 1990s, granted no free trade but preferential treatment instead. Some of them (Ukraine, Moldova, Georgia) have recently been replaced by bilateral association agreements comprising Deep and Comprehensive Free Trade Areas (DCFTAs) in the framework of the European Neighbourhood Policy (ENP). Armenia had completed negotiations on such an agreement but then instead joined the Russia-led Eurasian Economic Union in 2015, and Azerbaijan is also looking for an alternative legal basis for its bilateral relationship. Regarding the EU's old PCA with the Russian Federation, any resumption of negotiations on a new trade agreement requires overcoming the sanctions that were imposed after Russia's annexation of Crimea in 2014 and the interference in eastern Ukraine.

Beyond Europe, the FTAs with Mexico, Chile and South Africa provide for reciprocal liberalization of trade in goods and services, public procurement, competition, intellectual property rights, investment and dispute settlement. Even the more recent Economic Partnership Agreements (EPAs) with the countries in the African, Caribbean and Pacific (ACP) group are to progressively establish WTO-compatible free trade areas in the context of the Cotonou Agreement (see Chapter 6). The EU also aimed at agreements with other regional integration schemes. While negotiations with Central America and Cariforum were successfully concluded, those with Mercosur and the Gulf Cooperation Council (GCC) have been stagnating for years. When the bloc-to-bloc negotiations with the Andean Community and the Association of Southeast Asian Nations (ASEAN) failed, the EU launched bilateral negotiations with some of their member states, such as Colombia and Peru, or Singapore, Vietnam and Malaysia (Sahakyan, 2016). In addition, the EU embarked on free trade negotiations with heavy weights such as India, Japan, Canada and the United States. Whereas the FTAs with industrialized partners are based on symmetric reciprocity, asymmetric reciprocity applies to emerging economies and developing countries; that is, the EU liberalizes more rapidly and broadly than the trading partner (Woolcock, 2014). The titles of these FTAs can vary, taking into account the partners' preferences.

Since the Lisbon Treaty bestowed the EU with legal competence on foreign direct investment (FDI), this area is included in the newer FTAs, and a stand-alone investment agreement is, for instance, under negotiation with China. Although such a bilateral investment treaty with China is sometimes referred to as a step towards an EU–China FTA, this is currently still very unlikely. In fact, EU–China trade relations in the stricter sense have mostly been concerned with China's future 'market economy status' at the WTO (see Chapter 3 on anti-dumping in this regard).

Table 7.1 classifies the EU's trade agreements according to their degree of integration. It should be kept in mind that many countries have over time moved up in this 'pyramid' of preferences. For instance, the ACP countries, or other developing countries under the EU's autonomous Generalized System of Preferences (GSP), shifted from non-reciprocal

TABLE 7.1 *Typology of EU Trade Agreements, with Examples (June 2017)*

Type	Examples
Internal market association	European Economic Area (Norway, Iceland, Liechtenstein)
Customs union	Turkey, Andorra, San Marino
Free trade agreement	
– symmetric reciprocity	Switzerland, Israel, South Korea, Canada, Singapore, *Japan, United States*
– asymmetric reciprocity	Mexico, Chile, South Africa, Stabilization and Association Agreements (Western Balkans), Central America, Economic Partnership Agreements (ACP countries), DCFTAs (ENP countries like Ukraine, Moldova, Georgia), Vietnam, *India, Malaysia, Indonesia, Thailand, Philippines*
Partnership and Cooperation Agreement	Russia, Armenia, Azerbaijan, Central Asian republics, Iraq
Investment-only agreement	*China, Myanmar*

Source: DG Trade website. Agreements with countries in *italics* are still under negotiations.

trade preferences to a reciprocal FTA (see Chapter 6). Other countries moved from PCAs or from MFN treatment as a WTO member to an FTA with the EU (such as South Korea, Singapore or Canada). The withdrawal of the United Kingdom from the EU expected in 2019 implies that the country will leave these trade agreements and would have to negotiate similar ones itself if it wants to continue trading on the same level of preferences.

A 'strategic turn' in EU trade policy

In the wake of the collapse of communism and the triumph of liberal economic policies, the EU pursued a policy of 'managed globalization' in the late 1990s, aiming at the adoption of global rules and the strengthening of international regimes. It thus strongly advocated the launch of a new multilateral trade round in the still young WTO. Trade Commissioner Pascal Lamy announced in 1999 a moratorium on new bilateral and plurilateral trade negotiations for the Round's duration (Melo Araujo, 2016, pp. 32–40). The 'Millennium Round' to be opened in Seattle in 1999 failed due to differences between and among developed and developing countries, accompanied by unexpectedly violent demonstrations. The subsequent Doha Development Round finally took off in 2001 (see Chapter 5).

A few years later, the 'Lamy doctrine' was questioned because of the stagnation of the Doha Round, the new assertiveness of the emerging economies and the 'competitive liberalization', the latter of which the United States and others engaged in by concluding ambitious bilateral FTAs. The growing integration of global supply chains made 'behind-the-border' issues such as competition policy, public procurement, FDI, intellectual property or labour and environmental standards more important. However, in the WTO the major 'Singapore issues' (competition policy, public procurement, investment protection) were already dropped from the agenda in 2003, and only a Trade Facilitation Agreement was concluded at the Bali Ministerial Conference in 2013 (see Chapter 5). The EU thus had an interest to incorporate them into bilateral trade agreements, where it enjoys more bargaining leverage.

In this context, trade became part of the EU's strategy for growth and jobs, the so-called Lisbon Strategy (2000–2010) and, reinforced by the economic and financial crisis that hit Europe in 2008, the Europe 2020 Strategy (2010–2020). Therefore, in 2006, the European Commission adopted the Global Europe trade strategy that singled out future FTA partners based on their market potential (economic size and growth), level of protection against EU export interests and trade negotiations with EU competitors (European Commission, 2006, p. 9). 'Global Europe' envisaged in particular agreements with ASEAN; Mercosur and the GCC; and South Korea, India and Russia. In 2010, a 'new generation' agreement with South Korea was signed, the EU's first FTA with an Asian country and the first to be ratified by the European Parliament under the Lisbon Treaty (see also Chapter 4).

The 2010 update of the Global Europe strategy, entitled 'Trade, Growth and World Affairs', further emphasized reciprocity, especially vis-à-vis the emerging economies. It also targeted Japan and the United States as free trade partners (European Commission, 2010b). In 2008 the United States had joined ongoing negotiations between a group of

11 Asian and Pacific countries on a Trans-Pacific Partnership (TPP), which was signed in 2016, yet from which the new Trump Administration announced to withdraw in early 2017. As an alternative to TPP, which did not include China and India, ten member states of ASEAN and the six states with which ASEAN already has FTAs, including China, India and Japan, launched negotiations on a Regional Comprehensive Economic Partnership (RCEP) in 2012. In response to the stalled Doha Round and the emergence of such 'mega-regional' trade areas, the EU and the United States opened negotiations on a Transatlantic Trade and Investment Partnership (TTIP) in 2013 – although a few years earlier the idea of such a transatlantic FTA had still been rejected. In the same year, they joined 21 other WTO members in negotiations on a plurilateral Trade in Services Agreement (TiSA), based on the WTO's General Agreement on Trade in Services (GATS). The global trade landscape was thus changing rapidly outside the WTO.

The EU's new FTAs are more ambitious regarding tariffs, rules of origin, services, non-tariff barriers and intellectual property rights, as well as regarding the 'Singapore issues' (see Melo Araujo, 2016). In addition, the EU seeks to include human rights clauses, sustainable development provisions and institutional provisions, including dispute settlement.

The internal market and trade policy

The completion of the internal market in the early 1990s affected the EU's capacity to shape its trade policy by making its market more attractive and enhancing its bargaining power (see also Chapter 2). Art. 26:2 of the Treaty on the Functioning of the European Union (TFEU) defines the internal market as 'an area without internal frontiers in which the free movement of goods, persons, services and capital is ensured'. The creation of such a market involves both national liberalization removing discrimination (negative integration) and the necessary positive integration or (re)regulation at the European level for the internal market to function properly. On the other hand, market integration and enlargement rounds can impose costs on third countries in the form of trade diversion, be they through the internal liberalization of services, the Common Agricultural Policy (CAP), the adoption of common product and process standards or other regulatory measures. This section looks into some of these issues and their links to the EU's trade policy.

A deep and comprehensive trade agenda

A deep trade agenda goes beyond the WTO requirement of non-discrimination and addresses domestic rules by promoting 'internationally compatible' regulatory frameworks. These range from harmonization (replacing national rules by a common rule), equivalence (keeping different national rules but recognizing foreign rules with the same regulatory objective as equivalent to one's own) and mutual recognition of conformity assessment (a general principle establishing that a product or service that can be sold lawfully in one country can also be sold freely in the partner country) to an adoption of the EU's *acquis*. Since only products that comply with all applicable technical regulations and standards can be placed on the EU market, conformity assessment procedures (such as testing or certification) have to be carried out beforehand. Mutual recognition agreements aim to facilitate market access by specifying the conditions under which countries accept the conformity assessment results performed by each other's designated conformity assessment bodies.

The EU also engages in regulatory dialogues (e.g. with the United States, Japan, China, India and Russia) that serve to make each other's regulatory and market surveillance systems more understandable and compatible. Deep and comprehensive FTAs thus enter the realm of 'law-making treaties'. Whereas many regulatory areas are covered by multilateral or plurilateral agreements in the WTO, the EU's bilateral practice further refines these rules and goes beyond them by adding new topics.

First, the inclusion of agricultural trade on the agenda of the General Agreement on Tariffs and Trade (GATT) during the Uruguay Round (1986–1994) and then again in the WTO's Doha Round (2001–) was an important driving force for the reform of the CAP. High agricultural tariffs and price support had resulted in substantial surplus production in the EU, which was then subsidized for export, lowering prices on the world market at the expense of otherwise competitive foreign exporters. GATT/WTO pressure has been an important catalyst for EU policy change, from price support towards less distorting direct payments to farmers. In addition, the Eastern enlargement, budgetary constraints and public concerns for the environment, food quality and animal welfare played a role. Daugbjerg (2017) argues that the CAP's reform trajectory from the early 1990s to 2008 was marked by the EU's endeavour to make it more WTO compatible, whereas the 2013 reform again prioritized domestic concerns as a result of the stalemate of the Doha Round. In particular, recent reforms focused on a more equitable distribution of support across member states and on 'greening' the CAP by linking environmental requirements to the direct farm payments. Agriculture had entered bilateral free trade negotiations because Art. XXIV GATT requires FTAs to cover 'substantially all the trade' between the contracting partners. Although no agreement has been reached yet in the WTO on how to quantify or define this concept, the European Commission usually interprets this provision as on average at least 90 per cent of all the trade in goods.

Second, the services commitments in EU FTAs consistently go beyond GATS. The EU thereby normally combines a positive listing of the sectors covered with a negative listing of subsectors that remain excluded. This has enabled the EU to exclude key public services like education, health and social services. Another politically sensitive sector is trade in cultural and audio-visual services. In order to protect cultural and linguistic diversity in Europe, and more specifically out of fear of being flooded by American audio-visual products, the European Commission has consistently resorted to the 'cultural exception' and largely excluded audio-visual services in the WTO's GATS and in bilateral trade agreements. This is in line with the principles of the 2005 Convention on the Protection and Promotion of the Diversity of Cultural Expressions of the United Nations Educational, Scientific and Cultural Organization (UNESCO), which aims to promote international cooperation for cultural diversity and the role of culture in development policies (see Psychogiopoulou, 2014). In bilateral FTAs, the EU has in recent years concluded a few specific protocols on cultural cooperation. The effectiveness of the seemingly benevolent 'cultural exception' might well be questionable, though, as it goes hand in hand with an exception from EU competition rules, for example for publishers of scientific and cultural products, enabling these multinationals to act in an entirely oligopolistic market.

Third, EU competition law aims to ensure that competition in the internal market is not distorted. It comprises rules on cartels, monopolies and state aid. The European Commission – primarily Directorate-General Competition – acts as a supranational competition authority and can investigate, prosecute, judge and execute cases. For example, it can impose fines on companies and prohibit mergers and acquisitions that threaten to significantly reduce competition. The fact that corporations and value chains have become more global implies that anti-competitive behaviour has potentially spread across different national jurisdictions. This development challenges the EU's ability to ensure fair competition in the internal market and for EU companies abroad (see Damro and Guay, 2016). Competition policy has thus become increasingly linked with trade and acquired an external dimension. The EU has pursued a multi-pronged strategy in order to prevent negative effects from anti-competitive practices abroad on its internal market and to ensure market access and fair antitrust treatment for EU companies in third countries (Aydin, 2012). On the multilateral level, the EU pursued binding rules on policies against anti-competitive practices in WTO negotiations, yet many negotiation partners were against it. The EU also participates in non-binding forums, such as the International Competition Network, which brings together national and regional competition agencies. The unilateral strategy consists in an extraterritorial application of EU competition provisions, but this is often hampered by legal and practical obstacles. In bilateral relations, the EU sought to conclude cooperation agreements focusing on enforcement with strong trade partners such as the United States, Canada and Japan. Moreover, it has attempted to transfer its own competition rules to third countries, such as by incorporating them in trade agreements, a strategy that has been most effective with neighbouring countries. The content of competition chapters in FTAs varies considerably, and they play a rather complementary role to competition cooperation in other venues (Demedts, 2015).

Fourth, for the EU's knowledge-based economy, intellectual property rights (such as patents, trademarks, geographical indications, designs and copyrights) are vital to ensuring that high standards are respected worldwide. In some areas, international conventions already sufficiently protect these interests. For instance, the rules in the EU's FTAs on patents and copyrights do not go far beyond what is already foreseen in the WTO's Agreement on Trade-Related Aspects of Intellectual Property Rights (TRIPs). However, the enforcement of these rules varies considerably. By contrast, internationally accepted standards are still very weak for geographical indications, which are important for European upmarket agricultural goods (e.g. French champagne, Scotch whisky, Parma ham). In the past decade, the EU has thus included more detailed provisions on intellectual property rights in bilateral trade agreements which generally aim to strengthen the protection of geographical indications, to extend the duration of copyrights and to clarify TRIPs rules and their enforcement (Cornides, 2013). The EU also includes the protection of intellectual property rights very prominently in its EPA negotiations, a policy which has resulted in a strong intellectual property rights chapter in the EU–Cariforum agreement (Moerland, 2013). Yet, the plurilateral Anti-Counterfeiting Trade Agreement (ACTA), which aimed at stronger enforcement of standards by targeting, in particular, counterfeit goods, generic medicines and copyright infringement on the Internet, was rejected by the European Parliament in 2012 and has not entered into force (Meissner, 2016a).

Fifth, public procurement – how public authorities spend public money when buying goods or services – affects a substantial share of trade flows and of economies' gross domestic product. The EU generally aims to set rules that increase the efficient use of public resources, fight corruption, increase legal certainty and provide better market access for EU suppliers abroad. While opening European markets to foreign bidders helps ensure that the state obtains the best offer, granting privileges to domestic companies to stimulate the national economy may also be tempting to politicians. Within the WTO, the EU had co-negotiated the 1994 plurilateral Government Procurement Agreement, which includes some fundamental rules on non-discrimination, transparency and judicial protection. Yet, it applies to only those procurements that are not excluded from the commitments. In 2014 a more far-reaching revision of the Government Procurement Agreement entered into force. The EU draws on this framework in its bilateral relations by including provisions on public procurement in FTAs. Overall, the EU procurement market is relatively open, which dampens its bargaining leverage in negotiations with countries less open in their public procurement. Another challenge that remains is the fact that each member state has a policy of its own allowing or excluding third-country bidders from its market (similar local prerogatives can also be found in federal states). At the unilateral level, the Commission therefore proposed a common approach based on a regulation (Hoffmeister, 2016) in 2012. The proposed international procurement instrument foresaw that in case of a lack of substantial reciprocity in the third country, the Commission could still reject a foreign bid. However, the regulation was not adopted by the member states and an amended proposal was put forward in 2016 (see Chapter 3).

Finally, the EU has extended the free movement of persons to the EFTA countries and some parts – such as the non-discrimination of workers as regards working conditions, remuneration and social security – to other neighbouring countries. In 2002, the European Council in Sevilla had suggested to include 'a clause on joint management of migration flows and on compulsory readmission in the event of illegal immigration' (European Council, 2002, p. 10) in trade agreements. However, the EU has negotiated readmission agreements outside of trade agreements and rather coupled them with visa facilitation agreements. As part of the GATS rules, EU trade agreements replicate the temporary mobility of persons for trading services across borders and in some cases go beyond in order to attract highly skilled professionals. With regard to the trade-migration nexus, Jurje and Lavenex (2014) find that the EU has not strategically used trade policy to pursue migration policy goals. Instead, EU migration policy, which remains an area of shared competence, has been developing separately – for instance, in so-called Mobility Partnerships under the Global Approach to Migration and Mobility launched in 2005, the results of which have so far remained rather limited (see Hampshire, 2016).

In sum, the expanding deep and comprehensive trade agenda requires regulatory convergence between the EU and its partner countries.

Regulatory convergence

The EU has been conceptualized as a 'market power' with the capacity to externalize a wide range of economic and social market-related policies and regulatory measures (Damro, 2012). The EU usually promotes rather broad regulatory principles underpinning market economies based on international legal instruments instead of exporting its own regulations (Young, 2015). In its neighbourhood, however, the deep and comprehensive FTAs may foresee regulatory alignment to EU standards or even an adoption of relevant EU *acquis*, for instance in the EEA and in the DCFTAs with some of the ENP countries (see Van der Loo, 2015).

The most contentious trade agreements, however, are not those based on exporting *acquis* to neighbouring countries but the transatlantic FTAs. Given its sheer size, the negotiations on a TTIP that began in 2013 became very controversial, and as a spillover, so did the EU–Canada Comprehensive Economic and Trade Agreement (CETA), which was signed in 2016. Both agreements, which are similar in substance and scope, were perceived as a strategic response to the changing global trading order, with the potential to counterbalance the ongoing deeper integration of the South-East Asian markets, to kick-start the WTO negotiations again, to shape the future regulatory global framework for trade and investment and to strengthen the transatlantic alliance between like-minded democratic powers (e.g. see Hamilton, 2016). Whereas TTIP and CETA benefit from wide business support, many civil society organizations have voiced strong opposition. TTIP covers three main pillars (ibid., p. 380): market access (for trade in goods, services, public procurement, investment protection), regulatory cooperation (technical barriers to trade, sanitary and phyto-sanitary standards, sectors like chemicals, medicines or vehicles) and rules (e.g. competition, investment protection, energy and raw materials, intellectual property rights, sustainable development, dispute settlement).

The goal of regulatory convergence in the TTIP negotiations fuelled public fears about losing control over the member states' and the EU's right to regulate, or at least about producing a 'chilling effect', which would dissuade governments from taking regulatory action (Young, 2016; De Ville and Siles-Brügge, 2016). The controversial notion of TTIP as a 'living agreement' – allowing regulators to identify new areas for convergence without reopening the treaty – had led to concerns that a joint regulatory cooperation body would take decisions beyond democratic control. The parties would keep each other informed on forthcoming regulatory initiatives with the possibility to comment on proposed regulations. The joint body could consider amendments to sectoral annexes and the addition of new ones. Regulatory cooperation, however, is more likely to happen in a piecemeal fashion rather than across the board, and most importantly a joint body would not be able to replace the contracting parties' respective administrative, regulatory or legislative procedures (De Bièvre and Poletti, 2016).

Yet the anti-TTIP campaign was characterized by a profound lack of trust in the regulators and their different approaches to risk assessment on both sides of the Atlantic. Whereas the EU has codified the so-called precautionary principle in primary treaty law, which excludes products if there is the possibility that they might cause harm and where there is no scientific consensus, the United States in some areas allows products on the market as long as they have not been proven to be dangerous. Different process standards and diverging societal preferences had in the past led to controversial WTO disputes, for instance about beef hormones and genetically modified organisms. In addition, the United States is the EU's biggest possible negotiating partner for an FTA and has thus been – rightly or wrongly – perceived as being able to impose its alleged neoliberal preferences (Eliasson and Garcia-Duran, 2016). With the new

US Administration under President Trump, however, TTIP was put on ice in 2017.

Another issue raised to the level of considerable controversy has been investor-to-state dispute settlement (ISDS) – although this had for decades been present in many of the more than 1400 bilateral investment agreements concluded by EU member states. Investment protection provisions provide guarantees against discrimination and expropriation that is not for a public policy purpose. An ISDS system allows investors to bring a claim against a host government in front of an international tribunal, composed of arbitrators applying the – often vague – rules set out in the agreement, normally behind closed doors. The EU has often argued that this may be necessary because in many countries investment agreements are not directly enforceable in domestic courts. Critics claimed that the ISDS mechanism would allow firms – and mainly big business – to sue EU governments for compensation outside the normal judicial process if they believe that their investor rights were curtailed by public policies. In response, the Commission proposed to transform the ISDS system based on arbitrators into a public Investment Court System composed of a Tribunal of first instance and an Appeal Tribunal operating like traditional courts with independent judges (see Dickson-Smith, 2016; Bronckers, 2015). Such an approach puts all EU investors on equal footing, introduces more transparency and allows for clearer rules. In the long run, the Commission aims to establish a permanent multilateral International Investment Court, and to support the incorporation of investment rules into the WTO. Although the negotiations with Canada were concluded in 2014, CETA was revised in line with the EU's TTIP proposal a year later, replacing the ISDS system with a new dispute settlement mechanism that has a permanent tribunal and an appellate body. Such a permanent investment court system has also been incorporated in subsequent EU agreements, for instance in the FTA with Vietnam.

In addition to the nexus between trade and various internal EU policies, trade also intersects with other external policies

Foreign policy and trade

The EU is not only a large internal market but also a community of values claiming to be founded, according to Manners (2002, pp. 242–243), on the 'core norms' of peace, liberty, democracy, rule of law and human rights, supplemented by the 'minor norms' of social solidarity, anti-discrimination, sustainable development and good governance. As a 'normative power', the EU attempts to diffuse these norms in its external action as well, including in trade policy (Manners, 2009; Gstöhl, 2010b; Orbie, 2011). As a trading power the EU would seem to wield considerable leverage to use access to its vast internal market as an incentive for third countries to comply with non-trade objectives that go beyond the internal market.

The idea that trade policy must take into account developmental goals occupies a singularly important place in the EU's common commercial policy. The intersection of trade and development policy as well as trade and humanitarian assistance was already dealt with in Chapter 6. This section addresses trade and human rights, labour and environmental standards, and restrictive measures under the Common Foreign and Security Policy (CFSP).

Human rights

Since the end of the Cold War, the EU has been promoting human rights, democracy and the rule of law through its trade policy (e.g. see Bartels, 2015). The first suspension or non-execution clauses – making the respect for human rights and democratic principles 'essential elements' of cooperation – appeared in the EU's agreements with Central and Eastern European countries in the early 1990s. The 1969 Vienna Convention on the Law of Treaties (Art. 60) allows to unilaterally terminate or suspend a treaty in case of a material breach consisting in the violation of a provision which is essential to the accomplishment of the treaty's purpose. On a proposal from the Commission, the Council may adopt a decision suspending the application of an agreement (Art. 218:9 TFEU), while the European Parliament is only informed.

A human rights clause was included in the Lomé IV Convention with the ACP countries signed in 1989. It became an 'essential element' with the 1995 revision. The 2000 Cotonou Agreement expanded the suspension clause to good governance, yet only as a 'fundamental element', except for serious cases of corruption. In the latter case, where the EU provides significant financial support, appropriate measures may be taken as well. Cooperation in fighting the proliferation of weapons of mass destruction was added as an 'essential element' in the 2005 revision of the agreement. The human rights clause consists of Art. 9 (essential elements clause) and Art. 96 (non-execution clause) and is the most elaborate example in any EU agreement (see Box 7.1).

Box 7.1   The human rights clause in the Cotonou Agreement

Art. 9 Essential elements regarding human rights, democratic principles and the rule of law, and fundamental element regarding good governance

2. The Parties refer to their international obligations and commitments concerning respect for human rights. They reiterate their deep attachment to human dignity and human rights, which are legitimate aspirations of individuals and peoples. Human rights are universal, indivisible and interrelated. The Parties undertake to promote and protect all fundamental freedoms and human rights, be they civil and political, or economic, social and cultural. In this context, the Parties reaffirm the equality of men and women.

   The Parties reaffirm that democratisation, development and the protection of fundamental freedoms and human rights are interrelated and mutually reinforcing. Democratic principles are universally recognised principles underpinning the organisation of the state to ensure the legitimacy of its authority, the legality of its actions reflected in its constitutional, legislative and regulatory system, and the existence of participatory mechanisms. On the basis of universally recognised principles, each country develops its democratic culture.

   The structure of government and the prerogatives of the different powers shall be founded on rule of law, which shall entail in particular effective and accessible means of legal redress, an independent legal system guaranteeing equality before the law and an executive that is fully subject to the law.

   Respect for human rights, democratic principles and the rule of law, which underpin the ACP–EU Partnership, shall underpin the domestic and international policies of the Parties and constitute the essential elements of this Agreement.

3. [...] Good governance, which underpins the ACP–EU Partnership, shall underpin the domestic and international policies of the Parties and constitute a fundamental element of this Agreement. The Parties agree that serious cases of corruption, including acts of bribery leading to such corruption, as referred to in Article 97 constitute a violation of that element.

Art. 96 Essential elements: consultation procedure and appropriate measures as regards human rights, democratic principles and the rule of law

2.(a) If, despite the political dialogue on the essential elements [...], a Party considers that the other Party fails to fulfil an obligation stemming from respect for human rights, democratic principles and the rule of law referred to in Article 9(2), it shall, except in cases of special urgency, supply the other Party and the Council of Ministers with the relevant information required for a thorough examination of the situation with a view to seeking a solution acceptable to the Parties. To this end, it shall invite the other Party to hold consultations that focus on the measures taken or to be taken by the Party concerned to remedy the situation in accordance with Annex VII. [...]

3. [...] If the consultations do not lead to a solution acceptable to both Parties, if consultation is refused or in cases of special urgency, appropriate measures may be taken. These measures shall be revoked as soon as the reasons for taking them no longer prevail. [...]

5. The 'appropriate measures' referred to in this Article are measures taken in accordance with international law, and proportional to the violation. In the selection of these measures, priority must be given to those which least disrupt the application of this agreement.

It is understood that suspension would be a measure of last resort.

Source: Cotonou Agreement, as revised in 2010.

Similar, less elaborate clauses have been added to other trade agreements, in recent cases sometimes by cross-referencing to already existing agreements with the same partner country. Regarding the application of such clauses, the EU has a longstanding, marked preference for positive measures (such as dialogue and incentives) over negative measures (or sanctions), and suspension has only been a measure of last resort. Already in its first resolution on this topic in 1991 the Council of Ministers proclaimed 'a positive and constructive approach' to human rights, but 'in the event of grave and persistent human rights violations or the serious interruption of democratic processes', appropriate responses would be considered (Council of the European Communities, 1991, para 6).

In practice, the only action under a human rights clause in trade agreements was in the context of the Lomé/Cotonou Agreements and only on the occasion of political coups, in some cases along with human rights abuses. Moreover, the EU's measures have been limited to delays in and suspension of financial cooperation with the ACP countries concerned (Bartels, 2015, p. 81; Holland and Doidge, 2012, pp. 208–212; Døhlie Saltnes, 2013). No sanctions in terms of disrupting trade with a contracting party have been implemented. An often heard claim is that the EU prioritizes the first generation of human rights (civil and political rights) over the second generation (economic, social and cultural rights) even though Art. 21:1 of the Treaty on European Union (TEU) underlines the universality and indivisibility of human rights (Kerremans and Orbie, 2009, p. 638).

Since the mid 1990s, the EU devoted increased attention to labour rights and trade, but it did not succeed in promoting a social clause in the WTO. Instead, the EU began to pursue a broader social agenda in partnership with the International Labour Organization (ILO) (Bossuyt, 2009). Since serious and persistent infringements of core labour standards constitute also violations of human rights, the EU could invoke the human rights clause to suspend an agreement, but it has never done so. Newer trade agreements set up mechanisms to monitor the commitments to core labour standards between the parties, including through – voluntary but in some cases also compulsory – civil society involvement. However, these obligations do not entail legally binding enforcement mechanisms. Both sides agree not to use labour standards for protectionist trade purposes and not to encourage trade or FDI by lowering their standards (see also Oehri, 2014; Postnikov and Bastiaens, 2014).

Environmental standards

In the same vein, the sustainable development chapters in recent FTAs reaffirm the parties' international commitments in the field of environmental protection, either in general terms or by mentioning specific agreements, which can be exhaustively listed and also include a duty to ratify and implement environmental treaties (see Marín Durán and Morgera, 2012, pp. 82–129). Since the 1990s, the EU has developed leadership on global environmental governance on a host of issues: from climate change to biodiversity, trade in toxic wastes, the regulation of persistent organic pollutants and the 'greening' of the world trade regime. The driving forces have been the rise of domestic environmental interests across Europe and international regulatory competition in favour of spreading similar standards to other jurisdictions (Kelemen, 2010; Poletti and Sicurelli, 2012).

Trade measures may also be used to pursue certain environmental protection policies (Eeckhout, 2011, pp. 39–57). The Cartagena Protocol on Biosafety, which was concluded in 2000 in the framework of the Convention on Biological Diversity, aims at the protection of biological diversity against the harmful effects of trans-boundary movement of living modified organisms. In its *Opinion 2/00* on the Cartagena Protocol, the Court specified that if a Community measure pursued a twofold purpose and 'if one is identifiable as the main or predominant purpose or component, whereas the other is merely incidental, the measure must be founded on a single legal basis, namely that required by the main or predominant purpose or component' (Court of Justice of the European Union, 2001). However, if in exceptional cases 'the measure simultaneously pursues several objectives which are inseparably linked without one being secondary and indirect in relation to the other', the measure may rely on more than one legal basis (ibid.). Since the Cartagena Protocol's main purpose was the protection of biological diversity, a single legal basis in environmental policy was considered sufficient, and the Protocol was considered to fall outside the scope of the common commercial policy.

The focus in the FTAs is on cooperation in the field of sustainable development and concrete commitments to respect and improve labour and environmental standards. Hence, paradoxically, the human rights clause is enforceable but has no specific monitoring bodies, while the sustainable development provisions come with monitoring procedures and civil society involvement but lack enforcement and must rely on 'naming and shaming'. Box 7.2 gives the example of the EU–Korea FTA, which establishes a duty of consultation in the field of social, labour and environmental standards, and commits both sides to comply with a number of international agreements and to a 'stand-still clause' that prevents them from lowering their standards. In addition to government consultations, the agreement puts in place a dialogue with social partners, yet without a genuine enforcement mechanism. A committee of experts may adopt recommendations, which the parties should then endeavour to implement.

Box 7.2   The sustainable development provisions in the EU–Korea FTA

Chapter 13 'Trade and sustainable development'

Each Party shall establish a **Domestic Advisory Group(s)** on sustainable development (environment and labour) with the task of advising on the implementation of this Chapter.

The Domestic Advisory Group(s) comprise(s) independent representative organisations of civil society in a balanced representation of environment, labour and business organisations as well as other relevant stakeholders. [...]

Members of Domestic Advisory Group(s) of each Party will meet at a **Civil Society Forum** in order to conduct a dialogue encompassing sustainable development aspects of trade relations between the Parties. [...]

A Party may request **consultations** with the other Party regarding any matter of mutual interest arising under this Chapter, including the communications of the Domestic Advisory Group(s). [...]

Unless the Parties otherwise agree, a Party may, 90 days after the delivery of a request for consultations [...], request that a **Panel of Experts** be convened to examine the matter that has not been satisfactorily addressed through government consultations. [...] The Panel of Experts should seek information and advice from either Party, the Domestic Advisory Group(s) or international organisations [...]

Unless the Parties otherwise agree, the Panel of Experts shall, within 90 days of the last expert being selected, present to the Parties a report. The Parties shall make their best efforts to accommodate advice or recommendations of the Panel of Experts on the implementation of this Chapter. The **implementation of the recommendations** of the Panel of Experts shall be monitored by the Committee on Trade and Sustainable Development. The report of the Panel of Experts shall be made available to the Domestic Advisory Group(s) of the Parties. [...]

Source: EU–Korea Free Trade Agreement.

At the unilateral level, the EU granted special incentives to countries respecting certain labour and environmental standards for the first time in its 1995 revision of the GSP. Yet, this policy was met with little success (see Chapter 6). These schemes were among the predecessors of what in 2006 became the special incentive arrangement for sustainable development and good governance ('GSP+'). As of 2014, the 'GSP+' has been strengthened by stricter monitoring and a reversed 'burden of proof'. The EU has withdrawn these unilaterally granted trade preferences in very few cases only: for violations of labour rights in Myanmar (1997–2013) and Belarus (2007–2014, because the country was removed by the GSP reform in 2014 anyway) and under the 'GSP+' for human rights abuses in Sri Lanka (2010–2017). In addition, a withdrawal was considered but not implemented for some beneficiaries, such as Pakistan, El Salvador, Bolivia, Guatemala, Cambodia and Bangladesh and in the 1990s also India, China and Russia (Portela and Orbie, 2014; Vogt, 2015).

In the framework of the CFSP, the Union may also impose trade-related restrictive measures, either by implementing binding resolutions of the UN Security Council or on an autonomous basis (see Portela, 2010, pp. 55–101).

Security policy

An arms embargo usually consists of a prohibition on the sale, supply, transfer or export of arms and related material of all types as well as of related financial and technical assistance. Economic sanctions can consist of export and/or import bans (which may also apply to specific products, such as oil, timber, conflict diamonds or seal products), bans on the provision of specific services, flight bans, prohibitions on investment, payments and capital movements, or the withdrawal of tariff preferences. They are used cautiously since they should respect WTO obligations.

As an instrument of the CFSP, the adoption of a Union position on such measures requires unanimity in the Council. For the implementation of economic and financial sanctions based on such a decision, the Council adopts the necessary measures by a qualified majority. Some sanctions are implemented by member states, in particular arms embargoes or restrictions on admission (such as visa or travel bans). Although arms trade has remained a national competence, the EU has adopted rules governing the control of exports of conventional arms and a regulation on dual-use goods (i.e. products and technologies which may be used for both civilian and military purposes). Moreover, all member states joined the UN Arms Trade Treaty, which entered into force in 2014. The jurisprudence of the Court of Justice of the EU has established that the rules restricting the export of dual-use goods to third countries fall within the scope of the common commercial policy (Eeckhout, 2011, pp. 35–39).

Member states should exercise their national competences in matters of foreign and security policy in a manner consistent with EU trade rules. The fact that a trade measure may have non-commercial objectives does not alter the trade nature of such measures. Overall, however, 'coherence between the trade and security realms is rather limited' (Bossuyt et al., 2013, p. 80).

Box 7.3 presents two cases in which the EU autonomously imposed sanctions when Russian and Chinese vetoes prevented UN sanctions. In both Myanmar and Zimbabwe, the Western sanctions were only partially effective as their neighbours – in particular China, India and South Africa – did not support them. Moreover, in the case of Myanmar, the EU's comprehensive sanctions regime omitted the country's key energy extraction industry. In the case of Zimbabwe, an ACP country, Western sanctions helped foster opposition, but in the end it was the Southern African Development Community, under the leadership of South Africa, that brokered a power-sharing agreement among the Zimbabwean political parties.

Box 7.3   Examples of EU sanctions

The case of Myanmar

The EU adopted sanctions because of severe human rights problems and the failure of the ruling military junta to accept the results of the 1990 elections won by the National League for Democracy. Measures against Myanmar built up over time, and as a result of democratic reforms, they were gradually eased again as of 2010. At their peak, the sanctions comprised

- an arms embargo, including a ban on the attachment of military personnel to the mutual diplomatic representations
- a suspension of non-humanitarian aid (with some exceptions)
- a withdrawal of tariff preferences under the GSP as a result of forced labour in breach of an ILO Convention
- no extension of the EU-ASEAN Cooperation Agreement to Myanmar when the country joined ASEAN
- a visa ban and a freezing of assets of members of the elites
- an investment and loan ban
- a suspension of high-level bilateral governmental visits

→

Positive conditionality promises benefits to a country for future desired action, while negative conditionality threatens punitive sanctions for not fulfilling crucial conditions. These incentives and negative measures may also be combined in a 'carrot and stick' policy. That is, the Union may grant certain benefits (such as trade preferences or development aid), which it is not obliged to award, in response to the recipient's positive human rights record and reduce or withdraw them in response to violations. Moreover, ex ante conditionality requires that certain conditions be fulfilled before entering a (contractual) relationship, while ex post conditionality means that conditions appear once the parties have concluded a relationship (e.g. through a human rights clause). The most obvious example of ex ante conditionality is the criteria for accession to the European Union. The ENP is also based on the principle of conditionality. For the three ENP countries that have no bilateral agreements in force yet (Belarus, Libya and Syria), the EU also applies ex ante conditionality. Another

- a ban on the import of round logs, timber products, metals, precious and semi-precious stones and an export ban on the equipment and technology for enterprises engaged in these industries.

The case of Zimbabwe

Sanctions against Zimbabwe were imposed in 2002 due to flawed elections and breaches of human rights and the rule of law. The crisis had its origins in an agrarian reform, which entailed the expropriation of land from white farmers and was accompanied by a wave of political violence. The EU adopted, in parallel, sanctions under Art. 96 Cotonou Agreement and the CFSP. The process of re-engagement started when in 2008 a government of national unity was formed after elections. Before the gradual phasing out began in 2011, EU sanctions against Zimbabwe consisted of

- an arms embargo
- a travel ban and assets freeze on elites
- a suspension of the application of the Cotonou Agreement under Art. 96 (freezing budgetary support and, with some exceptions, support for development projects under the European Development Fund).

Source: Based on Portela (2010, pp. 82–87, 139–141).

example of ex ante conditionality is the accession of Cuba – a member of the ACP group – to the Cotonou Agreement.

Table 7.2 summarizes possible EU trade-related instruments and responses to breaches of value-based requirements.

The EU is striving for coherence in its external action, as required by the Treaties and set out in its various strategies. Coherence is normally understood as both the absence of contradictions (consistency) and the establishment of synergy between different policies (Gebhard, 2011, p. 107). Horizontal coherence thereby applies between different EU policies and vertical coherence to issue-specific policies of the member states and the Union. In practice, the EU has an overall record of inconsistent application of political conditionality, be it with regard to human rights clauses in trade agreements, the withdrawal of preferences under the GSP or trade-related sanctions under the CFSP (Brummer, 2009; Orbie and Tortell, 2009; Del Biondo, 2011; Portela, 2010, 2015; Vogt, 2015). The reasons are manifold: there might be international legal constraints

TABLE 7.2   *Political Conditionality in EU Trade Relations*

Instrument	Possible EU action
ex ante conditionality	no agreement before compliance
development aid	suspension of aid
GSP: human rights and core labour standards	withdrawal of trade preferences
GSP+: human rights, core labour standards, good governance and environmental standards	withdrawal of trade preferences
sustainable development chapters in trade agreements	commitment to international conventions, monitoring but no enforcement
human rights clauses in trade agreements	suspension of trade preferences
trade-related CFSP sanctions: export or import bans, freezing funds, investment restrictions	Union implementation (Art. 215 TFEU)
trade-related CFSP sanctions: arms embargo	national implementation by member states (Art. 346 TFEU)

(such as WTO rules); a lack of consensus among the EU member states on the prospects of consultations or sanctions; disagreement on the historical, political or economic importance of states (and the domestic implications for the EU itself); or no systematic monitoring and reliable information about the situation on the ground or any clear-cut criteria to be applied. Regarding the negotiation of trade agreements, it is more difficult for the EU to impose conditionality on bigger partners and industrialized countries (Da Conceição-Heldt, 2014). The tension between values and commercial interests can also play out through turf battles between EU decision-makers with different preferences (the Commission, the member states, the European Parliament and the European External Action Service), especially in cases where values are contested by the negotiation partner (McKenzie and Meissner, 2017).

Finally, apart from (in)coherence, the EU's trade decision-making rules have in recent years also repeatedly represented a challenge for its trade policy.

Institutional challenges

The EU is based on a complex institutional setup, and although the common commercial policy is an exclusive competence, it involves a high number of actors (see Chapter 3). Policy change normally requires a qualified majority of all member states, even though in practice consensus is sought. Arguably, this has further enhanced the EU's clout in international trade negotiations, as long as other countries actively seek access to its internal market, but it may also have the effect of making EU positions rather rigid (see also Chapter 4). The Lisbon Treaty added a stronger parliamentary dimension to the shaping of trade policy with the European Parliament as a potential 'veto player'. Making use of its new competences under the Lisbon Treaty, the European Parliament voted, for instance, against the ratification of the ACTA Agreement in 2012 (Meissner, 2016a). In addition, deep and comprehensive trade deals take the form of mixed agreements, which empower national and regional parliaments as well – currently 38 parliaments in the 28 EU member states. As set out in Chapter 3, mixed agreements are to be signed and concluded jointly by the EU and its member states and need to be ratified by all parties. The Lisbon Treaty has rightfully extended democratic control by the European Parliament, but national or even regional parliaments might yet act as veto players, too. Opting for a mixed procedure avoids lengthy discussions on competence questions, but it prolongs the ratification process. This may well defeat the very purpose of wielding power together in international trade negotiations. Trade agreements are package deals within which negotiators construct a balance of concessions, calibrated in consultation with domestic constituencies. Yet, in case of mixed agreements, minor stakeholders have the potential to derail an entire package and take all other participants hostage in order to obtain particularistic benefits.

These legal-institutional developments offer additional opportunities to representatives of interests seeking to influence the negotiation and implementation of international trade agreements to lobby at both European and national levels. From a democratic point of view, this 'empowerment' constitutes the logical consequence of the fact that the provisions of FTAs currently affect citizens' rights and interests more than they did in the past. However, the new possibilities to monitor and intervene in the complex decision-making process leading to the conclusion of FTAs also raise new legitimacy concerns. Events in 2016 showed that less than 1 per cent of the EU's population could block the signature or ratification of landmark trade agreements supported by the other member states – and in case of referenda for reasons not necessarily linked to an agreement at hand but linked to domestic politics. In April 2016, Dutch voters – with a low turnout – rejected their country's ratification act of the Association Agreement between the EU and Ukraine. This advisory referendum was the first one under a 2015 consultative referendum law in the Netherlands. The Association Agreement can only fully enter into force when all EU member states have ratified it, although this does not affect the provisional application of some parts, in particular the DCFTA (see Van der Loo and Wessel, 2017). In order to obtain parliamentary approval, the Dutch government sought and obtained a decision by the European Council that clarifies the limits of the Association Agreement – stating the rather obvious, such as the fact that an association agreement is not an accession agreement paving the way to EU membership for Ukraine. The Netherlands finally ratified the agreement in May 2017.

Regarding CETA, the European Commission believed it was an EU-only agreement but under pressure from the Council – itself reacting to a growing politicization – proposed to conclude it as mixed agreement (Van der Loo and Wessel, 2017, p. 737). The insistence on CETA being a mixed agreement came not least from the German Bundestag. Public pressure from the well-organized anti-TTIP and anti-CETA movement was particular strong in Germany. However, in October 2016, the regional parliament of Belgium's French-speaking region of Wallonia voted by a large majority to reject CETA, as did the Federation of Wallonia-Brussels parliament, thus preventing the Belgian federal government from signing it (see Laird and Petillon, 2017). This unexpected turn of events became possible since a 1992 constitutional reform had made external trade policy a regional competence in the then newly established federal constitutional order in Belgium – even though trade policy had been delegated to the European level since 1958. The agreement was finally signed after the EU and Canada agreed on a Joint Interpretative Instrument on CETA that states, among other things, that the parties preserve the right to regulate economic activity in the public interest, that cooperation between their regulatory authorities is voluntary and that the new permanent investment tribunals provide fair and transparent dispute resolution. As part of the compromise, the Belgian federal government committed to request an opinion of the CJEU on the compatibility of CETA's Investment Court System with the EU Treaties.

The increasing mobilization of activists and politicization of trade policy, especially in the case of the two transatlantic FTAs, in combination with the new decision-making procedures, have thus posed new challenges to EU trade policymaking in the twenty-first century. The Commission strengthened the (electronic) public consultations which take place early on in the process, in addition to the regular civil society dialogues taking place in Brussels. Sustainability impact assessments are commissioned as independent studies that help scrutinize the economic, social, human rights and environmental implications of envisaged trade and investment agreements. In late 2015, the Commission issued the Trade for All strategy, which responded to some of the demands of critics as regards transparency, regulatory issues and dispute settlement in investment (European Commission, 2015).

Starting with TTIP, the European Commission has in an unprecedented effort been publishing virtually all the EU's negotiating positions and proposals, including a declassification of the negotiating mandate. The 2015 strategy made this greater transparency in trade negotiations standard practice and extended it to trade defence as well. With regard to regulatory cooperation, the strategy clearly states that no trade agreement will ever lower the levels of consumer, environmental or social and labour standards, nor constrain the ability of the EU and its member states to take measures in the future to achieve legitimate public policy objectives. Furthermore, the European Commission (2015, p. 20) has committed to ensuring a responsible management of supply chains and to pursue 'a trade policy based on values' that is more responsive to the public's expectations.

Beyond a more mobilized and critical civil society, the emergence of global value chains has led to realignments of interests between the traditional import-competing and export-oriented sectors by adding import-dependent firms, which rely on imports of intermediate products for their production process or as retailers (see Chapter 4). Import-dependent firms share an interest with export-oriented firms in trade liberalization through reciprocal trade agreements. The EU's high integration in global value chains has significantly contributed to its eagerness to pursue FTAs, and these trade agreements are in turn deepening the integration of global supply chains and the consolidation of company ownership. The benefits of economies of scale are likely to remain acceptable to the general public as long as public authority over multinational companies keeps pace with such developments. The affirmation of public authority over large firms will equally be required in the field of taxation and international tax cooperation, yet fiscal integration within the EU itself has met resistance against tax harmonization (Wasserfallen, 2014).

Conclusion

This chapter has placed the common commercial policy in the broader context of the changing global trade agenda and of the EU's internal and external policies. Trade policy today attracts more public attention than ever and mobilizes non-traditional actors.

The Lisbon Treaty has subordinated EU trade policy to the general foreign policy objectives of the Union. Art. 21:1 TEU stipulates that the EU shall pursue both interests and values in its external action, yet it does not institute a hierarchy for the different objectives (see Chapter 2). On the one hand, this could be seen as a substantive precondition for conducting a more comprehensive and coherent trade policy. The 2016 EU Global Strategy acknowledges that in a more connected, contested and complex world, the EU needs 'a joined-up approach to its humanitarian, development, migration, trade, investment, infrastructure, education, health and research policies' (European External Action Service, 2016, p. 26). EU policies should become more joined up across external policies, between member states and EU institutions, and between the internal and external dimensions of its policies (ibid., p. 11). On the other hand, however, trade policy could be taken hostage by competing 'unrelated' policy issues that some may consider as 'hidden protectionism'.

Other present and future challenges that EU trade policy faces are elaborated on in Chapter 8. Among them is the uncertainty surrounding US policy under President Trump, who pledged to put 'America First', thus opening the door to increasing protectionism. It is striking, however, that the withdrawal from TPP has been accompanied by a lot of fanfare in the Trump Administration's media campaigns, whereas TTIP has been quietly 'put on hold'. Moreover, the impact of Brexit on the common commercial policy remains to be seen. The UK has traditionally perceived itself as a supporter of free trade. Yet, when it leaves the EU in 2019, it will be quitting the largest internal market in the world, forcing it to forge a new arrangement for its future trade relations with the EU as well as with other trading partners.

Further reading

Meunier, S. and K. Nicolaïdis (2006) 'The European Union as a Conflicted Trade Power', *Journal of European Public Policy*, 13(6), 906–925.

Velluti, S. (2016) 'The Promotion and Integration of Human Rights in EU External Trade Relations', *Utrecht Journal of International and European Law*, 32(83), 41–68.

Young, A.R. and J. Peterson (2014) *Parochial Global Europe: 21st Century Trade Politics* (Oxford: Oxford University Press), 183–214.

Žvelc, R. (2012) 'Environmental Integration in EU Trade Policy: The Generalised System of Preferences, Trade Sustainability Impact Assessments and Free Trade Agreements', in Morgera, E. (ed.), *The External Environmental Policy of the European Union: EU and International Law Perspectives* (Cambridge: Cambridge University Press), 174–203.

Chapter 8

Conclusion: Future Prospects of EU Trade Policy

This book has shown that the trade policy of the European Union (EU) is a multifaceted and fascinating topic to study for political scientists, economists and lawyers alike. The EU's performance in trade policy is important for the economies of the EU member states and, indeed, of the world (see Chapter 1). Nevertheless, for a long time EU trade policy appeared to be a field reserved for practitioners, and it has only recently attracted more attention from a broader range of scholars and the public. This concluding chapter highlights again the special nature of the common commercial policy before it addresses some future prospects in light of recent internal and external events.

The multilevel character of EU trade policy

The EU's unilateral and bilateral trade policy tools are embedded in the multilateral rules of the World Trade Organization (WTO). Due to their different scopes, actors and decision-making procedures, not only are the tools on the different levels complementary, but they can also serve strategic linkages. Trade entails intertwined policy choices, and initiatives from the multilateral level can be 'downshifted' to the bilateral or unilateral levels or 'uploaded' from the lower levels to the multilateral one.

With the common commercial policy – an exclusive EU competence (see Chapter 2) – the EU by and large pursues the progressive liberalization of restrictions on international trade and foreign direct investment (FDI) while taking into account the more general objectives of EU external action. In short, according to the Treaties, the EU is to strive for prosperity, development and values, with as much consistency as possible. In practice, this task is often impossible to achieve because it encounters opposing preferences from a multitude of actors on different

204

levels. This section briefly recalls the uni-, bi- and multilateral levels of trade policy to underline that the EU is an important player on and across all levels.

The EU is a strong supporter of multilateralism and committed to the principles of the WTO (see Chapter 5). It generally plays by the rules of the global trading system, frequently uses the dispute settlement system and actively participates in multilateral trade rounds and plurilateral negotiations. The WTO allows for bilateralism under certain conditions, which aim to ensure that trade creation outweighs trade diversion, and the EU has been making ample use of this exception over the past decade. Since the Doha Round has not delivered the expected results, a growing part of EU trade is covered by new generations of bilateral or regional free trade agreements (FTAs) of a deep and comprehensive nature (see Chapter 7). The WTO also allows for unilateral trade measures in the form of trade defence (see Chapter 3) or non-reciprocal trade preferences for developing countries as long as the multilateral rules are respected. Moreover, the expanding WTO agenda and its dispute settlement have over time had a broadening feedback effect on the scope of the common commercial policy.

On the bilateral level, the EU has refocused its FTA policy on competitiveness, growth and more reciprocity in light of the international power shifts in the twenty-first century, an economic crisis and reconfiguring global supply chains. This shift in trade strategy led to negotiations with bigger and more strategic partners. At the same time, with the end of the WTO waiver in 2007, the EU's longstanding relationship with the African, Caribbean and Pacific (ACP) countries has undergone fundamental changes, with the negotiation of reciprocal Economic Partnership Agreements (EPAs). The relationship is still under discussion since the Cotonou Agreement will expire in 2020.

On the unilateral level, the shift to regional EPAs has been accompanied by a reform of the Generalized System of Preferences (GSP) in 2014, which profoundly reduced the number of beneficiaries of autonomous EU trade preferences and pushed a number of ACP countries to reluctantly sign up for EPAs (see Chapter 6). The GSP benefits had already been gradually eroded by both WTO rounds and the tariff reductions resulting from the EU's FTAs with non-GSP countries. In recent years the EU has also been engaged in a reform of its trade defence instruments and a more assertive market access strategy (e.g. a recent proposal for an International Procurement Instrument or the Strategy for the protection and enforcement of intellectual property rights in third countries).

Moreover, the EU has kept up another unilateral policy implemented since the 1990s: the use of political conditionality in its GSP and FTAs. The scope of political conditionality expanded from human rights clauses to labour standards and global environmental standards, the latter taking the form of (non-enforceable) sustainable development chapters in the case of FTAs (see Chapter 7).

As set out in Chapter 4 on the theoretical perspectives on trade policymaking, different political economy approaches locate the factors shaping EU trade policy on three different levels of analysis: the society, the state and the international system.

Societal level: trade moves into the limelight

For decades, a large share of society seemed indifferent to EU trade negotiations. In general, consumers in the EU were expected to benefit from lower prices and a larger choice of products, and civil society organizations were not perceived as exerting much influence, compared to business. With the advent of anti-globalization and anti-establishment movements in the mid 1990s, trade policy began and continued to undergo increased societal contestation (see Chapter 7). The mobilization of interest groups, non-governmental organizations (NGOs) and media have contributed to a politicization of certain EU trade negotiations. De Wilde (2011, p. 560) defines politicization as 'an increase in polarization of opinions, interests or values and the extent to which they are publicly advanced towards the process of policy formulation within the EU'.

By encroaching more and more on 'behind the border' issues, EU trade policy has increasingly attracted the attention of civil society action groups and generated legitimacy concerns. At the same time, the Lisbon Treaty has bestowed the European Parliament with increased power in this policy field, offering an additional lobbying venue. Among the most prominent topics of civil society mobilization and campaigning have been the Multilateral Agreement on Investment (1998); the WTO Ministerial Conference in Seattle (1999), which failed to launch the Millennium Round; the EPAs with the ACP countries (since 2002); the Anti-Counterfeiting Agreement (ACTA, 2012); and the Transatlantic Trade and Investment Partnership (TTIP, as of 2014). NGOs and ad hoc coalitions of action groups that have mobilized on trade may well remain active in this field in the foreseeable future. At times, but certainly not for all these groups and their campaigns, this has overlapped with wider anti-establishment attitudes, generating a rise of Euroscepticism and tip-toeing around the ups and downs of different national populist parties in a wide variety of EU member states (see Mudde 2013).

State level: populism vs solidarity

Many EU member state governments became very reluctant to defend trade agreements such as TTIP, the Comprehensive Economic and Trade Agreement (CETA) with Canada or the Deep and Comprehensive Free Trade Area (DCFTA) with Ukraine, for which they had unanimously given negotiation mandates to the European Commission. This lack of support contributed to difficulties in the ratification procedures in the national and subnational parliaments (see Chapter 7). While distinct from political cleavages in the eurozone crisis or the lack of solidarity in the EU as visible in the 2015 'migration crisis' and the failed reallocation of refugees entering the Union via the Mediterranean Sea, EU trade policy clearly also became a target of contestation and politicization on a much larger scale than had previously been the case.

Moreover, in June 2016 a narrow majority of UK citizens voted in favour of leaving the EU in the wake of a highly controversial referendum campaign. On 29 March 2017, the British government triggered Art. 50 TEU, starting the clock for two years to negotiate the conditions of its departure. Once the withdrawal and transitional arrangements are clarified, the United Kingdom seeks 'a deep and special partnership' with the EU in economic and security cooperation and 'a bold and ambitious FTA' (May, 2017). The British priorities concerning the internal market are 'taking back control', curbing immigration from Europe and conducting an own trade policy – that is, to no longer be part of the EU's customs union and common commercial policy. The United Kingdom will thus have to develop autonomous trade instruments such as own tariff rates, anti-dumping procedures, its own schedule of preferences for developing countries and independent membership in the WTO. Merely replicating the EU's commitments in the WTO will not work for all areas. The EU can start applying its normal external tariff on goods imported from the United Kingdom relatively easily, but regarding EU quotas, for instance, the Union and the United Kingdom must reach an agreement on the British share, and the other WTO members may object.

What would seem warranted, though, is that the United Kingdom must clarify its trade relations with the EU and in the WTO before entering negotiations on trade agreements with other countries

(Holmes et al., 2016). If the United Kingdom would aim to replace the current EU bilateral treaties, it would have to renegotiate hundreds of trade-related agreements (Financial Times, 2017). This would be a not only time-consuming but also a resource-intensive exercise, requiring many experienced trade negotiators in an area that was in the past decades left to EU officials. In this context it is worth mentioning that although EU member states may to some extent control the European Commission in trade negotiations, the capacity of their national administrations has declined because trade policy has been an exclusive EU competence and varies strongly across member states (Adriaensen, 2016). A Department for International Trade has quickly been established, but the British government might still need a network of advisory committees and a trade strategy for prioritization. A priority could be the attempt to (re)negotiate the EU's most important existing and future FTAs because the EU will become the United Kingdom's most important competitor. There is no guarantee, though, that such agreements would largely consist of a copy-and-paste process given that the EU possesses much more bargaining power than the United Kingdom does alone. The British government may also eye the negotiation of an FTA with the United States, although it is unclear whether the Trump Administration would be willing to give priority to that and whether such bilateral trade talks would take place in parallel with or only after a possible resumption of the EU–US trade and investment talks currently on hold. Should the global trade regime shift back towards more power-based relations, regaining trade policy autonomy may make the post-Brexit trade policy of the United Kingdom as a 'middle power' more cumbersome than expected (Trommer, 2017).

Brexit will also have an impact on EU trade policy more broadly as the EU will shrink, turning into a smaller trade power (as well as a smaller donor in development aid) with potentially less bargaining power too. The British share in the European Development Fund and in the other EU financial instruments and programmes will certainly be missed. The balance between generally more liberally minded and some southern, sometimes more protectionist member states may shift. The EU may become less oriented around free trade and less Atlanticist than it has been. The Union is also likely to act more decisively in its use of anti-dumping and anti-subsidy measures against goods from China, as well as entertain a more defensive and reciprocity-based attitude in matters of government procurement liberalization and investor rights in its relations with China.

Not coincidentally, some of the above controversies about EU trade policy have also been brought to the fore in the form of legal proceedings in front of the Court of Justice of the European Union (CJEU). *Opinion 2/15* on the EU–Singapore FTA is also relevant to the United Kingdom's withdrawal from the EU. The broad interpretation of the EU's exclusive competences in trade facilitates the negotiation of the new generation of FTAs, as long as portfolio investment and investor-to-state dispute settlement are not included (see Chapter 2). In view of the time constraints, the United Kingdom might want to consider a less ambitious trade deal when it comes to FDI. Investment could still be covered in a separate agreement, similar to the case of the ongoing bilateral negotiations between the EU and China on a Comprehensive Agreement on Investment.

Systemic level: the West in a multipolar world

The negotiation deadlock in the Doha Round has demonstrated the need for WTO members to abandon the 'single undertaking' negotiation technique that has to varying degrees characterized most General Agreement on Tariffs and Trade (GATT) and WTO rounds. This technique (nothing is agreed until everything is agreed) implies that negotiations proceed simultaneously, not sequentially, and that all members must accept all the results. Relaxing this principle in recent years has opened the door to 'early harvest' deals like the Trade Facilitation Agreement and new plurilateral negotiations such as the Trade in Services Agreement (see Chapter 5).

Another effect of the Doha Round's stalemate was the shift of major economies towards not only bilateral FTAs but also mega-regional trade deals, in particular the Trans-Pacific Partnership (TPP), signed in February 2016 by 12 Asia-Pacific countries, including the United States and Japan; the negotiations between the EU and the United States on a TTIP; and those on a Regional Comprehensive Economic Partnership (RCEP), involving 16 East Asian countries. In addition, the Chinese President in 2013 launched the 'One Belt, One Road' (OBOR) initiative, which calls for massive investment in and development of trade routes – ports, roads, airports and railways. The Silk Road Economic Belt is envisioned as three routes connecting China to Europe (via Central Asia), the Persian Gulf, the Mediterranean (through West Asia) and the Indian Ocean (via South Asia). The 21st Century Maritime Silk Road is planned to create connections among regional waterways. OBOR could also become the foundation for future free trade areas (Holslag, 2017). Given their size, these mega-regional agreements, if successful, risk undermining the multilateral trade system by leading to competition between trade blocs. They also represent geopolitical undertakings with competing visions of economic governance and future global trade rules (Hamilton, 2016).

In January 2017, however, new US President Trump withdrew the United States from TPP. He also asked Canada and Mexico to renegotiate the North American Free Trade Agreement (NAFTA), which has been in effect since 1994. The fate of TTIP is still uncertain. The new US Administration appears to favour a rather neo-mercantilist view on trade policy: exports are good for growth and jobs, whereas imports are bad, and the United States needs to rectify its trade deficits with China and the EU (or even particular member states like Germany). It has threatened punitive taxes and tariffs on US companies that plan to move jobs abroad as well as on foreign imports. If trade relations are perceived as a 'zero-sum game' and the merits of the WTO are questioned, the potential revival of protectionism is within reach, and bilateral trade deals might at best consist of mutual sectoral concessions. At the G20 in March 2017 and the G7 summit in May 2017, the US President blocked statements condemning protectionism. He also announced the United States' withdrawal from the Paris Agreement, which builds on the United Nations Framework Convention on Climate Change. Meanwhile the Chinese government is presenting itself as a pro-globalization alternative to the United States and seeking closer relations with the EU. Such a rapprochement still faces a number of obstacles, for instance the question of China's market economy status and its relationship with the nature of EU anti-dumping investigations on Chinese firms, trade disputes in the WTO, the discriminatory nature of government procurement in China, the establishment of reciprocity in investment rights and obligations, and security concerns and human rights issues.

Conclusion

The EU has for many years been the world's largest market and trader, but China has been catching up fast. A post-Brexit EU27 will still hold the world's largest share of trade in services but only the third biggest share of trade in goods and of gross domestic product, behind China and the United States. In addition to the relative power shifts between the West and the emerging economies, the United Kingdom's withdrawal and the change of the United States Administration in 2017 appear to be leaving the Western world less unified. For decades the United States has championed an open global economy but is now looking into limiting imports and favouring domestic production. Europe may thus also have to realign its external relations to some extent. At the same time, the common commercial policy has undergone significant legal and institutional changes, and it has politically mobilized more, and more diverse, stakeholders. The years to come are therefore bound to be very interesting times for the study of EU trade policy and politics.

Further reading

As international and EU trade policy are currently undergoing many changes, readers might want to keep up to date via online resources such as the ones listed below.

Brussels-based think tanks:

- http://bruegel.org
- https://www.ceps.eu
- http://ecipe.org

DG Trade, European Commission

- http://ec.europa.eu/trade

Newswires and blogs bringing EU trade policy news and analysis:

- https://efilablog.org
- http://voxeu.org
- https://insidetrade.com
- http://americastradepolicy.com
- https://blogs.sussex.ac.uk/uktpo
- https://piie.com/blogs/trade-investment-policy-watch
- http://worldtradelaw.typepad.com

Bibliography

ACEA (2009) 'Trade deal with Korea goes against the interest of major European industries and their workforce', *Press Release*, Brussels, 15 October.

Ackrill, R.W. (2000) *The Common Agricultural Policy* (Sheffield: Sheffield Academic Press).

Adriaensen, J. (2016) *National Administrations in EU Trade Policy: Maintaining the Capacity to Control* (London: Palgrave Macmillan).

Ahnlid, A. (2005) 'Setting the Global Trade Agenda: The European Union and the Launch of the Doha Round', in O. Elgström and C. Jönsson (eds), *European Union Negotiations: Processes, Networks and Institutions* (London: Routledge), 130–147.

Ahnlid, A. and O. Elgström (2014) 'Challenging the European Union: The Rising Powers and the USA in the Doha Round', *Contemporary Politics*, 20(1), 77–89.

Alt, J.E. and M. Gilligan (1994) 'Survey Article: The Political Economy of Trading States: Factor Specificity, Collective Action Problems and Domestic Political Institutions', *Journal of Political Philosophy*, 2(2), 165–192.

Arantza Gomez, A. (2015) 'The European Union and the Central American Common Market Signs an Association Agreement: Pragmatism versus Values?', *European Foreign Affairs Review*, 20(1), 43–63.

Aydin, U. (2012) 'Promoting Competition: European Union and the Global Competition Order', *Journal of European Integration*, 34(6), 663–681.

Baccini, L., P.M. Pinto and S. Weymouth (2017) 'The Distributional Consequences of Preferential Trade Liberalization: Firm-Level Evidence', *International Organization*, 71(2), 373–395.

Balassa, B. (1961) *The Theory of Economic Integration* (Homewood: Richard D. Irwin).

Baldwin, R.E. (1997) 'The Causes of Regionalism', *World Economy*, 20(7), 865–888.

Baldwin, R.E. (2014) 'WTO 2.0: Governance of 21st Century Trade', *The Review of International Organizations*, 9(2), 261–283.

Baldwin, R. and F. Robert-Nicoud (2015) 'A Simple Model of the Juggernaut Effect of Trade Liberalisation', *International Economics*, 143, 70–79.

Bartels, L. (2007) 'The Trade and Development Policy of the European Union', *European Journal of International Law*, 18(4), 715–756.

Bartels, L. (2015) 'Human Rights and Sustainable Development Obligations in EU Free Trade Agreements', in J. Wouters, A. Marx, D. Geraerts and B. Natens (eds), *Global Governance through Trade: EU Policies and Approaches* (Cheltenham: Edward Elgar), 73–91.

Barton, J.H., J.L. Goldstein, T.E. Josling and R.H. Steinberg (2006) *The Evolution of the Trade Regime: Politics, Law, and Economics of the GATT and the WTO* (Princeton: Princeton University Press).

Bauer, M. (2016) 'Manufacturing Discontent: The Rise to Power of Anti-TTIP Groups', *ECIPE Occasional Paper*, 02/2016 (Brussels: European Centre for International Political Economy).

Billiet, S. (2005) 'The EC and WTO Dispute Settlement: The Initiation of Trade Disputes by the EC', *European Foreign Affairs Review*, 10(2), 197–214.

Bollen, Y., F. De Ville and J. Orbie (2016) 'EU Trade Policy: Persistent Liberalisation, Contentious Protectionism', *Journal of European Integration*, 38(3), 279–294.

Bossuyt, F. (2009) 'The Social Dimension of the New Generation of EU FTAs with Asia and Latin America: Ambitious Continuation for the Sake of Policy Coherence', *European Foreign Affairs Review*, 14(5), 703–722.

Bossuyt, F., L. Drieghe and J. Orbie (2013) 'Living Apart Together: EU Comprehensive Security from a Trade Perspective', *European Foreign Affairs Review*, 18(4), 63–82.

Bourgeois, J.H.J. (1982) 'The Tokyo Round Agreements on Technical Barriers to Trade and on Government Procurement in International and in EEC Perspective', *Common Market Law Review*, 19(1), 5–33.

Bridges (2016) 'European Commission Releases Proposal for Updating Anti-Dumping Rules', 20(38), 10 November.

Bronckers, M. (2015) 'Is Investor–State Dispute Settlement (ISDS) Superior to Litigation Before Domestic Courts? An EU View on Bilateral Trade Agreements', *Journal of International Economic Law*, 18(3), 655–677.

Buonanno, L. and N. Nugent (2013) *Policies and Policy Processes of the European Union* (Basingstoke: Palgrave Macmillan).

Brummer, K. (2009) 'Imposing Sanctions: The Not So "Normative Power Europe"', *European Foreign Affairs Review*, 14(2), 191–207.

Bungenberg, M. (2010) 'Going Global? The EU Common Commercial Policy after Lisbon', in C. Herrmann and J.P. Terhechte (eds), *European Yearbook of International Economic Law* (Berlin: Springer-Verlag), 123–151.

Carbone, M. (2008) 'Mission Impossible: The European Union and Policy Coherence for Development', *Journal of European Integration*, 30(3), 323–342.

Carbone, M. and J. Orbie (2015) (eds) *The Trade-Development Nexus in the European Union: Differentiation, Coherence and Norms* (Abingdon: Routledge).

Cohn, T.H. (2012) *Global Political Economy*, 6th edn (New York: Pearson Longman).

Collinson, S. (1999) '"Issue-Systems", "Multi-level Games" and the Analysis of the EU's External Commercial and Associated Policies: A Research Agenda', *Journal of European Public Policy*, 6(2), 206–224.

Cornides, J. (2013) 'Exporting Legal Standards through Trade Negotiations: Intellectual Property Rights Chapters in Global Europe PTAs', in D. Kleimann (ed.), *EU Preferential Trade Agreements: Commerce, Foreign Policy, and Development Aspects* (Florence: European University Institute), 97–111.

Council of the European Communities (1991) 'Resolution on Human Rights, Democracy and Development', Council and Member States, meeting within the Council, 28 November.

Council of the European Union (2007a) 'Council Regulation (EC) No 1528/2007 of 20 December 2007 applying the arrangements for products originating in certain states which are part of the African, Caribbean and Pacific (ACP) Group of States provided for in agreements establishing, or leading to the establishment of, Economic Partnership Agreements', *Official Journal of the European Union*, L 348/1, 31 December.

Council of the European Union (2007b) *Code of Conduct on Complementarity and Division of Labour in Development Policy*, 9558/07, Brussels, 15 May.

Council of the European Union (2016) 'Trade defence instruments: Council agrees negotiating position', *Press Release* 740/16, Brussels, 13 December.

Council of the European Union (2017) 'Anti-dumping methodology: Council agrees negotiating position', *Press Release* 231/17, Brussels, 3 May.

Court of Justice of the European Union (1971) Case 22/70 *Commission v. Council* [1971] ECR 263, 31 March.

Court of Justice of the European Union (1975) Opinion 1/75 *Understanding on a Local Cost Standard* [1975] ECR 1355, 11 November.

Court of Justice of the European Union (1979) Case 120/78 *Rewe v. Bundesmonopolverwaltung für Branntwein* [1979] ECR 649, 20 February.

Court of Justice of the European Union (1994) Opinion 1/94 *WTO Agreement* [1994] ECR I-5267, 15 November.

Court of Justice of the European Union (2001) Opinion 2/00 *Cartagena Protocol on Biosafety* [2001] ECR I-9713, 6 December.

Court of Justice of the European Union (2017) Opinion 2/15 *Singapore Free Trade Agreement* (not yet reported), 16 May.

Cremona, M. (2000) 'EC External Commercial Policy after Amsterdam: Authority and Interpretation within Interconnected Legal Orders', in J.H.H. Weiler (ed.), *The EU, the WTO and the NAFTA: Towards a Common Law of International Trade?* (Oxford: Oxford University Press), 5–34.

Cremona, M. (2002a) 'The External Dimension of the Single Market: Building (on) the Foundations', in C. Barnard and J. Scott (eds), *The Law of the Single European Market: Unpacking the Premises* (Oxford: Hart Publishing), 351–393.

Cremona, M. (2002b) 'A Policy of Bits and Pieces? The Common Commercial Policy after Nice', in A. Dashwood, C. Hillion, J. Spencer and A. Ward (eds), *The Cambridge Yearbook of European Legal Studies*, vol. 4, 2001 (Oxford: Hart Publishing), 61–91.

Da Conceição Heldt, E. (2010) 'Who Controls Whom? Dynamics of Power Delegation and Agency Losses in EU Trade Politics', *Journal of Common Market Studies*, 48(4), 1107–1126.

Da Conceição-Heldt, E. (2013) 'Two-Level Games and Trade Cooperation: What Do We Now Know?', *International Politics*, 50(4), 579–599.

Da Conceição-Heldt, E. (2014) 'When Speaking with a Single Voice Isn't Enough: Bargaining Power (A)Symmetry and EU External Effectiveness in Global Trade Governance', *Journal of European Public Policy*, 21(7), 980–995.

Damro, C. (2012) 'Market Power Europe', *Journal of European Public Policy*, 19(5), 682–699.

Damro, C. and T.R. Guay (2016) *European Competition Policy and Globalization* (Basingstoke: Palgrave Macmillan).

Daugbjerg, C. (2017) 'Responding to Non-Linear Internationalisation of Public Policy: The World Trade Organization and Reform of the CAP 1992–2013', *Journal of Common Market Studies*, 55(3), 486–501.

Dawar, K. (2016) 'The 2016 European Union International Procurement Instrument's Amendments to the 2012 Buy European Proposal: A Retrospective Assessment of Its Prospects', *Journal of World Trade*, 50(5), 845–865.

De Bièvre, D. (2015) 'DG Trade and EU Trade Policy', in E. Drieskens, Å. Kalland Aarstad, K.E. Jørgensen, K. Laatikainen and B. Tonra (eds), *SAGE Handbook on European Foreign Policy* (London: SAGE), 277–290.

De Bièvre, D. (2006) 'Legislative and Judicial Decision Making in the World Trade Organization', in M. Koenig-Archibugi and M. Zürn (eds), *New Modes of Governance in the Global System: Exploring Publicness, Delegation and Inclusiveness* (Basingstoke: Palgrave Macmillan), 31–51.

De Bièvre, D. (2014) 'A Glass Quite Empty: Issue Groups' Influence in the Global Trade Regime', *Global Policy*, 5(2), 222–228.

De Bièvre, D. and A. Dür (2005) 'Constituency Interests and Delegation in European and American Trade Policy', *Comparative Political Studies*, 38(10), 1271–1296.

De Bièvre, D. and J. Eckhardt (2011) 'Interest Groups and EU Anti-dumping Policy', *Journal of European Public Policy*, 18(3), 339–360.

De Bièvre, D. and A. Poletti (2013) 'The EU in EU Trade Policy: From Regime Shaper to Status Quo Power', in G. Falkner and P. Müller (eds), *EU Policies in a Global Perspective* (London: Routledge), 20–37.

De Bièvre, D. and A. Poletti (2016) 'Why the Transatlantic Trade and Investment Partnership Is not (so) New, and Why It Is also not (so) Bad', *Journal of European Public Policy*, 24(10), 1506–1521.

Dee, M. (2015) *The European Union in a Multipolar World: World Trade, Global Governance and the Case of the WTO* (London: Palgrave Macmillan).

Del Biondo, K. (2011) 'EU Aid Conditionality in ACP Countries: Explaining Inconsistency in EU Sanctions Practice', *Journal of Contemporary European Research*, 7(3), 380–395.

Demedts, V. (2015) 'Which Future for Competition in the Global Trade System: Competition Chapters in FTAs', *Journal of World Trade*, 49(3), 407–436.

De Ville, F. and G. Siles-Brügge (2016) 'Why TTIP Is a Game-Changer and its Critics Have a Point', *Journal of European Public Policy*, 24(10), 1491–1505.

De Ville, F. and M. Vermeiren (2016) 'The Eurozone Crisis and the Rise of China in the Global Monetary and Trading System: The Political Economy of an Asymmetric Shock', *Comparative European Politics*, 14(5), 572–603.

Devuyst, Y. (2013) 'European Union Law and Practice in the Negotiation and Conclusion of International Trade Agreements', *Journal of International Business & Law*, 12(2), 259–316.

De Wilde, P. (2011) 'No Polity for Old Politics? A Framework for Analyzing the Politicization of European Integration', *Journal of European Integration*, 33(5), 559–575.

Dickson-Smith, K.D. (2016) 'Does the European Union Have New Clothes? Understanding the EU's New Investment Treaty Model', *The Journal of World Investment & Trade*, 17(5), 773–822.

Dimier, V. (2014) *The Invention of a European Development Aid Bureaucracy: Recycling Empire* (Basingstoke: Palgrave Macmillan).

Dimopoulos, A. (2008) 'The Common Commercial Policy after Lisbon: Establishing Parallelism between Internal and External Economic Relations', *Croatian Yearbook of European Law & Policy*, 4, 101–129.

Dimopoulos, A. (2010) 'The Effects of the Lisbon Treaty on the Principles and Objectives of the Common Commercial Policy', *European Foreign Affairs Review*, 15(2), 153–170.

Doctor, M. (2007) 'Why Bother with Inter-regionalism? Negotiations for a European Union–Mercosur Association Agreement', *Journal of Common Market Studies*, 45(2), 281–314.

Døhlie Saltnes, J. (2013) The EU's Human Rights Policy: Unpacking the Literature on the EU's Implementation of aid Conditionality, *ARENA Working Paper*, 2, (Oslo: ARENA).

Dordi, C. and A. Forganni (2013) 'The Comitology Reform in the EU: Potential Effects on Trade Defence Instruments', *Journal of World Trade*, 47(2), 359–389.

Dür, A. (2007) 'EU Trade Policy as Protection for Exporters: The Agreements with Mexico and Chile', *Journal of Common Market Studies*, 45(4), 833–855.

Dür, A. (2008) 'Bringing Economic Interests Back into the Study of EU Trade Policy-Making', *The British Journal of Politics & International Relations*, 10(1), 27–45.

Dür, A. (2010) *Protection for Exporters: Power and Discrimination in Transatlantic Trade Relations, 1930–2010* (Ithaca: Cornell University Press).

Dür, A. (2011) 'Fortress Europe or Open Door Europe? The External Impact of the EU's Single Market in Financial Services', *Journal of European Public Policy*, 18(5), 619–635.

Dür, A. and D. De Bièvre (2007) 'Inclusion without Influence? NGOs in European Trade Policy', *Journal of Public Policy*, 27(1), 79–101.

Dür, A. and M. Elsig (eds) (2011) *The European Union's Foreign Economic Policies: A Principal-Agent Perspective* (London: Routledge).

Eckhardt, J. (2015) *Business Lobbying and Trade Governance: The Case of EU-China Relations* (London: Palgrave Macmillan).

Eckhardt, J. and A. Poletti (2016) 'The Politics of Global Value Chains: Import-Dependent Firms and EU-Asia Trade Agreements', *Journal of European Public Policy*, 23(10), 1543–1562.

Eeckhout, P. (2011) *EU External Relations Law*, 2nd edn (Oxford: Oxford University Press).

Elgström, O. and M. Frennhoff Larsén (2010) 'Free to Trade? Commission Autonomy in Economic Partnership Agreement Negotiations', *Journal of European Public Policy*, 17(2), 205–223.

Eliasson, L.J. and P. García-Duran (2016) 'Why TTIP Is an Unprecedented Geopolitical Game-Changer, but not a Polanyian Moment', *Journal of European Public Policy*, 24(10), 1522–1533.

Elsig, M. (2002) *The EU's Common Commercial Policy: Institutions, Interests and Ideas* (Ashgate: Aldershot).

Elsig, M. (2007) 'The EU's Choice of Regulatory Venues for Trade Negotiations: A Tale of Agency Power?', *Journal of Common Market Studies*, 45(4), 927–948.

Elsig, M. (2010) 'European Union Trade Policy after Enlargement: Larger Crowds, Shifting Priorities and Informal Decision-Making', *Journal of European Public Policy*, 17(6), 781–798.

Elsig, M. and C. Dupont (2012) 'European Union Meets South Korea: Bureaucratic Interests, Exporter Discrimination and the Negotiations of Trade Agreements', *Journal of Common Market Studies*, 50(3), 492–507.

Elsig, M. and E. Eckhardt (2015) 'The Creation of the Multilateral Trade Court: Design and Experiential Learning', *Judicial Politics in International Trade Relations*, 14(51), S13–S32.

Erixon, F. and H. Lee (2010) 'Stepping into Asia's Growth Markets: Dispelling Myths about the EU-Korea Free Trade Agreement', *ECIPE Policy Briefs*, 3 (Brussels: European Centre for International Political Economy).

European Commission (1985) 'Completing the Internal Market: White Paper from the Commission to the European Council (Milan, 28–29 June 1985)', Brussels, COM(1985) 310 final, 14 June.

European Commission (1988) 'Europe 1992: Europe World Partner', *Information Memo* P-117, Brussels, 19 October.

European Commission (1996) *Green Paper on Relations between the European Union and the ACP Countries on the Eve of the 21st Century: Challenges and Options for a New Partnership*, COM(1996) 570, Brussels, 20 November.

European Commission (2006) *Global Europe: Competing in the World. A Contribution to the EU's Growth and Jobs Strategy*, COM(2006) 567 final, Brussels, 4 October.

European Commission (2010a) 'EU and South Korea sign free trade deal', *Press Release*, IP/10/1292, Brussels, 6 October.

European Commission (2010b) *Trade, Growth and World Affairs: Trade Policy as a Core Component of the EU's 2020 Strategy*, COM(2010) 612 final, Brussels, 9 November.

European Commission (2010c) *Special Eurobarometer 357: International Trade*, Summary, Brussels.

European Commission (2010d) *Towards a Comprehensive European International Investment Policy*, COM(2010) 343 final, Brussels, 7 July.

European Commission (2012) 'Working Arrangements between Commission Services and the European External Action Service (EEAS) in Relation to External Relations Issues', SEC(2012) 48, Brussels, 13 January.

European Commission (2013) *Statement of Estimates of the Commission for 2014 (Preparation of the 2014 Draft Budget), Document III: Figures by MFF Heading, Section and Budget Line*, SEC(2013) 370 final, Brussels, 26 June.

European Commission (2015) *Trade for All: Towards a More Responsible Trade and Investment Policy*, COM(2015) 497, Brussels, 14 October.

European Commission (2016) 'Amended proposal for a Regulation of the European Parliament and of the Council on the access of third-country goods and services to the Union's internal market in public procurement and procedures supporting negotiations on access of Union goods and services to the public procurement markets of third countries', COM(2016) 34 final, 2012/0060 (COD), Brussels, 29 January.

European Commission (2017a) 'EU Official Development Assistance reaches highest level ever', *Press Release* IP/17/916, Brussels, 11 April.

European Commission (2017b) *DG Trade Statistical Guide*, Brussels, June.

European Commission (2017c) 'The European Commission imposes duties to counter Chinese steel subsidies', http://trade.ec.europa.eu/doclib/press/index.cfm?id=1669 (accessed June 2017).

European Commission and European Parliament (2010) 'Framework Agreement on relations between the European Parliament and the European Commission', *Official Journal of the European Union*, L304, 20 November, 47–62.

European Commission and High Representative (2016) *A Renewed Partnership with the Countries of Africa, the Caribbean and the Pacific*, JOIN(2016) 52, Brussels, 22 November.

European Council (2002) 'Presidency Conclusions of the Seville European Council, 21 and 22 June 2002', 13463/02 POLGEN 52, 24 October.

European External Action Service (2016) 'Shared Vision, Common Action: A Stronger Europe – A Global Strategy for the European Union's Foreign and Security Policy', Brussels, June.

European Parliament, Council and Commission (2006) Joint Statement by the Council and the Representatives of the Governments of the Member States Meeting within the Council, the European Parliament and the Commission on European Union Development Policy: 'The European Consensus on Development', 20 December 2005, *Official Journal of the European Union*, C 46, 24 February, 1–19.

European Parliament, Council and Commission (2008) Joint Statement by the Council and the Representatives of the Governments of the Member States Meeting within the Council, the European Parliament and the Commission: 'The European Consensus on Humanitarian Aid', 18 December 2007, *Official Journal of the European Union*, C 25, 30 January, 1–12.

European Parliament, Council and Commission (2017) Joint Statement by the Council and the Representatives of the Governments of the Member States Meeting within the Council, the European Parliament and the Commission: 'The New European Consensus on Development: Our World, Our Dignity, Our Future', 8 June.

European Parliament (2010) *An Assessment of the EU-Korea FTA*, Directorate-General for External Policies of the Union, Brussels, July, EP/EXPO/B/INTA/ FWC/2009-01/Lot7/01-02-03.

European Parliament (2011) 'Recommendation on the draft Council decision on the conclusion of the Free Trade Agreement between the European Union and its Member States, of the one part and the Republic of Korea, of the other part (08505/2010 – C7-0320/2010 – 2010/0075(NLE))', Committee on International Trade, Rapporteur Robert Sturdy, 9 February.

European Parliament (2014) *African, Caribbean and Pacific (ACP) Countries' Position on the Economic Partnership Agreements (EPAs)*, Study PE 433.843, Brussels, April.

European Parliament and Council of the European Union (2011) 'Regulation (EU) No 182/2011 of the European Parliament and of the Council of 16 February 2011 laying down the rules and general principles concerning mechanisms for control by Member States of the Commission's exercise of implementing powers', *Official Journal of the European Union*, L 55/13, 28 February.

European Parliament and Council of the European Union (2012) 'Regulation (EU) No 978/2012 of the European Parliament and of the Council of 25 October 2012 applying a scheme of generalised tariff preferences and repealing Council Regulation (EC) No 732/2008', *Official Journal of the European Union*, L 303/1, 31 October.

European Parliament and Council of the European Union (2014a) 'Regulation (EU) No 37/2014 of the European Parliament and of the Council of 15 January 2014 amending certain regulations relating to the common commercial policy as regards the procedures for the adoption of certain measures', *Official Journal of the European Union*, L 18/1, 21 January.

European Parliament and Council of the European Union (2014b) 'Regulation (EU) No 654/2014 of the European Parliament and of the Council of 15 May 2014 concerning the exercise of the Union's rights for the application and enforcement of international trade rules and amending Council Regulation (EC) No 3286/94 laying down Community procedures in the field of the common commercial policy in order to ensure the exercise of the Community's rights under international trade rules, in particular those established under the auspices of the World Trade Organization', *Official Journal of the European Union*, L 189/50, 27 June.

European Parliament and Council of the European Union (2015) 'Regulation (EU) No 2015/1843 of the European Parliament and of the Council of 6 October 2015 laying down Union procedures in the field of the common commercial policy in order to ensure the exercise of the Union's rights under international trade rules, in particular those established under the auspices of the World Trade Organization (codification)', *Official Journal of the European Union*, L 272/1, 16 October.

European Parliament and Council of the European Union (2016a) 'Regulation (EU) No 2016/1036 of the European Parliament and of the Council of 8 June 2016 on protection against dumped imports from countries not members of the European Union (codification)', *Official Journal of the European Union*, L 176/21, 30 June.

European Parliament and Council of the European Union (2016b) 'Regulation (EU) No 2016/1076 of the European Parliament and of the Council of 8 June 2016 applying the arrangements for products originating in certain states which are part of the African, Caribbean and Pacific (ACP) Group of States provided for in agreements establishing, or leading to the establishment of, economic partnership agreements', *Official Journal of the European Union*, L 185/1, 8 July.

European Voice (2010) 'EU-Korea: Parliament delays vote on free-trade safeguards', 21 October.

Evans, P.B., H.K. Jacobson and R.D. Putnam (1993) (eds) *Double-Edged Diplomacy: International Bargaining and Domestic Politics* (Berkeley: University of California Press).

Evenett, S.J. and M. Meier (2008) 'An Interim Assessment of the US Trade Policy of "Competitive Liberalization"', *The World Economy*, 31(1), 31–66.

Faber, G. and J. Orbie (2009) (eds) *Beyond Market Access for Economic Development: EU–Africa Relations in Transition* (Abingdon: Routledge).

Financial Times (2009) 'Free trade auto deal stalls', 3 April.

Financial Times (2010) 'EU agrees trade deal with South Korea', 16 September.

Financial Times (2017) 'After Brexit: the UK will need to renegotiate at least 759 treaties', 31 May.

Frennhoff Larsén, M. (2007) 'Trade Negotiations between the EU and South Africa: A Three-Level Game', *Journal of Common Market Studies*, 45(4), 857–881.

Furness, M. (2012) 'The Lisbon Treaty, the European External Action Service and the Reshaping of EU Development Policy', in S. Gänzle, S. Grimm and D. Makhan (eds), *The European Union and Global Development: An 'Enlightened Superpower' in the Making?* (Basingstoke: Palgrave Macmillan), 74–93.

García, M. (2015) 'The European Union and Latin America: "Transformative Power Europe" versus the Realities of Economic Interests', *Cambridge Review of International Affairs*, 28(4), 621–640.

GATT (1947) *The General Agreement on Tariffs and Trade* (Geneva: GATT Secretariat).

GATT (1979) 'Differential and more favourable treatment reciprocity and fuller participation of developing countries (Enabling Clause)', Decision of 28 November 1979 (L/4903), https://www.wto.org/english/docs_e/legal_e/enabling1979_e.htm (accessed June 2017).

Gebhard, C. (2011) 'Coherence', in C. Hill and M. Smith (eds), *International Relations and the European Union*, 2nd edn (Oxford: Oxford University Press), 101–127.

Gereffi, G., J. Humphrey and T. Sturgeon (2005) 'The Governance of Global Value Chains', *Review of International Political Economy*, 12(1), 78–104.

Gilligan, M.J. (1997) 'Lobbying as a Private Good with Intra-industry Trade', *International Studies Quarterly*, 41(3), 455–474.

Giumelli, F. (2010) 'New Analytical Categories for Assessing EU Sanctions', *The International Spectator*, 45(3), 131–144.

Goldstein, J. (1988) 'Ideas, Institutions and American Trade Policy', *International Organization*, 42(1), 179–217.

Greenwood, J. (2017) *Interest Representation in the European Union*, 4th edn (Basingstoke: Palgrave).

Greenwood, J. and J. Dreger (2013) 'The Transparency Register: A European Vanguard of Strong Lobby Regulation?', *Interest Groups & Advocacy*, 2(2), 139–162.

Gstöhl, S. (2008) 'Blurring Economic Boundaries? Trade and Aid in the EU's Near Abroad', in D. Mahncke and S. Gstöhl (eds), *Europe's Near Abroad: Promises and Prospects of the EU's Neighbourhood Policy* (Brussels: P.I.E. Peter Lang), 135–161.

Gstöhl, S. (2010a) 'Uneven Legalization of Non-Trade Concerns in the WTO: Blurring Regime Boundaries', *Journal of International Trade Law and Policy*, 9(3), 275–296.

Gstöhl, S. (2010b) 'The Common Commercial Policy and Political Conditionality: "Normative Power Europe" through Trade?', *Studia Diplomatica*, LXIII(3–4), 23–41.

Gstöhl, S. (2014) 'No Strings Attached? The EU's Emergency Trade Preferences for Pakistan', in I. Govaere and S. Poli (eds), *EU Management of Global Emergencies: Legal Framework for Combating Threats and Crises* (Leiden: Brill), 47–73.

Gstöhl, S. (2015) 'The European Union's Different Neighbourhood Models', in J.E. Fossum and E.O. Eriksen (eds), *The European Union's Non-Members: Independence under Hegemony* (Abingdon: Routledge), 17–35.

Guth, E. (2012) 'The End of the Bananas Saga', *Journal of World Trade*, 46(1), 1–32.

Hamilton, D. (2016) 'Rule-Makers or Rule-Takers? An American Perspective on Transatlantic Trade and Investment Partnership', *European Foreign Affairs Review*, 21(3), 365–382.

Hampshire, J. (2016) 'Speaking with One Voice? The European Union's Global Approach to Migration and Mobility and the Limits of International Migration Cooperation', *Journal of Ethnic and Migration Studies*, 42(4), 571–586.

Hanegraaff, M., C. Braun, D. De Bièvre and J. Beyers (2015) 'The Domestic and Global Origins of Transnational Advocacy: Explaining Lobbying Presence during WTO Ministerial Conferences', *Comparative Political Studies*, 48(12), 1591–1621.

Hannah, E., J. Scott and R. Wilkinson (2017) 'Reforming WTO-Civil Society Engagement', *World Trade Review*, 16(3), 427–448.

Hanson, B.T. (1998) 'What Happened to Fortress Europe? External Trade Policy Liberalization in the European Union', *International Organization*, 52(1), 55–85.

Heron, T. (2014) 'Trading in Development: Norms and Institutions in the Making/Unmaking of European Union-African, Caribbean and Pacific Trade and Development Cooperation', *Contemporary Politics*, 20(1), 10–22.

Heron, T. and G. Siles-Brügge (2012) 'Competitive Liberalization and the 'Global Europe' Services and Investment Agenda: Locating the Commercial Drivers of the EU-ACP Economic Partnership Agreements', *Journal of Common Market Studies*, 50(2), 250–266.

Hiscox, M.J. (2001) 'Class Versus Industry Cleavages: Inter-Industry Factor Mobility and the Politics of Trade', *International Organization*, 55(1), 1–46.

Hoekman, B.M. and P.C. Mavroidis (2015) 'WTO "à la carte" or "menu du jour"? Assessing the Case for More Plurilateral Agreements', *The European Journal of International Law*, 26(2), 319–343.

Hoffmeister, F. (2015a) 'The European Union as an International Trade Negotiator', in J.A. Koops and G. Macaj (eds), *The European Union as a Diplomatic Actor* (Basingstoke: Palgrave), 138–154.

Hoffmeister, F. (2015b) 'Modernising the EU's Trade Defence Instruments: Mission Impossible?', in C. Herrmann, B. Simma and R. Streinz (eds), *Trade Policy between Law, Diplomacy and Scholarship: Liber Amicorum in Memoriam Horst G. Krenzler, European Yearbook of International Economic Law* (Cham: Springer), 365–376.

Hoffmeister, F. (2016) 'The EU Public Procurement Regime on Third-Country Bidders – Setting the Cursor between Openness and Reciprocity', in H. Kalimo and M.S. Jansson (eds), *EU Economic Law in a Time of Crisis* (Cheltenham: Edward Elgar), 76–88.

Holden, P. (2009) *In Search of Structural Power: EU Aid Policy as a Global Political Instrument* (Farnham: Ashgate).

Holland, M. and M. Doidge (2012) *Development Policy of the European Union* (Basingstoke: Palgrave Macmillan).

Holmes, P., J. Rollo and L.A. Winters (2016) 'Negotiating the UK's post-Brexit Trade Arrangement', *National Institute Economic Review*, 238(1), R22–R30.

Holslag, J. (2017) 'How China's New Silk Road Threatens European Trade', *The International Spectator*, 52(1), 46–60.

Hwang, K.S. and H.J. Kim (2015) 'Three-Level Game Theory and the Strategy of EU-Korea FTA Negotiations', *The Journal of East Asian Affairs*, 28(1), 85–130.

Ikenberry, G.J., D.A. Lake and M. Mastanduno (1988) 'Introduction: Approaches to Explaining American Foreign Economic Policy', *International Organization*, 42(1), 1–14.

Jensen, J.B., D.P. Quinn and S. Weymouth (2015) 'The Influence of Firm Global Supply Chains and Foreign Currency Undervaluations on US Trade Disputes', *International Organization*, 69(4), 913–947.

Johnson, M. and J. Rollo (2001) 'EU Enlargement and Commercial Policy: Enlargement and the Making of Commercial Policy', *Working Paper*, 43 (Brighton: Sussex European Institute).

Jurje, F. and S. Lavenex (2014) 'Trade Agreements as Venues for 'Market Power Europe'? The Case of Immigration Policy', *Journal of Common Market Studies*, 52(2), 320–336.

Kelemen, R.D. (2010) 'Globalizing European Union Environmental Policy', *Journal of European Public Policy*, 17(3), 335–349.

Kerremans, B. (2004) 'What Went Wrong in Cancun? A Principal-Agent View on the EU's Rationale Towards the Doha Development Round', *European Foreign Affairs Review*, 9(3), 363–393.

Kerremans, B. (2011) 'The European Commission in the WTO's DDA Negotiations: A Tale of an Agent, a Single Undertaking, and Twenty-Seven Nervous Principals', in S. Blavoukos and D. Bourantonis (eds), *The EU Presence in International Organizations* (London: Routledge), 132–149.

Kerremans, B. and J. Orbie (2009) 'The Social Dimension of European Trade Policies', *European Foreign Affairs Review*, 14(5), 629–641.

Kerremans, B. and J. Orbie (2013) 'Towards Engaged Pluralism in the Study of European Trade Politics', *Journal of Contemporary European Research*, 9(4), 659–674.

Khorana, S. and M. García (2013) 'European Union–India Trade Negotiations: One Step Forward, One Back?', *Journal of Common Market Studies*, 51(4), 684–700.

Laird, I. and F. Petillion (2017) 'Comprehensive Economic and Trade Agreement, ISDS and the Belgian Veto: A Warning of Failure for Future Trade Agreements with the EU?', *Global Trade and Customs Journal*, 12(4), 167–174.

Lanz, R. and S. Miroudot (2011) 'Intra-firm Trade: Patterns, Determinants and Policy Implications', *OECD Trade Policy Papers*, 114 (Paris: OECD).

Larik, J. (2015) 'No Mixed Feelings: The post-Lisbon Common Commercial Policy in *Daiichi Sankyo* and *Commission* v. *Council (Conditional Access Convention)*', *Common Market Law Review*, 52(3), 779–800.

Mandelson, P. (2005) 'European Member States back new EU Generalised System of Preferences (GSP)', *Press Release* IP/05/772, Brussels, 23 June.

Manners, I. (2009) 'The Social Dimension of EU Trade Policies: Reflections from a Normative Power Perspective', *European Foreign Affairs Review*, 14(5), 785–803.

Manners, I. (2002) 'Normative Power Europe: A Contradiction in Terms?', *Journal of Common Market Studies*, 40(2), 235–258.

May, T. (2017) 'The government's negotiating objectives for exiting the EU: PM speech', London, Prime Minister's Office, Lancaster House, 17 January, https://www.gov.uk/government/speeches/the-governments-negotiating-objectives-for-exiting-the-eu-pm-speech (accessed June 2017).

Maresceau, M. (1993) 'The Concept of "Common Commercial Policy" and the Difficult Road to Maastricht', in M. Maresceau (ed.), *The European Community's Commercial Policy after 1992: The Legal Dimension* (Dordrecht: Martinus Nijhoff Publishers), 3–20.

Maresceau, M. (2010) 'Mixed Agreements Revisited: The EU and its Member States in the World', in C. Hillion and P. Koutrakos (eds), *Mixed Agreements Revisited: The EU and Its Member States in the World* (Oxford: Hart Publishing), 11–29.

Marín Durán, G. and E. Morgera (2012) *Environmental Integration in the EU's External Relations* (Oxford: Hart Publishing).

Matthews, A. (2008) 'The European Union's Common Agricultural Policy and Developing Countries: The Struggle for Coherence', *Journal of European Integration*, 30(3), 381–399.

Mavroidis, P.C. (2011) 'Doha, Dohalf or Dohaha? The WTO Licks its Wounds', *Trade, Law and Development*, 3(2), 367–381.

McKenzie, L. and K.L. Meissner (2017) 'Human Rights Conditionality in European Union Trade Negotiations: The Case of the EU-Singapore FTA', *Journal of Common Market Studies*, 55(4), 832–849.

Meissner, K.L. (2016a) 'Democratizing EU External Relations: The European Parliament's Informal Role in SWIFT, ACTA, and TTIP', *European Foreign Affairs Review*, 21(2), 269–288.

Meissner, K.L. (2016b) 'A Case of Failed Interregionalism? Analyzing the EU-ASEAN Free Trade Agreement Negotiations', *Asia Europe Journal*, 14(3), 319–336.

Melo Aruja, B.A. (2016) *The EU Deep Trade Agenda* (Oxford: Oxford University Press).

Melitz, M. J. (2003) 'The Impact of Trade on Intra-Industry Reallocations and Aggregate Industry Productivity', *Econometrica*, 71(6), 1695–1725.

Messerlin, P. (2001) *Measuring the Costs of Protection in Europe: European Commercial Policy in the 2000s* (Washington: Peterson Institute for International Economics).

Meunier, S. (2005) *Trading Voices: the European Union in International Commercial Negotiations* (Princeton: Princeton University Press).

Meunier, S. (2017) 'Integration by Stealth: How the European Union Gained Competence over Foreign Direct Investment', *Journal of Common Market Studies*, 55(3), 593–610.

Meunier, S. and K. Nicolaïdis (2006) 'The European Union as a Conflicted Trade Power', *Journal of European Public Policy*, 13(6), 906–925.

Moerland, A. (2013) *Why Jamaica Wants to Protect Champagne: Intellectual Property Protection in EU Bilateral Trade Agreements* (Nijmegen: Wolf Legal Publishers).

Molle, W. (2006) *The Economics of European Integration: Theory, Practice, Policy* (Aldershot: Ashgate).

Moravcsik, A. (1998) *The Choice for Europe: Social Purpose and State Power from Messina to Maastricht* (Ithaca: Cornell University Press).

Mortensen, J.L. (2009) 'The World Trade Organization and the European Union', in K.E. Jørgensen (ed.), *The European Union and International Organization* (London: Routledge), 80–100.

Mudde, C. (2013) 'Three Decades of Populist Radical Right Parties in Western Europe: So What?', *European Journal of Political Research*, 52(1), 1–19.

Nicolas, F. (2009) 'Negotiating a Korea–EU Free Trade Agreement: Easier Said than Done', *Asia Europe Journal*, 7(1), 23–42.

Nugent, N. (2017) *The Government and Politics of the European Union*, 8th edn (Basingstoke: Palgrave).

Oatley, T. (2012) *International Political Economy*, 4th edn (New York: Pearson).

Oehri, M. (2014) 'Comparing US and EU Labour Governance 'Near and Far' – Hierarchy vs Network?', *Journal of European Public Policy*, 22(5), 731–749.

Olson, M. (1965) *The Logic of Collective Action: Public Goods and the Theory of Groups* (Cambridge: Harvard University Press).

Orbie, J. (2007) 'The Development of EBA', in G. Faber and J. Orbie (eds), *European Union Trade Politics and Development: 'Everything but Arms' Unravelled* (London: Routledge), 20–42.

Orbie, J. (2011) 'Promoting Labour Standards through Trade: Normative Power or Regulatory State Europe?', in R.G. Whitman (ed.), *Normative Power Europe: Empirical and Theoretical Perspectives* (Basingstoke: Palgrave Macmillan), 161–184.

Orbie, J. and L. Tortell (2009) 'The New GSP Beneficiaries: Ticking the Box or Truly Consistent with ILO Findings', *European Foreign Affairs Review*, 14(5), 663–681.

Orbie, J., P. Van Elsuwege and F. Bossuyt (2014) 'Humanitarian Aid as an Integral Part of the European Union's External Action: The Challenge of Reconciling Coherence and Independence', *Journal of Contingencies and Crisis Management*, 22(3), 158–165.

Orefice, G. and N. Rocha (2014) 'Deep Integration and Production Networks: An Empirical Analysis', *The World Economy*, 37(1), 106–136.

Osgood, I. (2017) 'The Breakdown of Industrial Opposition to Trade: Firms, Product Variety, and Reciprocal Liberalization', *World Politics*, 69(1), 184–231.

Pelkmans, J. (2006) *European Integration: Methods and Economic Analysis*, 3rd edn (Harlow: Pearson Education).

Poletti, A. (2010) 'Drowning Protection in the Multilateral Bath: WTO Judicialisation and European Agriculture in the Doha Round', *The British Journal of Politics & International Relations*, 12(4), 615–633.

Poletti, A. (2012) *The European Union and Multilateral Trade Governance: The Politics of the Doha Round* (London: Routledge).

Poletti, A. and D. De Bièvre (2013) 'The Political Science of European Trade Policy: A Literature Review with a Research Outlook', *Comparative European Politics*, 12(1), 101–119.

Poletti, A. and D. De Bièvre (2014) 'Political Mobilization, Veto Players, and WTO Litigation: Explaining European Union Responses in Trade Disputes', *Journal of European Public Policy*, 21(8), 1181–1198.

Poletti, A. and D. Sicurelli (2012) 'The EU as Promoter of Environmental Norms in the Doha Round', *West European Politics*, 35(4), 911–932.

Poletti, A., D. De Bièvre and J.T. Chatagnier (2015) 'Cooperation in the Shadow of WTO Law: Why Litigate When You Can Negotiate', *World Trade Review*, 14(S1), 33–58.

Poletti, A., D. De Bièvre and M. Hanegraaff (2016) 'WTO Judicial Politics and EU Trade Policy: Business Associations as Vessels of Special Interest?', *The British Journal of Politics and International Relations*, 18(1), 196–215.

Pollack, M. (1997) 'Delegation, Agency and Agenda Setting in the European Community', *International Organization*, 51(1), 99–134.

Portela, C. (2010) *European Union Sanctions and Foreign Policy: When and Why Do They Work?* (London: Routledge).

Portela, C. (2015) 'Member States Resistance to EU Foreign Policy Sanctions', *European Foreign Affairs Review*, 20(2/1), 39–62.

Portela, C. and J. Orbie (2014) 'Sanctions under the EU Generalised System of Preferences and Foreign Policy: Coherence by Accident?', *Contemporary Politics*, 20(1), 63–76.

Postnikov, E. and I. Bastiaens (2014) 'Does Dialogue Work? The Effectiveness of Labor Standards in EU Preferential Trade Agreements', *Journal of European Public Policy*, 21(6), 923–940.

Psychogiopoulou, E. (2014) 'The External Dimension of EU Cultural Action and Free Trade: Exploring an Interface', *Legal Issues of Economic Integration*, 41(1), 65–86.

Putnam, R.D. (1988) 'Diplomacy and Domestic Politics: The Logic of Two-Level Games', *International Organization*, 42(3), 427–460.

Ravenhill, J. (1985) *Collective Clientelism: The Lomé Conventions and North-South Relations* (New York: Columbia University Press).

Richardson, D.J. (1990) 'The Political Economy of Strategic Trade Policy', *International Organization*, 44(1), 107–135.

Rogowski, R. (1989) *Commerce and Coalitions: How Trade Affects Domestic Political Alignments* (Princeton: Princeton University Press).

Ruggiero, R. (1998) 'From Vision to Reality: The Multilateral Trading System at Fifty', Address to the Brookings Institution and the World Affairs Council Forum 'The Global Trading System; a GATT 50th Anniversary Forum', San Jose, US, 26 February.

Sahakyan, D. (2016) 'EU Trade Policy Responses to the Proliferation of Preferential Trade Agreements in Latin America and East and Southeast Asia', *Politics & Policy*, 44(1), 74–96.

Scharf, T. (2015) 'Decision-Making in EU Trade Defence Cases after Lisbon: An Institutional Anomaly Addressed?', in C. Herrmann, B. Simma and R. Streinz (eds), *Trade Policy between Law, Diplomacy and Scholarship: Liber amicorum in memoriam Horst G. Krenzler, European Yearbook of International Economic Law* (Cham: Springer), 395–406.

Scharpf, F. (1988) 'The Joint-Decision Trap: Lessons from German Federalism and European Integration', *Public Administration*, 66(3), 239–278.

Schelling, T. (1960) *The Strategy of Conflict* (Cambridge: Harvard University Press).

Schuknecht, L. (1992) *Trade Protection in the European Community* (Chur: Harwood Academic Publishers).

Siles-Brügge, G. (2011) 'Resisting Protectionism after the Crisis: Strategic Economic Discourse and the EU-Korea Free Trade Agreement', *New Political Economy*, 16(5), 627–653.

Siles-Brügge, G. (2014a) 'EU Trade and Development Policy beyond the ACP: Subordinating Developmental to Commercial Imperatives in the Reform of GSP', *Contemporary Politics*, 20(1), 49–62.

Siles-Brügge, G. (2014b) *Constructing European Union Trade Policy: A Global Idea of Europe* (London: Palgrave Macmillan).

Singer, J.D. (1961) 'The Level-of-Analysis Problem in International Relations', *World Politics*, 14(1), 77–92.

Steinberg, R. (2002) 'In the Shadow of Law or Power? Consensus-Based Bargaining and Outcomes in the GATT/WTO', *International Organization*, 56(2), 339–374.

Tannous, I. (2013) 'The Programming of EU's External Assistance and Development Aid and the Fragile Balance of Power between EEAS and DG DEVCO', *European Foreign Affairs Review*, 18(3), 329–354.

Trebilcock, M. (2015) 'Between Theories of Trade and Development: The Future of the World Trading System', *The Journal of World Investment & Trade*, 16(1), 122–140.

Trommer, S. (2017) 'Post-Brexit Trade Policy Autonomy as Pyrrhic Victory: Being a Middle Power in a Contested Trade Regime', *Globalizations*, DOI:10.1080 /14747731.2017.1330986

Tullock, P. (1975) *The Politics of Preferences: EEC Policy Making and the Generalised System of Preferences* (London: Overseas Development Institute).

UNCTAD (1968) Resolution 21(II) 'Preferential or free entry of exports of manufactures and semi-manufactures of developing countries to the developed countries, 77th plenary meeting, 26 March 1968', in United Nations, *Proceedings of the United Nations Conference on Trade and Development, Second Session, New Delhi, 1 February-29 March 1968, Volume I: Report and Annexes*, TD/97 (New York: United Nations), 38.

Van den Bossche, P. and W. Zdouc (2013) *The Law and Policy of the World Trade Organization: Text, Cases and Materials*, 3rd edn (Cambridge: Cambridge University Press).

Van den Putte, L., F. De Ville and J. Orbie (2015) 'The European Parliament as an International Actor in Trade: From Power to Impact', in S. Stavridis and D. Irrera (eds), *The European Parliament in International Relations* (London: Routledge), 52–69.

Van der Loo, G. (2016) *The EU-Ukraine Association Agreement and Deep and Comprehensive Free Trade Area: A New Legal Instrument for EU Integration without Membership* (Leiden: Brill Nijhoff).

Van der Loo, G. and R.A. Wessel (2017) 'The Non-Ratification of Mixed Agreements: Legal Consequences and Solutions', *Common Market Law Review*, 54(3), 735–770.

Velluti, S. (2016) 'The Promotion and Integration of Human Rights in EU External Trade Relations', *Utrecht Journal of International and European Law*, 32(83), 41–68.

Vermulst, E., M. Pernaute and K. Lucenti (2004) 'Recent EC Safeguards' Policy: "Kill Them All and Let God Sort Them Out"?', *Journal of World Trade*, 38(6), 955–984.

Versluys, H. (2008) 'European Union Humanitarian Aid: Lifesaver or Political Tool?', in J. Orbie (ed.), *Europe's Global Role: External Policies of the European Union* (Aldershot: Ashgate), 91–116.

Vogt, J. (2015) 'A Little Less Conversation: The EU and the (Non) Application of Labour Conditionality in the Generalized System of Preferences (GSP)', *The International Journal of Comparative Labour Law and Industrial Relations*, 31(3), 285–304.

Wasserfallen, F. (2014) 'Political and Economic Integration in the EU: The Case of Failed Tax Harmonization', *Journal of Common Market Studies*, 52(2), 420–435.

Winters, A. (2001) 'European Union Trade Policy: Actually or Just Nominally Liberal?', in H. Wallace (ed.), *Interlocking Dimensions of European Integration* (Basingstoke: Palgrave), 25–44.

Woll, C. (2009) 'Trade Policy Lobbying in the European Union: Who Captures Whom?', in D. Coen and J. Richardson (eds), *Lobbying in the European Union: Institutions, Actors, and Issues* (Oxford: Oxford University Press), 277–297.

Woolcock, S. (2012) *European Union Economic Diplomacy: The Role of the EU in External Economic Relations* (Farnham: Ashgate).

Woolcock, S. (2014) 'Differentiation within Reciprocity: The European Union Approach to Preferential Trade Agreements', *Contemporary Politics*, 20(1), 36–48.

Woolcock, S. (2015) 'Trade Policy: Policy-Making after the Treaty of Lisbon', in H. Wallace, M.A. Pollack and A.R. Young (eds), *Policy-Making in the European Union*, 7th edn (Oxford: Oxford University Press), 388–406.

WTO (2004) *European Communities – Conditions for the Granting of Tariff Preferences to Developing Countries*, AB-2004-1, Report of the Appellate Body Report, WT/DS246/AB/R, Geneva, 7 April.

WTO (2008) *China – Measures Affecting Imports of Automobile Parts*, AB-2008-10, Reports of the Appellate Body, WT/DS339/AB/R, WT/DS340/AB/R, WT/DS342/AB/R, Geneva, 15 December.

WTO (2016) *European Union – Measures Related to Price Comparison Methodologies*, DS 516, Geneva, 2 December.

Yildirim, A.B. (2016) 'Domestic Political Implications of Global Value Chains: Explaining EU Responses to Litigation at the World Trade Organization', *Comparative European Politics*, https://link.springer.com/article/10.1057/s41295-016-0085-3 (accessed June 2017).

Yildirim, A.B., J. Tyson Chatagnier, A. Poletti and D. De Bièvre (2017) 'The Internationalization of Production and the Politics of Compliance in WTO Disputes', *The Review of International Organizations*, https://link.springer.com/article/10.1007/s11558-017-9278-z (accessed June 2017).

Young, A.R. (2002) *Extending European Cooperation: The European Union and the 'New' International Trade Agenda* (Manchester: Manchester University Press).

Young, A.R. (2003) 'What Game? By Which Rules? Adaptation and Flexibility in the EC's Foreign Economic Policy', in M. Knodt and S. Princen (eds), *Understanding the European Union's External Relations* (London: Routledge), 54–71.

Young, A.R. (2006) 'Punching its Weight? The EU's Use of WTO Dispute Resolution', in O. Elgström and M. Smith (eds), *The European Union's Roles in International Politics: Concepts and Analysis* (London: Routledge), 188–207.

Young, A.R. (2007) 'Trade Politics Ain't What It Used to Be: The European Union in the Doha Round', *Journal of Common Market Studies*, 45(4), 789–811.

Young, A.R. (2010) 'Effective Multilateralism on Trial: EU Compliance with WTO Law', in S. Blavoukos and D. Bourantonis (eds), *The EU's Presence in International Organisations* (Abingdon: Routledge), 114–131.

Young, A.R. (2011) 'The Rise (and Fall?) of the EU's Performance in the Multilateral Trading System', *Journal of European Integration*, 33(6), 715–729.

Young, A.R. (2015) 'Liberalizing Trade, not Exporting Rules: The Limits to Regulatory Co-ordination in the EU's 'New Generation' Preferential Trade Agreements', *Journal of European Public Policy*, 22(9), 1253–1275.

Young, A.R. (2016) 'Not Your Parents' Trade Politics: The Transatlantic Trade and Investment Partnership Negotiations', *Review of International Political Economy*, 21(3), 345–378.

Young, A.R. and J. Peterson (2013) '"We Care about You, but…:' The Politics of EU Trade Policy and Development', *Cambridge Review of International Affairs*, 26(3), 497–518.

Young, A.R. and J. Peterson (2014) *Parochial Global Europe: 21st Century Trade Politics* (Oxford: Oxford University Press).

Zimmermann, H. (2007) 'Realist Power Europe? The EU in the Negotiations about China's and Russia's WTO Accession', *Journal of Common Market Studies*, 45(4), 813–832.

Žvelc, R. (2012) 'Environmental Integration in EU Trade Policy: The Generalised System of Preferences, Trade Sustainability Impact Assessments and Free Trade Agreements', in E. Morgera (ed.), *The External Environmental Policy of the European Union: EU and International Law Perspectives* (Cambridge: Cambridge University Press), 174–203.

Index

Please note: page numbers in **bold type** indicate boxes, those in *italics* indicate tables.

Druck:
Canon Deutschland Business Services GmbH
im Auftrag der KNV-Gruppe
Ferdinand-Jühlke-Str. 7
99095 Erfurt